D0422864

THE NEW APOSTOLIC CHURCHES

EDITED BY C. PETER WAGNER

Regal

A Division of Gospel Light
Ventura, California, U.S.A.

141664

Published by Regal Books
A Division of Gospel Light
Ventura, California, U.S.A.
Printed in U.S.A.

Regal Books is a ministry of Gospel Light, an evangelical Christian publisher dedicated to serving the local church. We believe God's vision for Gospel Light is to provide church leaders with biblical, user-friendly materials that will help them evangelize, disciple and minister to children, youth and families.

It is our prayer that this Regal book will help you discover biblical truth for your own life and help you meet the needs of others. May God richly bless you.

For a free catalog of resources from Regal Books/Gospel Light please contact your Christian supplier or call 1-800-4-GOSPEL.

All Scripture quotations, unless otherwise indicated, are taken from
the *New King James Version*. Copyright © 1979, 1980, 1982
by Thomas Nelson, Inc. Publishers. Used by permission. All rights reserved.

Other versions used are:
KJV—*King James Version*. Authorized King James Version. (Chapter 3)
NIV—Scripture quotations are taken from the *Holy Bible, New International Version®*.
NIV®. Copyright © 1973, 1978, 1984 by International Bible Society.
Used by permission of Zondervan Publishing House. All rights reserved.

© Copyright 1998 by C. Peter Wagner
All rights reserved.

Cover Design by Barbara LeVan Fisher
Interior Design by Britt Rocchio
Edited by Virginia Woodard

Library of Congress Cataloging-in-Publication Data
The new Apostolic churches / edited by C. Peter Wagner.
    p. cm.
    ISBN 0-8307-2136-3
    1. Independent churches—United States. 2. Pentecostal churches—United States. 3. Independent churches. 4. Pentecostal churches.
    I. Wagner, C. Peter.
    BR516.N45 1998   98-11789
    289.9—dc21   CIP

1 2 3 4 5 6 7 8 9 10 11 12 13 14 15 16 17 / 05 04 03 02 01 00 99 98

Rights for publishing this book in other languages are contracted by Gospel Literature International (GLINT). GLINT also provides technical help for the adaptation, translation and publishing of Bible study resources and books in scores of languages worldwide. For further information, contact GLINT, P.O. Box 4060, Ontario, CA 91761-1003, U.S.A., or the publisher.

Dedicated to
John Wimber
1934-1997

A molder of a generation
And a pioneer of the
New Apostolic Reformation

CONTENTS

PART TWO:
BASED IN OTHER NATIONS

FOREWORD

We live in changing times—new churches are born as old ones die; new evangelistic methods emerge as old ones become ineffective; new worship expressions take center stage as old ones become empty traditions. The focus of this book is to consider this time for new denominations as old ones collapse.

Some Christians are frightened by changing times—they are threatened because of time changes for church meetings, or a change to a new Bible version, or a canceled program. When their denominations collapse around them, some people despair. Is it because their denominations propped up their faith, or maybe their whole lives were attached to their denomination, and when it deflated so did their Christianity?

America is moving into postmodernism—a time when the Church no longer drives culture, nor does the Church have much influence on society. Our culture is going beyond its past Christian influence to the neutralization of Christianity. We have become open to all religions; and at times our culture seems to be anti-Christian. Is that because so many churches and denominations have become ineffective? Is it because Christians live the same way as the heathen and "sin" the same as the folks with whom they work? Whatever the reason, the culture in which we worship is now different. What is happening is that old churches and denominations are collapsing, and new ones are arising.

We can learn a few things from history. We know that change is inevitable. Church names will change, church music expressions will change and church schedules will change. This book is about change. We see the emergence of new church expressions and new church alliances. As old church expressions pass from the scene, some new church models are arising. New babies are born as grandparents die. New church paradigms are being born into the world of change as past denominational paradigms die around us.

Years ago I asked myself the perplexing question, Why do churches and denominations die? The answer is simple. Because they change the wrong things and hang on to the wrong things. They die because they change their loyalty to the Word of God, which is the only permanent thing in life. They die because they hang on to their methods and traditions. When they confuse what to change and what not to change, they die.

Today, I see new churches sprouting that have adopted new names, new methods and new worship expressions. I see a new alliance of churches, but these new alliances are not called denominations. Yet they have some of the same features that originally attracted old churches into the old denominations. The glue that binds these new denominations together is the Great Commission, winning people to Christ, worshiping God, small-group Bible studies, energetic worship, gifted leadership and strong personal relationships. These new alliances are held together by the glue of biblical methods, not their particular doctrinal statements nor their traditions.

Most old denominations were formed by doctrinal distinctives. Some old denominations were born when they split because of doctrinal technicalities, others were founded on new doctrinal allegiances. The old denominations were allied to Calvinistic or Armenian or dispensational or Pentecostal or Wesleyan doctrines or some unique interpretation of Scripture. The new denominations are really movements or, to describe them in postmodern business terminology, they are like franchises. They are Willow Creek Associates, Calvary Chapels, Vineyard Fellowships or other names that describe a new movement for God in the postmodern world of new challenges.

C. Peter Wagner once called this new movement "Postdenominational Churches," but the term was rejected because some thought it linked them to past failures, or even worse, implied that some effective evangelical denominations were not in fact effective. So Wagner changed the title to "The New Apostolic Reformation."

This book is about change, thus many readers may not like it because they do not want to change anything. Do not close your mind; read it carefully to see what is being changed. These churches are not changing the essentials of Bible doctrine. They are as committed to the fundamentals of the faith as the originators of past conservative denominations were committed to the essentials of Christianity. They are merely changing the methods of evangelism, worship, Bible study and leadership.

Years ago I wrote a book called *Is the Day of the Denomination Dead?* (Thomas Nelson, 1973). The title asks a question about church groups. The answer to the question is yes, denominations are dying and will always die, because they are man made (only the Word of God is eternal). The answer to that book title, however, is also no! Denominations will never die, because those who love God will always plant new, vibrant churches, and when they excel in the work of the Lord, they will naturally be attracted to fellowship with others of like faith and like passion. Thus, like embryonic seeds, new movements will always be planted to replace dying movements.

May we see the churches described in this book as God sees them, and may we look beyond these churches to see God's work in the world. May we study the churches portrayed in this book to see how they minister in the growing anti-Christian world of modernity. Thus, may we learn from them to help us serve Christ better wherever we minister.

Elmer L. Towns
Liberty University
Lynchburg, Virginia

INTRODUCTION

What Is an
Apostolic Church?

1

THE NEW APOSTOLIC REFORMATION

professor c. peter wagner
colorado springs, colorado

Dr. C. Peter Wagner is cofounder of the World
Prayer Center in Colorado Springs and coordinator of the United Prayer Track of the A.D.
2000 and Beyond Movement. He is also a professor at Fuller Theological Seminary. He is the
author/editor of more than 40 books.

I will soon complete 30 years as a professor of church
growth on the graduate level. During these 30 years, I have studied
countless Christian churches of all sizes, in all kinds of locations, from
new church plants to those hundreds of years old, spanning virtually
every theological tradition, and rooted in varieties of cultures on six
continents. I have reported my research the best I have known how in
an average of one or two books a year.

I have never been more excited about a book dealing with church
growth than I am about this one, *The New Apostolic Churches*. Because
I suggested to the other 18 authors that they begin their chapters with
personal testimonies of how God has brought them to the places where
they are now, I will follow suit. It will explain why I am so excited.

SEASONS OF RESEARCH

During my decades as a scholar, God has seen fit to focus my research energies on certain aspects of church growth for certain periods of time. As I have done that, I have tried to use what I have learned to develop new courses for my students at Fuller Theological Seminary, and many of the lessons eventually become books.

My mentor in church growth research was Donald A. McGavran, the founder of the whole field of church growth. He is now with the Lord, but for years I have had the singular privilege of carrying the title of the Donald A. McGavran Professor of Church Growth. One of the most basic lessons I learned from McGavran was that the best way to discover what makes churches grow is to study growing churches. As a result, my first season of research, spanning the 1970s and into the 1980s, was spent doing exactly that. In retrospect, I now look at this as researching the *technical* principles of church growth.

During that time, I began to notice something I obviously did not have the mental equipment to understand or to assimilate into my analysis of church growth. I noticed that the churches worldwide that seemed to grow the most rapidly were, for the most part, those that outwardly featured the immediate present-day supernatural ministry of the Holy Spirit.

My mentor for helping me make a paradigm shift into what I now call the *spiritual* principles of church growth was John Wimber, founder of the Association of Vineyard Churches and Vineyard Ministries International, to whom this book is dedicated. This began my second season of research, focusing first of all on the relationship between supernatural signs and wonders and church growth, then on prayer and spiritual warfare. This began in the early 1980s and continued to the mid-1990s.

My third season of research is now focusing on the New Apostolic Reformation, the subject of this book. I am very excited because the new apostolic churches, better than any I have previously studied, combine, on the highest level, solid *technical* principles of church growth with solid *spiritual* principles of church growth. I will tell more about that later.

UNITY + GIFTS = GROWTH

One of the most explicit Scripture verses about church growth is Ephesians 4:16, which says that the Body of which Jesus is the head, "joined and knit together by what every joint supplies, according to the effective working by which every part does its share, causes *growth* of the body" (italics added). A formula for growth, then, is: Unity (joined together) + Gifts (every part does its share) = Growth.

Paul tells us in verse 7 that each one of us has a "measure" of grace, just as Romans 12:3 says we have a "measure" of faith, the measure being our spiritual gifts. Then Ephesians 4:8 says that Jesus, when He ascended, "gave gifts to men," and it goes on to tell us that He gave gifted people to the Church on two levels: (1) the government level (apostles, prophets, evangelists, pastors, teachers) in verse 11, and (2) the ministry of the saints in general in verse 12. When the government is in its proper place, biblical unity of the saints emerges and "every part can do its share."

How do these biblical principles unfold in real life? For 2,000 years, the Church of Jesus Christ has grown and spread into every continent. Jesus said, "I will build My church," and He has been doing it. As we review those 2,000 years, however, it is quite obvious that Jesus does not always build His Church in the same ways. He did it one way in the Roman Empire before Constantine; another way after Constantine; another way in the Middle Ages; another way following the Reformation; another way during the era of European colonization; and yet another way post-World War II, just to name a few.

GROWTH: A STORY OF NEW WINESKINS

Every time Jesus began building His Church in a new way throughout history, He provided new wineskins. While He was still on earth, He said that such a thing would be necessary: "Nor do they put new wine into old wineskins, or else the wineskins break, the wine is spilled, and the wineskins are ruined. But they put new wine into new wineskins, and both are preserved" (Matt. 9:17). The growth of the Church through the ages is, in part, a story of new wineskins.

Because this is the case, a crucial question not only for professors of church growth, but also for Christians in general, is this: *What are the new wineskins Jesus is providing as we move into the twenty-first century?*

FOUR CRUCIAL QUESTIONS

My experience as a church growth scholar has led me constantly to ask four crucial questions:

1. Why does the blessing of God rest where it does?
2. Churches are not all equal. Why is it that at certain times, some churches are more blessed than others?
3. Can any pattern of divine blessing be discerned?
4. Do those churches that seem to be unusually blessed have any common characteristics?

As I have tried to answer these questions, it is important to realize that I am a very traditional Christian. For decades I have been an ordained Congregational minister, and I still am. We Congregationalists came over on the *Mayflower!* I find myself in one of the oldest wineskins on record. Furthermore, I am a *conservative* Congregationalist (ordained in the Conservative Congregational Christian Conference). This was definitely an obstacle to my early church growth research because while I was a missionary in Bolivia I was anti-Pentecostal, and the fastest-growing churches in Latin America at the time happened to be Pentecostal churches.

I finally overcame my biases, however, and, in 1973, wrote *Look Out! The Pentecostals Are Coming!* (Creation House). At that time, Pentecostal churches were one of the new wineskins, and their growth was showing it.

WINESKINS OF THE 1990S

That was back in the 1970s. What, however, are the new wineskins of the 1990s? Where does the blessing of God seem to be resting today?

The answer to this question began coming into focus in 1993. As a professional missiologist, I had picked up certain bits and pieces of information through the years, but until then, at least in my mind, these bits and pieces were unrelated. Then, however, I did begin to see a pattern among three amazing church growth movements:

1. *The African Independent Churches.* These roots go back to the turn of the century when large numbers of contextualized African churches began breaking away from the traditional mission churches. Throughout the century, the growth of the independent churches in Africa has far exceeded the growth of the traditional churches.
2. *The Chinese house churches.* Particularly since the end of the Cultural Revolution in the mid-1970s, the multiplication of house churches under a hostile Marxist government in China has been a missiological phenomenon.
3. *Latin American grassroots churches.* During the past 20 years, the largest churches that have been launched in virtually every metropolitan area of Latin America are largely those that are pastored by individuals who have had no formative experience with foreign missionaries or mission-initiated institutions.

I would put these three together with the rapid growth of the American independent charismatic churches I researched for the *Dictionary of Pentecostal and Charismatic Movements*, published by Zondervan in 1987. My article, entitled "Church Growth," pointed out that this was the fastest-growing segment of Christianity in the United States in our times.

What happened in 1993, then, was the realization in my mind that, indeed, a pattern of divine blessing today on certain identifiable groups of churches is discernible (Question #3). The next question then becomes (Question #4): What are their common characteristics?

A CHURCHQUAKE!

In the balance of this chapter, I will outline the nine most common characteristics of these churches I have been able to discern to date. My exposition and comments about each will, of necessity, be brief so as to keep the size of this chapter proportionate to the others in this book.

I am simultaneously working on my textbook about the subject, which will provide abundant details. The title I am considering for the textbook is *Churchquake!*, which, to me, reflects the magnitude of change these new wineskins are bringing to the Body of Christ. In fact, I am sure we are seeing before our very eyes the most radical change in the way of doing church since the Protestant Reformation.

Let's take a brief look at nine components of the new wineskins that are shaping the Church for the twenty-first century.

1. A NEW NAME

When I began researching the Pentecostal movement years ago, it already had a name. This new movement, however, did not have a name. Because I was planning to teach a seminary course based on it, I needed a name for my course. For a couple of years I experimented

> **The New Apostolic Reformation *is an extraordinary work of God at the close of the twentieth century that is, to a significant extent, changing the shape of Protestant Christianity around the world.***

with "postdenominationalism," but strong protests from my denominational friends persuaded me that it might not be the best name. Besides, many of the new apostolic churches have remained within their denominations. "Independent charismatic" does not seem to fit either because (1) these churches see themselves as *interdependent*, as opposed to *independent*, and (2) they are not all charismatic in orientation.

The name I have settled on for the movement is the New Apostolic Reformation, and individual churches being designated as new apostolic churches.

I use "reformation" because, as I have said, these new wineskins appear to be *at least as radical as those of the Protestant Reformation almost 500 years ago.* "Apostolic" connotes a strong focus on outreach plus a recognition of present-day apostolic ministries. "New" adds a contemporary spin to the name.

Although many people were begging for a definition of the New Apostolic Reformation from the beginning, I resisted formulating one until I believed I had a more mature grasp of the movement. Now that I have taught my first Fuller Seminary course about the subject, I believe it is time to take the risk of a definition, hoping that it will not have to be revised too frequently in the future:

The New Apostolic Reformation is an extraordinary work of God at the close of the twentieth century that is, to a significant extent, changing the shape of Protestant Christianity around the world. For almost 500 years, Christian churches have largely functioned within traditional denominational structures of one kind or another. Particularly in the 1990s, but having roots going back for almost a century, new forms and operational procedures are now emerging in areas such as local church government, interchurch relationships, financing, evangelism, missions, prayer, leadership selection and training, the role of supernatural power, worship and other important aspects of church life. Some of these changes are being seen within denominations themselves, but for the most part they are taking the form of loosely structured apostolic networks. In virtually every region of the world, these new apostolic churches constitute the fastest-growing segment of Christianity.

Infinite creativity seems to be the watchword for assigning names to local churches. The "Crystal Cathedral" and "Community Church of Joy" are among the most prominent congregations in our country. "Icthus" churches are multiplying in England. On a recent visit to the Philippines I came in contact with "The Warm Body of Jesus Church." One of my favorite churches in Argentina is "Waves of Love and Peace." In Kenya, Thomas Muthee pastors "The Prayer Cave." A friend told me of a church in Zimbabwe called the "Dodge the Devil and Go Straight to Heaven Church"!

2. NEW AUTHORITY STRUCTURE

In my judgment, views of leadership and leadership authority constitute the most radical of the nine changes from traditional Christianity. Here is the main difference: *The amount of spiritual authority delegated by the Holy Spirit to individuals.* I have attempted to use each word in that statement advisedly. We are seeing a transition from bureaucratic authority to personal authority, from legal structure to relational structure, from control to coordination and from rational leadership to charismatic leadership. This all manifests itself on two levels: the local level and the translocal level.

On the local church level, the new apostolic pastors are the *leaders* of the church. In traditional Christianity, the pastors are regarded as *employees* of the church.

It is a question of trust. New apostolic congregations trust their pastor. Traditional congregations trust boards and committees. The difference between the two is enormous. The most passionate description of this difference I have yet seen is Lawrence Khong's chapter (15) in this book.

On the translocal level, one of the most surprising developments for those of us who are traditionalists is the growing affirmation of contemporary apostolic ministries. Our English "apostle" is a transliteration of the Greek *apostolos*, which means one who is sent out with a commission. This is an important dimension of what we are seeing, but the more surprising feature is the reaffirmation, not only of the New Testament *gift* of apostle, but also of the *office* of apostle. This is one of the first books I have seen that includes a chapter by one who designates himself "Apostle John Kelly," much like the apostle Paul did in most of his Epistles.

3. NEW LEADERSHIP TRAINING

Although new apostolic pastors are fervently dedicated to leading their churches, they are equally dedicated to releasing the people of their congregations to do the ministry of the church. A characteristic of many new apostolic churches is an abundance of volunteers. Church members are normally taught that part of being a good Christian is to discover the spiritual gifts God has given them and to minister to others through those gifts as well as through any natural talents they might also have.

Members of the paid pastoral staff of typical new apostolic churches are usually homegrown. As all the believers in the congregation become active in ministry, certain ones tend to rise to the top like cream on fresh milk, and they are the ones who are then recruited for the staff. Because for many this involves a midlife career change, the possibility of their enrolling for two or three years in the residence program of a traditional seminary or Bible school is extremely remote. Therefore, academic requirements for ordination, so long the staple in traditional churches, are being scrapped. New apostolic ordination is primarily rooted in personal relationships, which verify character, and in proved ministry skills.

> *Traditional Christianity starts with the present situation and focuses on the past. New apostolic Christianity starts with the present situation and focuses on the future.*

Continuing education for leaders more frequently takes place in conferences, seminars and retreats rather than in classrooms of accredited institutions. Little aversion is noticed for quality training, but the demands are many for alternate delivery systems. A disproportionate number of new apostolic churches, especially the large ones, are establishing their own in-house Bible schools.

One of the most notable features of new apostolic churches, which traditional church leaders soon discover to their amazement, is the absence of nominating committees (to place lay leaders within the congregation) and of search committees (to locate and recruit new staff members).

4. New Ministry Focus

Traditional Christianity starts with the present situation and focuses on the past. New apostolic Christianity starts with the present situation and focuses on the future.

Many traditional churches are *heritage driven*. "We must get back to our roots. We need to pray for renewal"—meaning that we should once again be what we used to be. The founders of the movement are often thought of as standing shoulder to shoulder with the 12 apostles.

On the other hand, new apostolic church leaders are *vision driven*. In a conversation with a new apostolic senior pastor about his church, I once asked, "How many cell groups do you have?" I think that was sometime in 1996.

He replied, "We will have 600 by the year 2000!"

I can't seem to recall ever finding out how many cells he did have in 1996. As far as the pastor was concerned, though, that apparently didn't matter at all. In his mind, the 600 cells were not imaginary, they were real. The 600 was what really mattered.

5. NEW WORSHIP STYLE

In only a few exceptions, new apostolic churches use contemporary worship styles. Contemporary worship is the one characteristic of the New Apostolic Reformation that has already penetrated the most deeply into traditional and denominational churches across-the-board. Many churches that would not at all be considered new apostolic are now using contemporary worship in at least one of their weekend services.

Worship leaders have replaced music directors. Keyboards have replaced pipe organs. Casual worship teams have replaced robed choirs. Overhead projectors have replaced hymnals. Ten to 12 minutes of congregational singing is now 30 to 49 minutes or even more. Standing during worship is the rule, although a great amount of freedom for body language prevails.

As you scan a new apostolic congregation in worship, you will likely see some sitting, some kneeling, some looking at the ceiling, some lying prostrate on the floor, some holding up hands, some closing their eyes, some clapping their hands, some wiping tears from their eyes, some using tambourines, some dancing and some just walking around.

"Performance" is a naughty word for new apostolic worship leaders. Their goal is to help every person in the congregation become an active "participant" in worship. Frequent applause is not congratulating those on the platform for their musical excellence, but it is seen as high tribute to the triune God.

6. NEW PRAYER FORMS

Prayer in new apostolic churches has taken forms rarely seen in traditional congregations. Some of this takes place within the church and some takes place outside the church.

The actual number of prayer times and the cumulative number of minutes spent in prayer during the worship service of new apostolic churches far exceeds the prayer time of the average traditional church. Worship leaders weave frequent times of prayer into singing worship songs. Many of them argue that true worship is, in itself, a form of prayer, so blending the two seems natural. A considerable number of new apostolic churches practice *concert prayer*, in which all worshipers are praying out loud at the same time, some in a prayer language and some in the vernacular. At times in some churches, each one will begin singing a prayer, creating a loud, harmonious sound not unlike the sound of the medieval Gregorian chant.

New apostolic leaders have been among the first to understand and put into practice some of the newer forms of prayer that take place in the community itself, not in the church. For many, praise marches, prayerwalking, prayer journeys and prayer expeditions have become a part of congregational life and ministry. Just as a matter of interest, as I am drafting this chapter, 55 members of one local church, New Life Church of Colorado Springs, are preparing to leave three weeks from now for Nepal, high in the Himalayas, to pray on-site for each of the 43 major, yet-unreached people groups of the nation.

7. NEW FINANCING

New apostolic churches experience relatively few financial problems. Although no vision-driven church believes it has enough resources to fulfill the vision adequately, and although financial crises do come from time to time, still, compared to traditional churches, finances are abundant. I think at lease three discernible reasons explain this situation.

First, generous giving is expected. Tithing is taught without apology, and those who do not tithe their incomes are subtly encouraged to evaluate their Christian lives as subpar.

Second, giving is beneficial, not only to the church and its ministry in the kingdom of God, but also to the giver. Tithes and offerings are regarded as seeds that will produce fruit of like kind for individuals and families. Luke 6:38, which says that if we give, it will be given to us in greater measure, is taken literally.

Third, giving is cheerful. It is not yet a common practice, but I have been in new apostolic churches in which the congregation breaks out into a rousing, athletic-event kind of shouting and clapping the moment the pastor announces he is collecting the morning offering. They are cheerful givers and they want everyone else to know it. I rarely hear the complaint in new apostolic churches I often hear in traditional churches: The pastor talks about money too much.

8. NEW OUTREACH

Aggressively reaching out to the lost and hurting of the community and the world is part of the new apostolic DNA. These churches assiduously attempt to avoid the "bless me syndrome" as they try to live up to their apostolic nature and calling. They do seek personal blessings from God, but usually as means to the end of reaching others. A worship song I frequently hear in new apostolic churches says: "Let your glory fall in this room; let it go forth from here to the nations."

Planting new churches is usually an assumed part of what a local congregation does. The question is not whether we should do it, but when and how. The same applies to foreign missions. One of the more interesting developments for a missiologist like me is that a large number of congregations are becoming involved, as congregations, in foreign missions. This does not mean they are necessarily bypassing mission agencies, especially newer ones such as Youth With A Mission, but it does mean they are expanding their options for influencing their people to participate in a more direct and personal way in world outreach.

Compassion for the poor, the outcast, the homeless, the disadvantaged and the handicapped is a strong characteristic of most new apostolic churches. Many other churches do a lot of talking about helping unfortunate people, but new apostolic churches seem to find ways to actually do it. The Vineyard Christian Fellowship of Anaheim, California, for example, distributes almost $2 million worth of food to hungry people in their area every year. The Cathedral of Faith in San Jose, California, has constructed a million-dollar food distribution warehouse facility and it has become one of the largest food distribution centers in the state. Other local churches are doing similar things.

9. NEW POWER ORIENTATION

I mentioned earlier that the New Apostolic Reformation seems to be combining the technical principles of church growth with the spiritual principles of church growth better than any similar grouping of churches I have observed. Even those new apostolic churches that do not consider themselves charismatic usually have a sincere openness to the work of the Holy Spirit and a consensus that all the New Testament spiritual gifts are in operation today.

The majority of the new apostolic churches not only believe in the work of the Holy Spirit, but they also regularly invite Him to come into their midst to bring supernatural power. It is commonplace, therefore, to observe active ministries of healing, demonic deliverance, spiritual warfare, prophecy, falling in the Spirit, spiritual mapping, prophetic acts, fervent intercession and travail, and so on in new apostolic churches.

A basic theological presupposition in new apostolic, as contrasted to traditional, churches is that supernatural power tends to open the way for applying truth, rather than vice versa. This is why visitors will frequently observe in these churches what seems to be more emphasis on the heart than on the mind. Some conclude from this that new apostolic churches are "too emotional."

CONCLUSION

The more I have studied the New Apostolic Reformation during the past few years, the more convinced I have become that we have a major transformation of Christianity on our hands. Don Miller titles his excellent new book on the subject *Reinventing American Protestantism* (University of California Press). By extension, I believe we are witnessing a reinventing of world Christianity. If that is the case, it is all the more reason to give God thanks for allowing us to be alive and active in His kingdom in these enthralling days.

PART ONE:

Based in the
United States

2
ANTIOCH CHURCHES AND MINISTRIES

Apostle John P. Kelly
Southlake, Texas

Apostle Kelly has spent the past decade establishing and strengthening churches and ministries throughout the United States and overseas. Antioch Churches and Ministries has established more than 100 churches in the United States, and is helping to establish apostolic networks in more than 46 nations. He draws on a varied background that includes service in the United States Marines, real estate sales and management, professional education and athletics as well as 15 years in New Testament ministry. Apostle Kelly has earned a bachelor of arts degree in Education and Business, a master's degree in Human Potential and Development and holds an honorary doctorate of divinity.

The realization that I was falling to my death drew out a cry from my innermost being: "Jesus, save me!" I instantly recalled words I had once heard from Billy Graham, that Jesus has the power to save. I realized that my own physical strength, which was considerable, could do nothing in the situation.

As I was falling, I saw two hands larger than me reach out to catch me. When I came to consciousness, two men were reaching out to rescue me from the cross cables that had broken my fall. The mouth of the Hudson River loomed some 700 feet below. Although I had sustained several cracked ribs, I returned the next morning to my summer job as a structural steel ironworker on the Verranzano-Narrows Bridge in New York City. At 19, I knew without a doubt that Jesus had saved my life. Not until more than a decade later, however, would this realization come to fruition in my life.

In my athletic career I played college, semiprofessional and professional football. I was also involved in boxing, judo and various forms of martial arts. When my professional football career ended, I began my military career as an infantry officer. I was soon promoted into Force Recon and eventually Intelligence. After the Marine Corps, I worked to train high school boys who were emotionally disturbed, socially maladjusted and exhibiting violent behaviors. My career then turned to business, where I became a successful salesman and briefly managed a real estate company. At that time, I also owned and managed a cement and steel construction company.

IS GOD REAL?

During the early 1970s, the church was experiencing charismatic renewal. My wife, Helena, became an active member of our Catholic parish, and we were invited to a charismatic weekend retreat. After one of the night meetings at the retreat, my friend and I decided to return to the chapel to find out if God was real. We broke down the church doors, but when we did we were immediately hit by the power of God. We were hit with such force that we were both knocked to the ground. At this powerful point I surrendered my life totally to the Lord. He was real!

I began my ministry by establishing a Bible study in a New Jersey prison. This ministry, which I called The Bridge Ministries, grew to become one of the largest prison ministries on the east coast. My involvement in the prison ministry eventually opened doors for me to share my testimony at Christian banquets. I was then asked to speak at evangelistic meetings, tent revivals and camp meetings. I began traveling as an evangelist throughout the northeastern United States. At that time, I had developed three sermon topics: faith, healing and deliverance. Within each of those topics I had up to four separate sermons. By the grace of God, the ministry of the Word was almost always followed by supernatural signs and wonders. My ministry was exciting, and at that time I was considered by some as being "deep." Looking back, however, we were in reality what I would call a "charismatic traveling circus."

GOSPEL MINISTRY OR GOSPEL BUSINESS?

During this time, I came into great personal conflict about the direc-

LIBRARY
BRYAN COLLEGE
DAYTON, TENN. 37321

tion I was taking in my ministry. My wife, Helena, who is a prophetic intercessor, said to me, "What are we doing? Are we in the Gospel Ministry or the Gospel Business?" I found this statement upsetting and unsettling.

God began to show me that the ministerial relationships I had built while traveling were shallow at best. Pastors who knew nothing about me invited me to preach. It was a "hired-gun" mentality. Little Kingdom building for permanence or an underlying desire to establish and build significant personal relationships was taking place.

> **"Are we in the Gospel Ministry or the Gospel Business?" I realized I was on the road to becoming a ministerial entertainer.**

In a series of meetings, I was ministering in the daytime at a tent revival for a church in Long Island, New York. The main speaker did the large evening meetings. One night, when the crowd was very large, he used more time to take an offering than to minister the Word. After the meeting, he invited me to drive with him to New York City. I was glad for the opportunity and hoped to hear words of wisdom from this well-known evangelist. We went to a classy shop where he used the entire offering to buy himself a "pinkie" ring. He put it on his finger, showed it to me and said, "Look John, see how the Lord has blessed me!"

My wife's words reverberated through my spirit, "Are we in the Gospel Ministry or the Gospel Business?" I realized I was on the road to becoming a ministerial entertainer.

The following day I canceled every speaking engagement except one. A personal friend had invited me to conduct an evangelistic crusade involving several churches. We had a tremendous move of the Holy Spirit that night, especially among the youth. In my motel room that night, I asked the Lord about the reality of my ministry because I realized I had based it on the emulation of others. The Lord spoke to me and said, "As limited as the messages are that you are preaching, they are in My Word. But the method and function of your ministry cannot be found." This was a tremendous revelation to me.

THE LOCAL CHURCH IS CENTRAL

At that point, I began a concentrated study of the Word and read every book I could find regarding the function, structure and government of Christian ministry. I began to see the importance of the local church and how God views and uses it. After much prayer and discussion with my wife, we started a church built on our understanding of the Word, the anointing, evangelism and relationships. From this church we planted two other churches within three and a half years. All those churches were built on biblical principles, and today they are still healthy, thriving churches.

NEW TESTAMENT CHURCH GOVERNMENT

I soon saw that many of the churches I had been visiting up till that time were not based on what I understood to be the New Testament pattern of government. They were either a one-man show or they were governed by a church board. Some did not have elected elders, and when elders were present, they were often vying for positions or they were elders in name only. Overall, I sensed strongly that such churches were out of order, and that many traveling ministries were doubly out of order. I began to realize that many of us were copying a corporate America paradigm or a paradigm that came out of Greco-Roman philosophy rather than building on the biblical design.

In 1980, my family and I went to New Hampshire for summer vacation. We discovered a church that had been closed by a U.S. marshal. The church building was absolutely beautiful. It was built on the peak of a mountain and overlooked several mountaintops. One of the walls encompassed three picture windows.

The Lord spoke to me to come to this church each morning, to sit inside the pulpit overlooking the mountains and commune with Him. Each morning I would arise at 6:30 A.M. and drive the half hour to the building to pray and worship God. On the last morning, God spoke clearly and simply, saying, "My Church is like this beautiful building; it is beautiful and on a hill, but empty and captured by world systems." He then told me, "Go and wash the feet of the young men who will become the patriarchs of the coming move of My Spirit."

My family and the three pastors with whom I was then in relationship witnessed this word to be true, although none of us knew at the time exactly what it meant. That was 17 years ago and I still believe I am just now beginning to realize the significance of this call on my life.

PERSONAL RELATIONSHIPS ARE VITAL

In Antioch Churches and Ministries (ACM) we build relationally, person to person, rather than through conferences, publications and advertisements. At present, we have established more than 100 churches across America, which include 45 translocal ministers, 10 of whom function full time in apostolic ministries. We are partnering with 62 New Testament apostolic networks in 42 countries, embracing more than 4,000 churches, and we are continuing to grow in number and influence.

Our network is basically a network of leaders: builders of churches, missions and ministries. It is intended for those who believe they can make the same kind of commitment as an 18-year-old boy joining the military. We are not interested in having leaders in our network who cannot live up to a demanding level of commitment. It takes mature believers to build and maintain strong relationships. It takes strong character for so many individuals to come together, work together and stay together. Our network is for those who can build covenantally.

When the apostle Paul gave the qualifications for elders and deacons in 1 Timothy 3:1-13, he told the churches to choose a certain kind of man. He told them to handpick men they could trust and with whom they could build. ACM is looking for that kind of leader. Because of this, our network is growing resolutely and deliberately. Each one must have vision and integrity and be an emotionally healed individual in order to work hard in a team atmosphere. Our network is not for everybody who believes in the fivefold ministry. It is only for those men who believe that the fivefold ministry should function according to the New Testament pattern of government.

WHO IS IN CHARGE?

Antioch Churches and Ministries attempts to follow the New Testament pattern of government and, as a network, one of our main concerns relates to what we can do to benefit ministers and churches. We have recruited many apostles as well as traveling prophets, evangelists and teachers. All minister full time within their ministry function. We like to have one full-time apostle oversee every 10 to 15 churches.

We do not assign apostles to specific churches or geographic areas. Doing so takes away from spiritual and personal relationships among the pastors whom we call "set-men." The apostles provide spiritual covering to the pastors and give input regularly, but the local church remains autonomous. Church authority is in the plurality of local church elders, giving the set-man the final decision.

We do not have a central hierarchical headship. When we understand family, we understand how apostolic ministry is meant to function. For example, when a father goes to his son's house he does not take charge, he submits. The son is in charge of that home. When the son goes to his father's house, the father is in charge. Within the context of a person's ministry, mission or church, that person has the ultimate responsibility and authority.

APOSTLES AND PROPHETS TOGETHER

Within the local church, the apostle and prophet bring synergy because they are foundational ministries. Apostolic ministry focuses on *building* ministry; prophetic ministry focuses on *blessing*. For instance, prophets can often point out what is wrong, but they should not always be expected to do much to solve the problem. On the other hand, the apostles are the problem solvers.

I believe we will see greater blessing come to the Church when we see prophets joining with apostles and harmoniously working together. When we look at the hand of God, picturing the thumb as the apostle and the pointing finger as the prophet, we see that to make a fist, the thumb (the apostle) has to hold the pointing finger (the prophet). Then the evangelist, pastor and teacher (the other three fingers) will follow suit, and we will see the Body ready to fight the good fight of faith using all its God-given power. At present, it often seems as though the Body is trying to fight by using open fingers to slap. When the hand becomes a fist, we can then experience true knockout power to bring the revival and the great harvest God desires.

TRAINING LEADERS

God has set a vision bearer and a leader in every church. Our viewpoint of leadership is simply that leaders lead. They bear the vision, they point the way and they have a following. We call these individuals the "set-men." We have taken our biblical cues from when Joshua was "set" over the congregation by Moses all the way into the New

> *Certain leadership principles can be taught, but the anointing is something that must be caught.*

Testament where Jesus has "set" some to be apostles, prophets, evangelists, pastors and teachers in the Church. We believe that leadership must be anointed.

Certain leadership principles can be *taught*, but the anointing is something that must be *caught*. We believe that leadership development is transferable from those who are leading and building apostles, and not necessarily from those apostles who major more in the prophetic, evangelistic, pastoral or teaching functions. It is essential for ministers not only to have the anointing, but also the knowledge that comes from continuous education.

I have a tremendous burden to make certain ministers receive an excellent education within the context of the local church. If we were to research our Bible schools and seminaries, we would find that many are graduating, but a surprising number do not stay in the ministry. I think this is because we are trying to build the Church by following a flawed model of ministerial training. Upon considering this situation, we created Antioch University International (AUI). It has a standard of excellence and is specifically designed for ministerial development within the local church.

AUI was originally founded to educate our own leaders, but it is now open to anyone interested in pursuing continuing education. People of all ages can be educated and trained under the covering of their set-man and his leadership team. They can begin to apply their gifts and knowledge to building the local church as they complete their ministerial training courses.

Ordination

To be ordained in ACM, the person must already be known by a set-man (pastor) and be regarded as having vision, character and anointing. It is of the utmost importance that all those who join in covenant with us share the same vision. Before ordination, the set-man arranges a meeting with one of the apostolic leaders to review network guidelines. Once recommendation is made by both the set-man and the apostle, the candidate is ordained.

We are not interested in reading about a person on an ordination application form. We want to talk to him or her personally, meet the person's family and get to know what kind of an individual the person is. The only real members of the Antioch Network are full-time ordained ministers who lead either a church, a ministry or a mission. The actual churches, ministries and missions are not under the covering of the network; they are autonomous. The ordained ministers are, however, accountable to the network in all areas.

Accountability

"Accountability" is a cry we are hearing from many ministers today, but I regard much of it as more "talk than walk." For accountability to be truly effective, it must be based on strong personal relationships with other men and women in ministry. Within those relationships there must always be an openness to receive correction and discipline. Every group I have ever been close to has had certain requirements, yet many ministers shrug off accountability as if it were some yoke of bondage. It is essential that someone in the lives of all fivefold ministers can hold them accountable in their marriages, finances and ethics.

A self-ordained apostle, prophet, evangelist or teacher can cause problems and create division.

Many pastors have no one to turn to because they have never established a committed, transparent relationship with a father or a brother in the Lord. They may have friendly relationships with other ministers, but these frequently are not governmental. Some relationships must have a governmental aspect or else we may have the unfortunate situation of correction without discipline. If we do not have relationships that can bring discipline, there is no genuine accountability nor will there ever be.

We had a situation in our network for which discipline had to be enacted. A pastor was discovered to be in an immorality situation. We sent an apostle to the pastor's home within 24 hours, who then also assumed responsibility for the pastorate the following Sunday. The apostle shepherded the congregation through this grievous situation and not one church member left because of it. At the same time, we provided ministry gifts of counseling and deliverance, and full restoration was brought to the erring pastor's family.

We believe strongly in ministerial restoration after the minister has repented and has proved to be trustworthy. In this case, the apostles decided to relocate the fallen, but restored, minister and his family. Without adequate finances and governmental structure, a proper process of restoration would have never taken place, and the affected church more than likely would have carried a permanent scar.

FINANCIAL PRINCIPLES

Antioch Churches and Ministries believes strongly in the principle of tithing. When Malachi says bring your tithes into the storehouse, we think it means just that. I have found that the majority of believers in the new apostolic churches tithe correctly. Many of the ministers, however, tithe incorrectly. The two questions I ask ministers concerning tithes are as follows: Where is your storehouse? and Where do you feed from? If they tithe to their local church, they are tithing back into their own paychecks. Their church is not their storehouse. They have to feed from other sources. A minister's storehouse is what we call the "covering."

I view our ACM apostles as father figures in the lives of the set-men. Of equal importance to having fathers in the faith is to develop a brotherhood among the set-men. If the pastor of a local church does not desire to have such a covering, I would be leery about being in that church. Many pastors will declare they have a covering, but the question is, do they tithe to that covering? By tracking the tithe, we can literally track the order in the house of God.

THE ANTIOCH STEWARDSHIP COUNCIL

To maintain our financial integrity and assist our churches in financial matters, we have created the Antioch Stewardship Council (ASC). ASC provides individuals with financial services in the following areas: accounting, budgets, taxes, mutual funds, financial planning, mortgages, trusts, pensions, IRAs, CDs and insurance.

Our local churches also tithe, but they tithe for a different purpose. Instead of tithing to their spiritual covering, they tithe to the network for global impact and a global harvest.

GLOBAL OUTREACH

We are partners with and develop key national leaders around the globe, teaching them how to build and develop new apostolic networks. Our missions movement is based largely upon training and enlisting nationals. We then become partners to develop and strengthen apostolic networks in their countries. Our method for reaching unreached people groups is to enlist a person most closely related to the culture of that people group, who then works through apostolic networking with nationals.

Let me further explain our mission strategy by sharing an example. In 1991 we held a ministerial conference in Mexico City. Another network was also having a ministerial conference there at the same time. That group went back to Mexico twice and the third time planted a church in Mexico City. Today that church is a successful mission plant consisting of approximately 450 people.

Our network took a different approach. We did not plant a church. Instead, we began to build relationships with three Mexican pastors. Each one of them was the pastor of a church of more than a thousand members as well as of a small apostolic network of churches, so we knew we had discovered truly strong leaders. We recognized and affirmed their apostolic calling, and then we began to send teams of ministers to their churches to strengthen and expand their networks. Today those three networks have a total of more than 200 churches.

Our financial cost for doing this was one tenth that of the other network, and our net results were something like four times bigger than theirs. The other network had to raise money for the pastor and his family as well as for two other families, eight individuals and the cost of travel between the United States and Mexico. We have been sending four teams a year to our various Mexican apostolic networks and the amount of fruit in this field has been tremendous.

CHURCH PLANTING

ACM network is supportive of church plants. We do not believe, however, they should be birthed from the network itself. It is unnatural for an apostolic network to birth a church. New church plants must be birthed out of local churches. Our church-planting strategy is similar to our missions strategy. As a network, we do not plant churches. We do, however, provide spiritual covering and structure to facilitate and assist in church plants. The person planting the church must be an experienced elder and must be sent from his local church. Unfortunately, space prohibits explaining our church-planting strategy in more detail.

RESTORING THE ROLE OF MANHOOD

I believe one of the main things the current apostolic movement will restore is biblical manhood in the leadership of the Church. Men have been experiencing an incredible amount of attack, to the point that it seems some pathological gender blending is taking place in their minds. You may have noticed that, in addressing principles of church leadership, I have used masculine pronouns more than others may like. This is because I believe the Church has been overly influenced by an effeminate spirit and, especially during the last few decades, our society has experienced an increase of adult men who have been raised primarily by mother figures in single-parent households. Consequently, a proper lack of understanding about patriarchalism exists.

Patriarchalism is confused with male abuse and chauvinism to such a point that many men who read what the Scriptures say about church government may not remember what they have read. Many do not know the scriptural guidelines for elders, the purpose of elders or how to disciple and train them.

If someone were to hold a loaded revolver to the head of the average pastor and say, "I'm going to shoot you unless you can give me four Scriptures on local church government and tell me how your church conforms to them," many of them would die. Ministers who are graduating from Bible schools and seminaries are being called to establish, build and pastor local churches, but they have little comprehension of what the Bible says regarding local church government.

If you were to take the Bible into a primitive culture and ask the people to put on paper how the local church should function governmentally, they will almost always do it correctly. The Scriptures speak clearly about male government, elders, apostles, prophets, evangelists, pastors, teachers and women in ministry. The apostle Paul said, "The husband is the head of the wife, as also Christ is head of the church" (Eph. 5:23).

The Church today is largely dysfunctional. It is dysfunctional because many people in today's churches are also dysfunctional. Comprehension of church government is as hard for some present-day churches as it was for the Church of old. One of the problems in the Church today is that it has been unduly influenced by the radical feminist movement. As a result, we are seeing an increase in the number of matriarchal churches.

WOMEN IN MINISTRY

When it comes to women in ministry, there are two schools of thought. Some believe that men can and should do everything and that there is no need for women in ministry. Others believe that women are equally redeemed and should not only be in ministry, but can also hold governmental positions. It seems to me that both of these positions are extremes and that both neglect the difference between biblical *government* and biblical *ministry*. Those in the extreme patriarchal position equate government and ministry as being strictly for men. Those in the extreme matriarchal position think that because a woman has ministerial gifts she should also be eligible for a governmental position.

Ministerial giftings do not equate with governmental giftings, in my understanding of the Scriptures. All believers are called to ministry, although only a small percentage will ever stand behind a pulpit. Among those who are called, not everyone is called to government. Scripture is clear about ministry and government. God's government is patriarchal. ACM believes that women can function in ministerial gifts, but should not hold a governmental position.

> **The restoration of the Church and its government is largely dependent upon the restoration of the family. This will take place only after the biblical relationships between men and women have been restored.**

ACM believes in the ordination of women. For example, more than 100 ordained women are part of the network. Many women are in full-time ministry, including many who travel outside their local churches. The difference between the women in ACM and many other women ministers is they have male covering and male support. I have observed instances when a woman thought she had *covering* when all she really had was male *permission*. She, therefore, did not have male protection or provision.

We believe that if the covering is genuine, women ministers will have the protection, provision and permission that will open the way to optimum ministry. It is our desire not only to ensure that the government of the church is restored, but also to ensure that all relationships, especially the family, are restored to the fullness of Christ. We believe the restoration of the Church and its government is largely dependent upon the restoration of the family. This will take place only after the biblical relationships between men and women have been restored.

WHERE DO WE GO FROM HERE?

Our vision for the foreseeable future is to establish a prototype of apostolic networking. One of my greatest burdens is to ensure the continuance of great revivals such as the Argentina revival and the Pensacola revival. I believe that without the biblical wineskin of God's government, this wine of revival may spill forth and dry up; but if kept in the proper wineskin, the wine will not run dry.

We are beginning to reap the harvest of revival both in the United States and abroad. To continue reaping the harvest of revival, however, we must have the best of equipped workers in the field. Many men and women have great gifting, but they are not adequately equipped to reap in fullness. My vision for Antioch Churches and Ministries is that we be a network committed to training and enlisting the highest-quality workers for the harvest.

In conclusion, I want to emphasize that the principle of apostolic ministry is not new. We have had apostles on earth throughout Church history. Apostolic networking in the United States is not new either, although I realize it is a new concept for many readers. I believe ACM to be at least a third-generation apostolic network.

The apostolic movement is no longer in the *formulation* phase; it is currently going through a *maturation* process. The key to apostolic building is through relationships and for this to happen, we must have a certain kind of people. These people must be secure enough to build and maintain relationships. They must understand that being balanced is not doing a little bit of this and a little bit of that; it is being radical about everything God's Word says. That requires a certain kind of leader, the kind of leader with whom I want to walk.

- Those who can be troopers.
- Those who can walk on the head of a serpent, preach with anointed power and go to the nations.
- Those who have the strength and empowerment to endure to the end.

I have been blessed by God since the beginning of ACM network's establishment to work with large numbers of brothers and sisters in Christ just like them.

John P. Kelly, Overseeing Apostle
Antioch Churches and Ministries
P.O. Box 92790
Southlake, TX 76092
Phone: 817-284-3693
Fax: 817-284-3825
E-mail: ACM@aol.com

3

CRUSADERS CHURCH AND INTERNATIONAL MINISTRIES OF PROPHETIC AND APOSTOLIC CHURCHES

Apostle John Eckhardt
Chicago, Illinois

Pastor and overseer of Crusaders Ministries located in Chicago, John Eckhardt is gifted with a strong apostolic call and has traveled throughout the United States and overseas to 21 nations, imparting biblical truths that include deliverance and spiritual warfare. He is dedicated to "perfecting the saints" to do the works of Jesus Christ through solid teaching, training and demonstrating. He has authored several publications and also produces a daily television program and radio broadcast in the Chicago area.

In 1988, I became the pastor of Crusaders Church of God in Christ, located on the south side of the city of Chicago. This occurred after the death of my pastor, Timothy Longley, who had founded the church in 1976. He was a great leader who had served the Lord for almost 60 years before passing away at the age of 78. I was 31 at the time and had been saved since the age of 20. I was now pastoring the church I had been a member of for 11 years.

After becoming the pastor of Crusaders Church, I began to teach a daily radio program in Chicago on the subject of deliverance. The response to this teaching was phenomenal. Our church membership quadrupled within two years. This led us to plant another church on the west side of Chicago, which also began to experience the same rate of growth. To this we added a daily television program in Chicago, which in turn caused both churches to grow even more. Our emphasis on deliverance drew multitudes of people who recognized their need for this kind of ministry. At the same time, we began to train hundreds of workers to minister to the thousands of people who came through our church doors for deliverance every year. Our emphasis became "perfecting the saints for the work of the ministry," based on Ephesians 4:12.

AWAKENING TO THE ROLE OF APOSTLES

The first year I began to think about apostolic ministry was 1989. I was privileged to take a ministry team to Nigeria, West Africa, to be a part of a conference focusing on deliverance and spiritual warfare. Another minister from the United States who attended the conference was teaching about the ministry gifts of Ephesians 4. He taught about the characteristics of each gift, and then he turned to me and began to prophesy that I had been called to be an apostle and that my ministry would not be limited to serving as a pastor. I was both shocked and challenged. I had never thought seriously in those terms.

Previously, I had limited my ministry to pastoring. Most of the little I had read about the subject of apostleship argued that apostles do not exist today. Not much serious discussion of this subject was available in the literature at that time. I therefore went to prayer and asked the Lord for the wisdom I lacked, based on His promise in James 1:5. Since then I have continued to ask the Lord for increased revelation concerning the role of apostles, and much of what I have learned has come as an answer to those prayers. I believe it is important to share some of that wisdom in this chapter.

Upon returning to Chicago from Nigeria, I submitted the prophecy I had been given to my church. I would not start calling myself an apostle based solely on one prophetic word. I therefore asked the church to pray about this prophecy and, that if it were judged to be true, to pray for me that I would begin to operate properly as an apostle. Many of the saints in our fellowship began to receive me as an apostle. I believe that having the full support of our local assembly has been one of the strengths of my ministry through the years. It has given me the confidence and boldness I have needed to launch out into apostolic ministry with full force.

I have never been inhibited by doubt, because my calling has been fully confirmed both by prophetic ministry and by the local church. I would never try to force this ministry upon a church that was unwilling to receive it. I needed the church to accept me and to release me as an apostle. I needed the congregation's ongoing prayers and support. I believe this is based on Paul's words to the Corinthian church, "If I be not an apostle unto others, yet doubtless I am to you: for the seal of mine apostleship are ye in the Lord" (1 Cor. 9:2, *KJV*).

> **The Holy Spirit was given for power to go to the uttermost parts of the earth. In other words, the anointing of the Spirit is not a local anointing, but an international anointing.**

One of the first truths the Lord taught us is that the saints could not be fully perfected without the ministry of the apostle. The five ministry gifts given for equipping the saints (see Eph. 4:11) include apostles and prophets. It takes all five of these ministry gifts operating in the church to properly mature God's people for the work of the ministry. When the apostle is absent, the saints will lack the apostolic character they need to fulfill the Great Commission.

A VISION FOR THE WORLD

Another truth the Lord taught us is that the Holy Spirit was given for power to go to the uttermost parts of the earth. In other words, the anointing of the Spirit is not a local anointing, but an international anointing. This gave us a vision for the nations, which, at that time, was somewhat unusual for an inner-city church. The inner city faces so many problems that most churches don't want to think about taking care of the problems of the rest of the world.

When I first started teaching about the 10/40 Window in our church, some people commented, "I live in the 10/40 Window!" To be apostolic implies being a pioneer, breaking new ground and leading people into new territories. To be a mission-minded church in the inner city is to be a pioneer church.

The Great Commission is an apostolic commission. It was first given to apostles, and it will take an apostolic church to fulfill it. This Commission involves more than evangelism. Nations must also be discipled. The multitudes must be healed and delivered. Churches must be planted. Elders and church government must be established. Certain truths and mysteries must be revealed. The saints must be perfected for the work of the ministry.

This is why there is a need for restoration. The Church has been experiencing restoration for centuries. God is restoring the years the locust has eaten. The harvests that were lost in previous generations will be reaped in these last years. Peter spoke of the times of restitution of all things as spoken by the prophets (see Acts 3:21). The restoration of the apostolic is a fulfillment of Bible prophecy. We are living in a time of restoration and prophetic fulfillment.

TEAMS FOR THE NATIONS

Our vision has been to enlist teams to send to the nations. This includes intercessory prayer teams, prophetic teams, praise and worship teams, deliverance teams and apostolic church-planting teams.

As Crusader Church began to grow, I noticed that many who came to us were ministers. At first I wondered what I was to do with so many people who felt called to minister. Then I began to understand that apostolic ministries tend to attract a large number of people who have ministry callings. This is because apostles have been given a special ability to establish teams and activate people into their callings and giftings.

Apostolic ministry is a ministry of great grace (see Acts 4:33); therefore, it has no lack of gifts (see 1 Cor. 1:7). This is because the apostolic anointing is a resource anointing. It takes an abundance of resources to fulfill the tasks and responsibilities given to apostles. People are our greatest resource. They will come in large numbers and bring the abilities needed to do what the Lord has assigned. It is important to train and release them to minister. They will help the apostle carry the burden of this ministry.

In 1991, the Spirit of the Lord began to put the word "reformation" in our hearts. We then sponsored a conference called REFORMATION 91. We began to understand that the apostolic Spirit is a reforming Spirit. God had throughout history enlisted apostolic men to bring reformation to the church. Reformers are also change agents. They bring necessary correction to the way the church functions. This can apply to church government as well as to the whole way of "doing church." When the church methods become outmoded, the Lord raises apostles to challenge the status quo and to update and change the church in accordance with the Scriptures. They develop new models that can be seen by others and initiated elsewhere. Apostolic churches tend to be unique because they don't copy old models, but rather they release new ones.

"God hath set some in the church, first apostles" (1 Cor. 12:28, *KJV*). The word "first" is the Greek word *proton*, meaning first in time order or rank. The apostle is first and foremost a pioneer. Apostles are the first to go into a territory or the first to present a new truth. The inner cities of the United States need pioneers. We cannot take old models to this generation and expect to reach them. Outmoded and outdated methods of ministry will not influence the inner cities of the United States.

Every generation needs apostles who bring a fresh approach to ministry. They discover and restore truths and ministries that have been hidden or been dormant within the Church. They build new models and implement new philosophies of ministry. The exciting thing is that these new models and philosophies work. They have tremendous success in spite of a measure of initial misunderstanding and opposition.

PULLING DOWN STRONGHOLDS

Another truth the Lord taught us was concerning strongholds. Paul talked about the "weapons of warfare" (see 2 Cor. 10:4). The word for "warfare" is *strateia*, which, according to *Strong's*, carries the figurative meaning of "apostolic career." The strongholds Paul is referring to are the mind-sets that prevent people of a city, nation or culture from obeying and submitting to the truth. These mind-sets can be cultural, religious or political. They are the philosophies by which people govern their lives.

Apostles are called to challenge and confront those mind-sets that are in opposition to the Word of God. They change our philosophy of ministry because the wrong philosophy of ministry can produce an inability to reach certain people. Entire generations can be unreachable by using a wrong philosophy of ministry. Wrong philosophies are strongholds that need to be pulled down. When these strongholds fall, entire cities and regions can be opened to the truth.

Warfare is therefore an integral part of our philosophy of ministry. A word related to *strateia* is *strateuomai*, which means "to serve in a military campaign"; that is, to execute the apostolate with its arduous duties and functions. The apostle is like a military commander who is able to muster sufficient numbers of soldiers to fight in a military campaign. This is done by mobilizing large numbers of people to pray against the strongholds that grip a region or territory. Teaching people to pray and training them in the ministry of deliverance are two of the ways we mobilize the army of God to pull down strongholds.

The first thing the Lord gave the Twelve when He sent them out was "power against unclean spirits" (Matt. 10:1, *KJV*). The apostolic anointing is therefore recognized in the spirit realm. A level of power—an authority that is released through apostles and apostolic churches—must be acknowledged by the demonic and angelic realm. This is important if we are to be successful. What happens in the natural realm is governed by the spirit realm. After the Seventy were sent out they rejoiced, saying, "even the devils are subject unto us through thy name" (Luke 10:17, *KJV*). The Lord said unto them, "I beheld Satan as lightning fall from heaven" (v. 18, *KJV*).

This understanding is especially necessary for significant breakthroughs in the inner cities of America, as well as in the nations of the 10/40 Window. The principalities and powers that have gripped multitudes of people for so long must be challenged by implementing this kind of power and authority. This will end the frustration of many ministers who have labored for so long with so little success. Jesus told the Twelve that He had ordained them to "bring forth fruit" (John 15:16, *KJV*). Apostolic power will release fruitfulness for churches and ministries.

THE MODEL OF ACTS

The book of Acts provides a model of what the Church is expected to do. What many fail to realize is that the dominant anointing in Acts is apostolic. If the Church wants to have the same results the Early Church experienced in growth, power and impact, we need the same kind of spirit released today. This is a key to understanding the book of Acts.

The book of Acts is an apostolic book that records the deeds of an apostolic church—a network of churches and ministries related to one another. They encouraged each other and shared in the ministry to touch the known world. Different churches were established by different apostles. They recognized apostolic authority and submitted to it. During a period of time, however, the early apostles died and the Church began to lose this apostolic dynamic.

It was never the will of God for the Church to go without the apostolic dimension. Because of tradition and unbelief, this dynamic did not continue from generation to generation. The good news is, though, that we are now living in times of restoration. We view ourselves as being a part of prophetic fulfillment. What we are doing is based upon the Word of God. It is not extrabiblical or heretical. It is something that was a part of the original plan of God and is still valid for today.

In other words, the concept of apostolic ministry has become a part of our theology. Therefore, it affects the way we live and conduct our lives and ministries. We believe an understanding of it is essential if we are to fulfill our ministries. We are living in the days of increased knowledge and communication. We call it "the age of information." This is also true concerning the Church. We are living in the day of increased spiritual knowledge. A new wisdom is being released to the Church. This wisdom is to be manifested to the "principalities and powers in heavenly places" (Eph. 3:10, *KJV*).

We must constantly rethink our philosophy of ministry. Apostles and apostolic networks help challenge our philosophies of ministry and they suggest new ones to replace them. They replace old philosophies with new ones that are given by the Lord for a new time and season. This is a process that should continue from generation to generation. New apostolic churches will always be organized, and new networks will be formed. Other ministries will be attracted to the new models that surface.

AN APOSTOLIC NETWORK

One aspect of our ministry was that pastors from the Chicago area began to come to our services. They came to build relationships as well as for fresh insights and impartation. Networks invariably form around an apostle as a variety of ministers begin to relate to the new model. For example, churches from within the Chicago area, as well as from other parts of the United States, began to recognize the apostolic call upon my life and the church. Our model of doing church then began to be reproduced in other cities and now in many nations. It is based on the principle of "perfecting the saints." The laity must be mobilized to operate the work of the ministry. Believers are trained in prayer, deliverance, healing, prophecy, church planting and a desire to reach the nations. This is done both through preaching and demonstration. People must not only *hear* it, but they must also *see* it.

Developing an apostolic network is based on what we refer to as "Cornelius Connections." This is a term we borrowed from Dr. Noel Woodroffe of the Breakthrough Network from the nation of Trinidad. It is based on the story of Cornelius being connected to Peter as a result of his praying and giving (see Acts 10).

Divine connections are important in forming and operating apostolic networks. God will sovereignly join ministries to a faithful apostle for the purpose of relationship. A network of churches and ministries will be formed that reflects the model and philosophy of ministry given to the apostle.

WHAT IS IMPAC?

IMPAC is a network of churches and ministries that has a vision to establish apostolic and prophetic ministries around the world. Our vision is to help develop young apostles and prophets in the nations of the 10/40 Window. This is accomplished by teaching about the subjects of the apostolic and prophetic ministry. This is also done by identifying emerging apostolic and prophetic ministries overseas and imparting to them what the Lord has given us.

We believe that the apostolic ministry is a ministry of impartation (see Rom. 1:11). We also believe in prophetic presbytery, especially at the time of ordination (see 1 Tim. 4:14), something that many emerging ministries have lacked. We provide the necessary encouragement and accountability for these emerging ministries.

We also believe that evangelists, pastors and teachers need to receive and operate in an apostolic and prophetic dimension. This will release

> **New things are birthed because apostles are catalysts to new moves of God. They are spiritual igniters who stir up the gifts of God.**

a greater amount of power and authority in their ministries. The apostolic will only increase and add to what a church has, not take away from it. New things are birthed because apostles are catalysts to new moves of God. They are spiritual igniters who stir up the gifts of God.

IMPAC facilitates relationships between ministers and churches that strengthen and help build up the individual ministries that are involved. This is especially true for ministries that might not be comfortable in some of the more traditional organizations, because they sense that the Lord is doing something new. They have a strong need to build relationships with people of like spirit.

Apostles reveal certain truths and establish these truths throughout a region. One of the truths the Lord gave us to preach and establish was deliverance. Being an inner-city church requires deliverance. New truths tend to be controversial, but by grace they can be preached and established. A grace is placed upon apostles to preach and defend the truth. Some would say that the truth does not need to be defended, but it does. Paul said he was "set for the defence of the gospel" (Phil. 1:17, *KJV*). Paul's gospel had to be defended against those who did not understand it. We not only preach that Christians need deliverance, but we also defend the message of deliverance.

At the time the Lord gave us the ministry of deliverance, we had no idea that the message was apostolic. The Lord gave us the grace to preach this truth in spite of opposition and misunderstanding. As a result, thousands of believers have come into a knowledge of deliverance. Many churches have also been released into this ministry.

The same is true concerning prophetic ministry. Our church has a vision to see that believers are released to prophesy. This comes through training and activation. As a result, hundreds of believers have been trained and released to prophesy. Prophetic teams have been formed in the church to minister to thousands of people regularly. Apostles are graced to present new truths such as this, and to release the saints to operate in them.

RELEASING NEW APOSTLES

We also know that networks will be birthed from within IMPAC as the Lord develops other apostolic ministries within our circles. This will prevent our network from becoming too large to adequately provide the kind of covering and personal relationships individual ministries need. Many of the ministers involved have come from larger organizations where they felt lost in the vastness of the group. Emerging apostles need to be encouraged and released to walk in the fullness of their call rather than being locked into a structure that hinders them from being everything God wants them to be. Our goal is to multiply well-functioning apostolic networks throughout the world. It is our desire to maintain fruitful relationships with these new networks, but not to control them.

PASSPORT SUNDAY

Many inner-city pastors have never traveled to the "nations," as instructed in Matthew 28:19. I believe this has been because of a lack of vision. To stir our members to go to the nations, awhile ago I encouraged every member of Crusaders Church to obtain a passport. We then had a "Passport Sunday" when all the members brought their passports to church for us to pray over. What a glorious Sunday when hundreds of believers came to church bringing their passports to receive prayer for the Lord to open the way for them to go to the nations! As a result, many of our members have taken prayer journeys to nations of the 10/40 Window and have joined teams for other mission trips.

We have a vision to take large numbers of inner-city pastors to the nations. This will help give them a biblical burden for the nations. For too long a time, inner-city churches have had an "import" mentality. They have been looking for someone to come into the inner city to

> **Apostolic leadership...develops an "export" mentality. It stresses sending rather than receiving.**

help them. Apostolic leadership, however, develops an "export" mentality. It stresses sending rather than receiving.

Because they have an abundance of resources, apostolic churches are able to "send out." We are exporting ministry to the nations. We are identifying the areas of lack and helping to supply them out of our abundance. We have a vision to impart to leaders overseas through teaching and prophetic ministry. This includes church planting and helping to organize the nationals to influence their own nations. It is a pioneering work for us because it is new to the mind-sets of many inner-city pastors and churches.

THE MODEL OF ANTIOCH

The Antioch church is a model church for us because it was a sending church (see Acts 13:1-4). Barnabas and Saul were both sent out after a period of ministering to the Lord and fasting.

They were sent not only by the Church, but also by the Holy Spirit. In other words, the Holy Spirit works through and with the Church to release ministries. This is important because ministries must be released properly. Prophets were present at Antioch who were involved in this release. I believe that thousands of new ministries will be released through apostolic churches and networks in the days to come. We are only seeing the beginning. These ministries in turn will have an ability to influence the world, just as Barnabas and Saul did.

PLANTING NEW CHURCHES

A revelation and understanding of apostolic ministry has affected the way we plant and build local churches. We believe that it takes apostolic wisdom to properly build local churches (see Prov. 24:3). We have also come to learn that the principal anointing and spirit of the Church should be apostolic. This is because the Holy Spirit is first and foremost an apostolic Spirit. He is a "sent" Spirit before He is anything

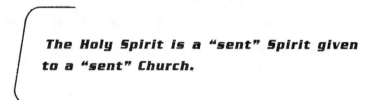

The Holy Spirit is a "sent" Spirit given to a "sent" Church.

else. The Church has also been "sent" into the world even as Jesus was sent by the Father (see John 20:21). After Jesus sent them, He breathed on them to receive the Holy Spirit. The Holy Spirit is a "sent" Spirit given to a "sent" Church.

When the Church begins to operate and minister in this "sent" dimension, it begins to have a sense of purpose and destiny. People begin to discover their individual callings and ministries. Churches begin to walk in a greater degree of purpose. The apostolic Spirit affects everything the Church does. It affects the preaching, teaching, worship, prayer and giving of the local church. It causes churches and individuals who may have felt insignificant to realize their importance in the kingdom of God.

Apostles are important because they release and stir up this dimension of the Holy Spirit within the local church. Our philosophy of ministry has been changed by this understanding. We would not attempt to build local churches without the apostles' input. Our pastors and leaders are taught the importance of impartation and are expected to draw from apostolic ministries. We do not teach that every pastor has to be an apostle, but we do believe that every minister needs an apostolic dimension. In other words, a minister cannot be fully successful without being "sent" and having a "sent" one's anointing.

WHERE ARE WE HEADED?

This understanding has also developed our focus and vision for the future of the Church. Where are we headed? I believe the Lord is restoring the apostolic dynamic to the Church. The Church will once again be an apostolic Church. This does not mean the other anointings and giftings will not operate. Every gift should operate within the local church. The apostolic provides a framework within which all of the ministries are released. The framework is large enough to contain and make room for all. Any other framework will not be large enough. Without the apostolic foundation, the Church will not have the capacity to do everything God has purposed to be done. Therefore, a rise of apostolic ministries and networks have appeared around the world. This is not surprising to us, nor are we afraid of it. It is God's present-day plan for the Church. We are simply identifying and praying for it to fully manifest.

PRAYING FOR APOSTOLIC MINISTRIES

The worldwide prayer movement has helped initiate the restoration of apostolic ministry. A strong relationship exists between prayer and the apostolic. We are told to pray to "the Lord of the harvest, that he will send forth labourers into his harvest" (Matt. 9:38, *KJV*). These "sent" ones refer to an apostolic company of believers. Jesus prayed all night before He chose the Twelve (see Luke 6:12,13). The result of prayer is a release of the apostolic Spirit. Apostolic networks and Cornelius Connections have been birthed through prayer.

CONCLUSION

Through the years, we have seen an increase in the number of ministries identifying themselves as apostolic. I believe the Lord is giving us more revelation concerning this ministry so that we will be able to operate fully in these offices. Leaders have not walked fully in these ministries in the past because they did not understand these giftings and anointings. We tend to draw back from what we don't understand. The Lord desires for us to walk boldly and confidently in the ministries with which He has graced us. I believe that many will once again walk in the fullness of these biblical offices and have a much better understanding of who they are and what they are called to do. We are learning the function and purpose of the office of the apostle. The Lord is calling us to walk fully in the power and authority of this ministry He has set in the Church.

John Eckhardt, Apostle
Crusaders Ministries
P.O. Box 7211
Chicago, IL 60680
Phone: 773-637-2121
Fax: 312-637-3357

Resource List—Books
Deliverance and Spiritual Warfare Manual
Identifying and Breaking Curses
Behemoth and Leviathan
The Ministry Anointing of the Prophet
Let Us Alone

Resources may be ordered through:
Crusaders Ministries
P.O. Box 7211
Chicago, IL 60680

4

GRACE PRESBYTERY

Pastor Michael P. Fletcher
Fayetteville, North Carolina

Senior pastor of Manna Church for 11 years, Michael founded ARC Ministries (Assisting Romanian Churches), which has, to date, planted or partnered in planting 20 churches in Romania and distributed more than $1,000,000 in humanitarian aid. He has long had a vision for revival and reconciliation, which led to founding "Unified 2000" along with pastors Al Brice and Larry Jackson. Church Network Coordinator for the A.D. 2000 United Prayer Track "Pray Through the Window III" project, he has mobilized 17,390 churches to pray for the world's 1,739 unreached people groups.

Their numbers had dwindled to only six in recent weeks. Who could accept this crazy teaching? Glenn "Dad" Ewing, a Presbyterian, believed with all his heart that the ministry gifts he read about in Ephesians 4 still operated today, although no one he knew had ever seen what they considered an apostle or a prophet. He also believed that the operation of the Church in Acts should be normative for the operation of the Church today.

Who could accept this teaching? Who had seen a miracle, heard "speaking in tongues" or received a prophecy? What was a "word of knowledge"? Still, Dad Ewing believed and taught that if they sought the present-day manifestation of the Spirit, and if they patterned their church after the New Testament, they would eventually see New Testament results.

GOD'S POWER FELL IN WACO!

Then it happened, in that little white building in Waco, Texas, in 1946. The power of God fell. People began to speak in tongues, to see visions and to receive and give prophecies. Miracles began to happen and new people began to come into the church. They came from everywhere. Most, like Dad Ewing, were from traditional settings who, for one reason or another, had become dissatisfied with their present experience of Christianity; they wanted more. Some had been awakened in the night feeling a strong impression to go to this little Texas town to receive what they were looking for in their hearts. Dad Ewing would teach them of what he called the "fivefold ministry" and the "New Testament" vision.

"Walk in purity," Dad Ewing would say. "Follow the New Testament pattern and you'll find New Testament power!"

For years people came and received the vision, and from that little place in Waco they went out to minister. They weren't sent out in the modern ecclesiastical sense of being sent out. They went out with nothing but faith and the call of God. They believed that God would provide for them and that He would open doors for ministry. They went throughout the world, planting churches and doing things that, formerly, they had only dreamed about. From day one, the movement was a strong missionary movement.

In the years to follow, literally hundreds of churches had been established, all small, all following the "New Testament pattern," but none of them linked together. Linking together would be the first step toward denominationalism, they believed, which would destroy the New Testament pattern. Most of them had been there and done it, so to speak. Instead, they would gather in convention settings, usually in Waco or in New Covenant Church in Virginia, to hear what God was doing around the world, including behind the iron curtain where the Spirit of God had miraculously been opening doors. They would hear of crusade meetings in India or Mexico where thousands had turned to Christ and where the deaf heard, the blind saw and the lame walked.

Others would hear of the New Testament vision from those who went out from Waco and began to plant churches themselves. Eventually, pools of churches formed because of the "apostolic" church-planting activity of those who would put their vision into practice. Some would gravitate to those who had apostolic anointing, seeking their counsel and covering.

Now, pools of churches tied to "Waco" roots are located across the United States and in various parts of the world. One such pool is a group we now call Grace Presbytery. It started when a group of like-minded ministers began gathering in a pastor's house for fellowship in the early 1980s, and it has continued ever since. The name, Grace Presbytery, came 10 years later.

WHY "GRACE PRESBYTERY"?

A "presbytery" is a gathering of leaders. "Grace" is our central theological emphasis. The interesting thing about our particular pool of churches is that not one of the pastors involved has ever been to Waco! We all adhere to the basic ideas put forth in those early years by Dad Ewing, however: that the New Testament pattern is for today; that Jesus, not a human being, is the head of the Church; and that the power of that day is intended for us as well. We have all been influenced strongly by the movement started in Waco.

In the past, Grace Presbytery has been resistant to structuring itself in any formal way, fearing the pitfalls of denominationalism. In recent years, however, the desire to work more effectively has led us to the conclusion that working together is better than just fellowshipping together, but working alone. Predictably, not all in our group believed that way and some chose to part company with us, preferring not to be formally united with any structured company of churches. The rest of us, though, have continued to evolve into a coalition that preserves local church autonomy, but at the same time incorporates the benefits of translocal ministry and cooperative effort. In our present form, the presbytery is only a little more than two years old.

In keeping with the influence we received from Waco, Grace Presbytery has a strong missions emphasis. Grace not only focuses on church planting in the United States, but, at the time of this writing, we are also actively engaged with missionary presence in more than 20 countries, including many in the 10/40 Window. In Romania alone, for example, we have planted or partnered in planting 21 churches and we have distributed more than 1 million dollars in humanitarian aid in the last five years. We are rapidly learning that cooperative effort can far outstrip individual initiatives.

WHAT IS OUR PRESBYTERY'S PHILOSOPHY OF MINISTRY?

Grace Presbytery is founded on four key biblical concepts:

1. Relationships are essential to the Body of Christ.
A great need exists in the Church today for church leadership to find fellowship and accountability with others of like mind. In our experience,

> *The central focus of our presbytery, the thing that holds us together, is not our allegiance to a key charismatic leader, but personal relationships.*

the relationships formed between pastors have strengthened the pastors personally, and they have also strengthened the overall ministry of the local church. The central focus of our presbytery, the thing that holds us together, is not our allegiance to a key charismatic leader, but personal relationships. We acknowledge the gift and Person of Christ in each other, applauding our differences and building on each other's strengths.

2. The kingdom of God advances best through the cooperative effort of the Church.
"One shall put to flight a thousand but two, ten-thousand." Much more is accomplished in the effort to advance the kingdom of God when pastors and local churches work together. We are more effective and efficient when we function as a team. In light of this, we abhor competition and "grandstanding." Spirituality, for us, is measured not in terms of church size, fame or the accomplishments of a single individual, but rather in terms of humility and serving the whole in furthering the cause of Christ. It isn't who you are, but *who you help others become* that makes the most difference.

3. Structure can both promote and inhibit life.
Having experienced both the limitations and blessings of structure, we have developed an environment that attempts to center not on hierarchical authority, but on relationships. The Leadership Team, which serves as a spiritual covering and helps direct the affairs of the presbytery, comprises seasoned leaders whose gifts and character have qualified them to serve the pastors and local churches in our association.

Some structure is required to work together effectively, of course, so we have endeavored to build our structure around the function of ministry in an attempt to *facilitate* ministry rather than to *hinder* it. To that end, we have created Grace Presbytery School of Ministry (GPSM) to help us equip future leaders, and Grace Missions to help us manage cooperative missions efforts domestically and abroad. The Leadership Team, GPSM and Grace Missions will be outlined in detail later.

4. The role of translocal ministry is to help each local church develop to its maximum potential.
Those in Grace Presbytery who have been called and gifted by God with translocal ministry gifts have as their goal to strengthen the local church and to make the pastor's job a delight. Central to the success of the individual churches is the local church leadership team. Translocal ministries operate as their servants.

We affirm the authority of local elders in governing the affairs of the church and also acknowledge the need of every local church to benefit from the input of the fivefold ministry as outlined in Ephesians 4:11. These apostles, prophets, evangelists, pastors and teachers exist to equip the saints so they might effectively fulfill the ministry of Christ and extend the kingdom of God. These translocal ministries are made available to every local church in the presbytery, but are never forced upon a local assembly. Again, we center not on hierarchical authority, but on relationships.

GRACE PRESBYTERY'S WORLD OUTREACH

Our mission is to spread a passion for God and to advance His kingdom by planting churches, developing leaders and helping churches grow. Every association of churches within the presbytery has a similar goal as a basis of its mission. In the process of carrying out our mission, we mostly discover the true distinctives of Grace Presbytery. We base our approach to advancing God's kingdom on five operative principles. We attempt to accomplish our mission by doing the following:

1. Fathering churches through translocal input from seasoned ministries.

The Body of Christ grows as each member does its part. God has set some individuals apart as "gifts" to the Body. They aren't gifts because they are better than others, but because their sole existence is to serve the Bride of Christ in the way God has equipped them. These gifts are clearly listed as such in Ephesians 4:7-12.

As these gifted people become more seasoned through experience in ministry, their input is of increasing value to the local churches they

> *By the time people in this apprenticeship setting finish the course of study, they haven't just learned about ministry, they have done it.*

serve. They are then able to act as a "father" to the local churches and to the younger ministers who are developing. This sense of heritage and wisdom creates an atmosphere in which emerging ministries can come forth and new churches can grow without fear.

"We are not alone. Someone has been here before who can help us through this situation."

2. Fostering leadership through practical and academic training in a formal setting (Grace Presbytery School of Ministry) and discipleship in the local church.

Whereas a number of pastors in our presbytery have received formal education in a traditional setting, and we affirm the role for traditional education in many circumstances, we also believe that the primary setting to receive training for ministry is in the local church. Combining academic preparation with the local church setting, we have created Grace Presbytery School of Ministry. GPSM is a combination of practical and academic training opportunities designed to equip believers, and those called to full-time ministry, for service.

We believe that character takes precedent over anointing in training a person, so we view discipleship in the context of the local church as essential to preparation for ministry. A person receives the influence of the local church leadership while serving alongside them and functioning in real ministry. By the time people in this apprenticeship setting finish the course of study, they haven't just *learned* about ministry, they have *done* it. We have many key leaders serving in all parts of the world who were trained in just this fashion. Some have gone on to engage in further training at a graduate level as their personal inclinations and callings have dictated.

3. Facilitating new church planting through cooperative efforts.
For years, our churches engaged in ministry projects around the world all by themselves. Each one of us did as we believed the Lord was calling us. At that time, we did have a missionary presence in many more places in the world than we do now.

We discovered, however, that each of us was struggling much too much to really be as influential as we desired. We had violated a major principle of war—"concentration of force." We were sending missionaries to foreign fields by the ones and twos, hoping they would conquer the world. Most of the time we planted churches here in the United States by sending one or two families to a location and letting them struggle on until they made it. We do have some wonderful churches in our presbytery that were started in just this manner. Our pastors would now agree, though, that this is far from the optimal method. As a result, today we are targeting specifically selected cities for what we call "cooperative church planting," and we are working on the foreign field using teams of people in fewer places, but having greater total effect.

Within the presbytery, certain bands of churches come together to pray for, and ultimately reach, unreached people groups according to our various burdens. Prayer journeys and mission projects are being undertaken by these bands of churches as they follow the collective leading of the Holy Spirit.

4. Furthering the kingdom of God in our cities and geographic regions through cross-denominational city-reaching efforts.
God loves cities because God loves people. The heaviest concentration

of people is in the cities. We believe that it will take the entire Body of Christ in a given city to reach that city for God. Each local church, regardless of its theological orientation, is a unique expression of Christ and, as such, plays an important role in reflecting God's will for that locality. The churches in Grace Presbytery are committed to working across racial and denominational lines along with other life-giving churches to reach the cities where they are located. Because united prayer provides the foundation for all city-reaching efforts, we seek to build coalitions of pastoral prayer in all the cities where our local churches minister.

5. Finishing the Great Commission through mission sending (Grace Presbytery Missions).

We believe that a New Testament church is a missions church. Although we applaud the efforts of the multitude of missions agencies that exist worldwide, we believe that the local church should be the basic building block of world missions. Our churches work with agencies and send missionaries to work with them, but our main emphasis

> *Every local church is called to participate in the mandate of Acts 1:8 to reach its city (Jerusalem) through evangelism, its geographic region (Judea and Samaria) through church planting, and the world (uttermost parts of the earth) through mission sending.*

is to train, fund and send missionaries ourselves. Even when we send a missionary through an agency, we maintain a close local church contact with that person.

We observe local churches in the New Testament working very closely with apostolic bands who were sent throughout the known world. Missionaries are seen as extensions of our local churches into the fields of the world. Every local church is called to participate in the mandate of Acts 1:8 to reach its city (Jerusalem) through evange-

lism, its geographic region (Judea and Samaria) through church planting, and the world (uttermost parts of the earth) through mission
sending. Grace Missions was created to equip missions committees to
function more intelligently, local churches to send more efficiently and
missionaries to work more effectively. In addition to these activities,
Grace Missions sponsors several short-term mission opportunities
each year for young people and adults.

LEADERSHIP

Grace Presbytery is led by a Leadership Team that comprises men who
have fivefold callings and exhibit proven translocal anointing. They
have wisdom and insight for more than the local church they pastor or
the ministry they lead. Others have recognized this grace and have
reached for these men to help in their local situations. Their anointing
and grace have been recognized by a consensus of the leaders who are
part of the presbytery and is generally confirmed through prophetic
ministry. It is clear to all that these men are called by God to this particular place of service.

Each year at our annual conference, the composition of the
Leadership Team is reviewed. Some members of the team may continue another year. Some may step down. Others may be replaced. A person's position on the Leadership Team is not a place of *prestige*, but
rather a place of *service* to the presbytery as a whole. Humility would
dictate that a person make room for other ministries as needed, to help
the whole function more effectively. Team members are replaced by
the appointment of a new member by the remaining members of the
Leadership Team and confirmed by the consensus of the presbytery. A
Leadership Team member who has stepped down or has been replaced
may be asked to serve at a later date as the need arises and as determined by the presbytery.

The Leadership Team has "direct" authority over the functions of
the presbytery (Grace Missions, GPSM, Grace Presbytery employees,
Regional Leadership Teams) and it has "relational" authority over
churches. Because the boards that govern Grace Missions and GPSM
are appointed, and their directors are hired by the Leadership Team,
the Leadership Team has a direct line of authority over them. At this
level, they have the power to hire and fire.

In reference to the local churches, however, the Leadership Team has only "relational" authority. As I have said, Grace Presbytery is built along relational, not hierarchical, lines. Churches receive ministry from the members of the Leadership Team through the personal relationships they form with each other. In this way, the churches themselves empower outside ministries to speak to their local churches. We affirm that the highest earthly authority in a local church is the eldership and the local pastor who are responsible to be in accountable relationships with outside ministries. The ministries to whom they are accountable do not necessarily have to be represented on the Leadership Team. The point is not to control or dominate a church, but to make sure it gets all the outside help it thinks it needs.

Local churches, led by men who are not on the Leadership Team, are encouraged to send out church-planting teams and then be faithful to oversee those new churches. Although these pastors may not be on the Leadership Team, they do serve in an apostolic relationship to the churches they plant and they function as their relational oversight. The function of the Leadership Team is to ensure that every local church in the presbytery enjoys the benefit of biblical fivefold relationships in one way or another.

IDENTIFYING AND TRAINING NEW LEADERS

Because the local church is the training ground for leadership, it is the responsibility of the pastor and elders to identify and disciple the next generation of leaders. The beauty of being in relationship with translocal ministry is that the processes of identification and discipleship are thereby enhanced.

For example, a prophet ministering in a local church may help the local leadership identify those called by God into specific ministries in that church. From time to time, a local pastor may send a budding leader to travel or work with a translocal ministry whose calling is seen as compatible with the church's philosophy of ministry. A young evangelist, for instance, may serve on a team with a seasoned evangelist for a period of time before striking out on his own.

Grace Presbytery School of Ministry comprises three schools, each designed to meet specific needs.

1. The School of Biblical Studies is the arm of GPSM that seeks to equip students with a solid biblical foundation along two tracks. The Certificate Track is an audit-level course of study designed to strengthen believers at a pace and depth determined by the student's own personal motivation. The Diploma Track seeks to provide the student with an undergraduate-level biblical education. Courses include: Teachings of Jesus, Systematic Theology I-IV, Old Testament History, Intertestamental History, New Testament History, Church History, and Principles of Biblical Interpretation.

2. The School of Worship is the arm of GPSM that seeks to strengthen the worship experience of the local church to the end that the presence of God may more fully influence the life and ministry of the whole church. Courses include: Worship Models for Generation X, Tapping Into Today's Tech, Tightening the Team, and Authoring Spiritual Songs.

3. The School of Leadership is the arm of GPSM that seeks to equip believers for effective leadership in the local church in 12 key areas, as indicated by the titles of the course offerings. Courses include: Releasing the Power of Mentoring, Releasing the Shepherd's Heart, Releasing Healthy Marriages, Releasing the Wisdom Gift, Releasing Unity into a City, Releasing a Passion for Souls, Releasing Mission in the Local Church, Releasing Growth in the Local Church, Releasing Small Group Leadership, Releasing a World Perspective, Releasing Intercessory Ministry, and Releasing Ministry to Children.

Whenever possible, GPSM seeks to bring in instructors who have authored the text we have chosen or who are recognized as national leaders in the particular subject matter covered in the course. In this way, we seek to expose those training for leadership to a cross section of the Body of Christ. GPSM is linked to Reformed Theological Seminary in that courses taken through GPSM can be transferred to the seminary for credit.

The exact criteria for ordination to full-time ministry is established by each local church in consultation with those with whom they have established an oversight relationship. Grace Presbytery does not *guarantee* anyone a place of ministry. Instead, we believe a person's gifts will provide the right qualifications and God will open the doors of opportunity.

FINANCING GRACE PRESBYTERY

Grace Presbytery operates as a 501(c)(3) corporation that serves to cover the various ministries and churches of the presbytery. Presbytery churches contribute 4 percent of their annual budget (less designated offerings) monthly to fund the operation of the presbytery ministries and offices. All moneys are sent to the Grace Presbytery Executive Assistant, who then distributes funds to the ministries according to the yearly budgetary allotment as determined by the Leadership Team.

Each year presbytery churches receive, and send to the presbytery office, a special offering for domestic and world missions during "Missions Month." These funds are not used for the monthly operating expenses of Grace Missions. Rather, they are designated for projects approved by the Grace Foreign and Domestic Missions Boards. The boards comprise pastors and mission-minded individuals from presbytery churches and are responsible, in conjunction with the Missions Director, for coordinating our corporate domestic and world thrusts.

HOW CAN NEW CHURCHES JOIN GRACE PRESBYTERY?

Because one of our core values is in reference to relationships being central to Kingdom advancement, we steadfastly avoid recruiting churches for the sake of swelling numbers. Instead, we require all churches desiring to join our presbytery to go through a "courtship period," during which time we encourage each individual church to develop relationships with members of the Leadership Team. To initiate the process, a local church may contact the office of the executive assistant for an application. Churches planted by existing presbytery churches are automatically considered to be part of our association. The 4 percent financial participation of local churches is phased in during the first year as a presbytery church.

Grace Presbytery
200 Sage Road
Chapel Hill, NC 27514
Phone: 1-800-556-1325
Fax: 919-968-0835
E-mail: admin@gracepresbytery.org
Web site:
http://www.gracepresbytery.org

Grace Presbytery Missions
5117 Cliffdale Road
Fayetteville, NC 28314
Phone: 910-867-9396
Fax: 910-864-8998
E-mail: missions@gracepresbytery.org

Grace Presbytery School of Ministry
200 Sage Road
Chapel Hill, NC 27514
Phone: 919-969-GPSM (4776)
Fax: 919-968-0835
E-mail: gpsm@gracepresbytery.org

5

WILLOW CREEK COMMUNITY CHURCH AND THE WILLOW CREEK ASSOCIATION

Pastor Bill Hybels
South Barrington, Illinois

Bill Hybels is the senior pastor of Willow Creek Community Church in South Barrington, Illinois, which he launched in 1975 with a vision of building a church that would reach unreached people. Today, Willow Creek is one of North America's largest churches, with weekend attendance of 16,000. Bill has authored a number of books, including *Rediscovering Church, Becoming a Contagious Christian, Fit to be Tied* and the recently released *The God You're Looking For*. Bill serves on the board of World Vision, and is the chairman of the Willow Creek Association, a growing network of 3,000 outreach-oriented churches from many different denominations and nations around the world.

The church is the hope of the world, and its renewal rests in the hands of its leaders.

I believe that statement to the core of my being. It has two parts, and they sum up the whole of what I have devoted my life to. Because I am thoroughly convinced that "the church is the hope of the world," I have given my last 23 years to building, growing and leading Willow Creek Community Church. After two-decades-plus of ministry, I can say with confidence that *the church is where the action is.* Nothing is more captivating, nothing more strategic, nothing more lasting and nothing more rewarding than investing your best in creativity, energy, hours and effort in the work of the local church.

Then consider the second half of the statement, "and its renewal rests in the hands of its leaders." God, in His wisdom and for His purposes, has chosen to direct the Church through those He has gifted and called to be its leaders. As the leaders go, so the church goes. That is why I am so committed to becoming the best leader I can possibly be and to enlisting, training and empowering more and more leaders at our church. It is also why, especially in the last five years, I have been pouring my energy into envisioning and encouraging church leaders around the country and around the world through the conferences and activities of the Willow Creek Association.

CHURCH USED TO BE A FAMILY OBLIGATION

I didn't always feel so positively about the church. Growing up, church attendance was something I did partly out of obligation, partly out of habit and partly because it seemed like the right thing to do. Whenever the church was open, our family went there. It wasn't really something I thought about much. To me, it certainly wasn't where the action was!

Besides, I had my eyes on other things. I had been groomed to run our family's produce business in Michigan, and I looked forward to enjoying all the toys and perks that would come with it. I loved on-the-edge adventure, and I got my fill of it through sailing, power boating, motorcycle racing, flying airplanes, parachuting out of airplanes and traveling around the world. Wherever there was a risk to be taken or a new experience to be enjoyed, there I would be, ready and willing to give it a try.

FIVE DEFINING MOMENTS

About the time I thought I had my future decided, I experienced a series of *five* defining moments that would change everything. The *first* was when, at age 17, I went to a Bible camp in Wisconsin and, for the first time in my life, really understood the message of the gospel. Prior to that time, I had been on the performance plan of trying to be good enough to somehow live up to God's standard—at least at a baseline level.

During that week at camp, however, Titus 3:5 hit me squarely between the eyes: "He saved us, not because of righteous things we had done, but because of his mercy" *(NIV)*. That simple message came crashing in on me as I realized simultaneously how far short my own efforts fell and how amazing God's grace really is! Thus, I gave my life to Christ at that camp, asking Him to forgive my sins and to lead my life.

The *second* defining moment came when, soon after committing my life to Christ, a man I respected deeply asked me a question I wouldn't be able to shake: "Bill, what are you doing with your life that will last for eternity?"

I'm busy doing all kinds of things, and a lot of them seem pretty important, I thought, *but put against the backdrop of eternity they seem awfully insignificant.*

That self-revelation started me down a track that helped me reevaluate everything in which I had been investing myself. Before long, it led me to the point where, at age 20, I got on my knees and told God I wanted to give the rest of my life to building things that really last. In almost no time, I sensed Him leading me to leave the family business and to move to Chicago.

CREATIVE APPROACHES
FOR UNCHURCHED PEOPLE

The *third* defining moment was when, soon after arriving in the Chicago area, God opened a door for me to help lead a youth ministry at South Park Church in Park Ridge, Illinois. There, in partnership with Dave Holmbo, the music director, we built the ministry that came to be known as Son City. During that era, I began to learn about reaching unchurched people through creative approaches to outreach, including the use of contemporary music, drama, multimedia and relevant, biblical teaching—many of the core elements Willow Creek is known for today. In spite of our lack of experience and expertise, God blessed those efforts as hundreds of students came to Christ and grew in their faith.

The *fourth* defining moment came during this same time, while I was attending school at Trinity College in Deerfield, Illinois. It was in one of my Bible classes where a middle-aged Bible professor named Gilbert Bilezikian was teaching us, often extemporaneously, about his favorite subject—the Church.

Dr. Bilezikian would stand in front of the lectern and look wistfully into the air as he poured out his heart about what he called the "Community of Oneness." He would also explain that this had been in the mind of God from eternity past and could be a reality today except that it was obscured by formalism in most churches. He would read from Acts 2:42-46, telling us about how radically devoted the people were to God and to each other, and about how relentless they were in their pursuit of people outside the community. He would tell us about how they were free with their worship, active with their servanthood, transformational with their teaching, expectant with their prayers and outrageous with their generosity.

> **We didn't want to play church; we really wanted to be the church to each other.**

"Dr. B," as we came to know him, raised my vision for how churches could be biblically functioning communities, and built into me a discontent for anything less. By God's grace, Dr. B became my friend and my mentor as well as one of my most important partners in ministry, even to this day.

I encountered my *fifth* defining moment after several years of putting into action at Son City what I was learning from Scripture and from Dr. B. I sensed that God was leading me to leave that student ministry and to start a church, applying the principles I had been learning to reaching and teaching adults and whole families. So in 1975, a small band of young ministry pioneers and I started a church in the Willow Creek Theater in Palatine, Illinois. That is where we got our name—Willow Creek Community Church.

LET'S NOT PLAY CHURCH, LET'S BE THE CHURCH

We set out having a vision of becoming a biblically functioning community—a modern-day Acts 2 church—the kind Dr. B had been challenging us to become. We didn't want to *play* church; we really wanted to *be* the church to each other. We also knew we couldn't keep community to ourselves; we needed to extend community to those out-side God's family. We believed deeply that lost people mattered to God and therefore they mattered to us, too. So we adopted a mission state-ment that was based on the Great Commission: We wanted to "reach irreligious people and turn them into fully devoted followers of Christ."

UNCHURCHED HARRY AND MARY

Then and today, the central thrust of Willow Creek has been to intro-duce wayward, unchurched people to Jesus Christ, and then to nur-ture them in the faith. How did we go about this? Through a *seven-step process* designed to walk irreligious men and women—whom we per-sonified as "Unchurched Harry and Mary"—all the way from spiritu-al indifference to radical commitment to Christ.

It is hard to describe how strongly we felt about the importance of finding ways to reach those outside the family. We would look at all the houses in the neighborhoods around our fledgling church and realize that many of the people living in them cared little about God or His desire for their lives. We knew that on Sunday mornings they weren't gathering their families to go to church—they were sipping their cups of

> **The kingdom of God advances one life at a time.**

coffee or cans of beer, reading their *Chicago Tribune* and wondering how the Bulls or the Bears would do in the game that day. They didn't watch Christian TV or radio; they didn't read Christian books or hang out with any Christians at work. They lived in a nation filled with churches, Christian media, Christian schools and Christian books and music; yet they were effectively insulated from any direct Christian influence.

These were people who were seemingly within our reach and yet who were, according to the Bible, headed for a Christless eternity. That thought was almost too much to bear. We knew from Scripture that it was almost too much for God to bear, too. He had gone to the greatest of lengths in sending His Son to die for these people, so we knew we had to prioritize them in our lives and in our church—to pray bold prayers, take big risks and try new approaches in an all-out effort somehow to reach them.

As we thought about all this, it was tempting to think of solutions in terms of big events, huge campaigns and high-visibility efforts. We wanted to "take our community for Christ" as much as the next church, and to do it as quickly as possible. We also remembered something we had learned during our Son City days: *The kingdom of God advances one life at a time.*

Large events certainly have their place, but they have maximum effect only when used as supplements to personal efforts. So the first step in our strategy, both then and today, was to challenge and equip our people to follow the example of Jesus and others in the Bible by moving outside their "holy huddles" to build relationships with unchurched people.

BEING A FRIEND TO SINNERS

I know it doesn't sound dramatic, and it isn't very glamorous, and you had better believe it won't be understood by a lot of fellow believers. I am convinced, though, that reaching irreligious people in a culture like ours requires a personal approach. Like Jesus, we need to become a "friend to sinners" and be like the doctor Jesus described who brought the medicine to the people who needed the cure.

Like Paul, we need to "become all things to all men" (1 Cor. 9:22) for the sake of the gospel, getting up close to relate to the men and women we hope to reach. That is the *first step* of our strategy, and it is the prerequisite to the *second*, which is to share a verbal witness with those friends concerning what Christ has done for us and can do for them. We knew that we as Christians first had to build a bridge of trust by establishing a genuine relationship, but we also knew we couldn't stop there.

Paul asks in Romans 10:14 (*NIV*), "How, then, can they call on the one they have not believed in? And how can they believe in the one of whom they have not heard? And how can they hear without someone preaching to them?" It is not enough to just live our faith; we have to articulate the content of our faith in ways other people can understand and to which they can respond.

So from the beginning of Willow Creek, I have done everything I can to encourage and train our core of believers in how they can enter into a relational context with people outside God's family and then put into words, concisely and clearly, the message of the Christian faith. I have done that through preaching various outreach-oriented series at our midweek worship services. We have done it through various classes and seminars, and I have tried to model this value in ways that set the pace for our congregation.

For example, I tell them about my crew with whom I race sailboats each year during the summer. When I first assembled that crew, not one of them was a believer—and that is a huge understatement! During the last few years, however, several of them have made commitments to Christ and had their lives radically transformed by Him. As our congregation hears about this, and as they have seen me baptize some of these friends in our pond, their hunger for that kind of activity just becomes stronger and stronger. They think, *What can I do to start seeing some of that action in my life?* To which we say: We're glad you asked!

BECOMING A CONTAGIOUS CHRISTIAN

That question prompted me to become partners several years ago with two of our evangelistically gifted leaders at Willow Creek, Mark Mittelberg and Lee Strobel. The purpose of our partnership was to develop a training curriculum called *Becoming a Contagious Christian Evangelism Course*, which we teach repeatedly at our church. We make it a basic expectation that every member will study it in its entirety, and some do so many times. As a result, we have been able to equip thousands of our people to communicate their faith in a style that fits them, and God is using them in countless ways to draw people to Himself.

GIVING SEEKERS PRIME TIME

That being said, it is important to add that I think it is a mistake to put all our eggs in the basket of relational evangelism and just send out our people to do the work in isolation. We need to find ways to be partners with them, and to give them ongoing encouragement and support. We do this in many ways, but primarily through the *third step* in our strategy: by providing a place every week where our people can bring their spiritually seeking friends.

I am talking about what has come to be known as our "seeker services," which present basic Christianity—at a 101 level—in ways that will be clear and relevant to any of the friends our people are able to bring. We conduct these seeker services Sunday mornings because we have found that most secular people who are willing to visit a church tend to come on a Sunday. So we decided at the inception of Willow Creek to prioritize Harry and Mary by giving them this prime time of Sunday mornings (we later added identical services on Saturday nights), and to be willing to inconvenience ourselves by meeting during the middle of the week for our believer-oriented worship services.

WEEKEND SEEKER SERVICES

What do these weekend seeker services look like?

- They are contemporary, using up-to-date Christian music to reach contemporary people.
- They are visual, using true-to-life drama and cutting-edge multimedia to reach TV-oriented generations.
- They are planned with as much creativity and excellence as we can muster, to reach people who are used to high standards in the secular marketplace.
- They are relevant, using present-day illustrations and applications, showing people that Christianity is for them, both today and tomorrow.
- They are biblical, teaching without apology the whole counsel of God, including the "hard" areas such as heaven and hell, the judgment day, the message of the cross and the fact that Jesus is the only way to the Father.

I might add that our seeker services have received more attention than anything else we do. The reactions from church leaders have varied widely, from wholesale rejection of something they might not really understand to wholesale adoption of something that may not really fit them. My advice? Carefully study what God has led us to do; come to our Church Leadership Conferences and see for yourself how we are applying biblical approaches to evangelism and how God is using those efforts to reach people. Then let Him lead you concerning how to apply transferable principles in ways that fit you and your leadership, your church and your surrounding community.

The *first three steps* form our *main evangelism strategy* and, as you can see, it is a team effort. Our believers form relationships of integrity with the friends they hope to reach, then they present a consistent verbal witness to them, and next they let us be partners with them as a whole church when they bring them to our weekend services. Usually at this point, after friends have been attending services for several months—taking in biblical teaching, asking questions and "counting the cost" of following Christ—they finally take the step of crossing the line of faith. Sometimes this happens at a service, but often it is with the friend who has been helping them along their spiritual journey.

MIDWEEK: THE "NEW COMMUNITY"

At that point *step four* is critically important: participation in our midweek worship service. We call this "New Community," and here our believers deepen their understanding of the Bible through expository teaching, expand their hearts through corporate worship and compound their gratitude through regular communion observances. These services are sometimes highly celebratory, other times intensely contemplative. They are all designed, however, to help us grow in our understanding and appreciation of God as we gather to worship Him, to learn from His Word and to be together as the Body of Christ.

GROWING BELIEVERS IN SMALL GROUPS

Step five is to join a small group. This is where the big church becomes small. Once a church grows beyond about 50 people, you can't hear each other's stories anymore, or track each other's progress or evaluate or encourage or hold each other accountable. That is why we have been committed from the very beginning to build small groups so that all participants in the life of Willow Creek can be relationally connected in a particular group that will help them grow, learn and flourish in the Body of Christ.

Although this is step five, it is really the backdrop to all other aspects of ministry as we increasingly move from being a church *with* small groups to a church *of* small groups. This is especially true during the last five years as we have adopted a modified version of Carl George's metamodel to our approach to building small groups. What that means is we are now set up with a system for developing our leaders with appropriately limited spans of care and with a formula for birthing new groups out of groups that grow beyond a certain size.

We also have a wide variety of groups, including evangelistic groups designed for spiritual seekers, serving groups for teams that minister together, study groups for deepening biblical understanding, accountability groups for maintaining spiritual progress, and the list goes on. These also include small groups of children, students, singles, seniors, men, women and couples.

MINISTRY THROUGH SPIRITUAL GIFTS

Step six is performing ministry according to spiritual giftedness. I am convinced that people don't just want to come to services, be part of small groups and observe what is going on in the ministries of the church. Deep inside, all Christians have longings to move out of the spectator stands and onto the playing field. They want to be part of the bigger team. They want to have a personal piece of the action. They want to invest their time and energy in something that really will make a difference—one that will last for eternity.

The only problem is that most Christians don't know how to get started serving in ways that will maximize their unique potential. That is why we teach regularly at our New Community services about the topic of spiritual gifts, and it is why we developed and repeatedly teach the *Network* serving seminar curriculum. We want to help all Christians unlock their unique combination of spiritual giftedness, ministry passion and personal style, and then match them with a ministry that will utilize and benefit from their contribution.

From my experience, churches often start with the task and then try to "get a person to fill it." This does not lead to effective ministry, fulfilled servers or longevity in the position. When we start with the people, however, determining who God made them to be and helping them become connected to a ministry that needs them, *watch out!*

They will set new performance standards, gain great satisfaction and stay in their serving post even when people try to move them!

Before I go to the next step, let me tell you that it is the thousands of sold-out, fired-up volunteers who make Willow Creek work. We have nearly 100 ministries in the church, and every one of them is dependent on "unpaid staff" to make them run. Not surprisingly, our heroic volunteers usually make the strongest impression on visitors to our church.

BECOMING KINGDOM BUILDERS

The *seventh and last step* is another one we teach and emphasize to people as they move along the seven-step process, but it doesn't tend to take root as a priority and life habit until later in the believer's development. I am talking about biblical stewardship, which is much more than just giving of one's finances; it is being completely com-

> **The characteristics we look for in a participating member are reflective of the elements of the seven-step process.... We call them the five Gs: Grace, growth, group, gifts and good stewardship.**

mitted, at a heart level, to building the church both locally and internationally, through our extensive missions efforts. *That* results in people giving generously of their resources, as well as their time, energy, creativity and passion. We call that kind of person a Kingdom Builder.

At this point, the person has moved all the way from being an unchurched Harry or Mary, to a friend of a Christian, to a spiritual seeker, to a weekend attender, to a new believer, to a midweek worshiper, to a small group learner, to a gift-based server, to a heart-driven builder, and now it is natural that he or she would become a participating member of the church that has helped throughout the whole journey. The characteristics we look for in a participating member are reflective of the elements of the seven-step process we have just described. We call them the five Gs:

Grace
The individual appropriation of the saving work of Christ (Eph. 2:8,9).

Growth
The ongoing evidence of a changing life and pursuit of Christlikeness (2 Pet. 3:18).

Group
Participation in the Body of Christ and connection with others in significant relationships (Acts 2:46).

Gifts
Serving Christ's Body according to spiritual giftedness and passion (Rom. 12:6-8).

Good Stewardship
Honoring God with one's material resources and supporting the church using the biblical precedent of the tithe as a goal to reach or exceed as God prospers (Phil. 4:11-19).

WILLOW CREEK COMMUNITY CHURCH

As people exhibit these five characteristics, we encourage them to now go and reinvest in yet more people outside the family—unchurched Larry and Sherry. They are to start the whole process again from step one, build an authentic relationship, then step two, share a verbal witness and so on. That is our philosophy of ministry, and I teach it again and again in a variety of ways and forums, especially at our annual January "Vision Night" at New Community. By God's grace, it is the approach He has used to grow Willow Creek in the last 23 years from a handful of inexperienced but enthusiastic high school students to our current attendance of 16,000 people each weekend, 6,000 at New Community, 11,000 in small groups and 5,500 in identifiable positions of service.

To answer a few other common questions about the church, we are interdenominational, both attenders and staff coming from many religious and nonreligious backgrounds. Our staff, which consists of more than 300 full- and part-time workers, is organized along the lines of the metamodel, having limited spans of care for each supervisor. At the top of the organization is our management team of 11, who lead the staff and manage the day-to-day operations. Supervising them is an elder board, which gives watch care to the entire church, handles spiritual concerns and questions, as well as church discipline, and prays for those who are sick or in need.

Finally, a board of directors oversees the business and financial aspects of the church and manages its properties. Financially, we are willing to invest in ministry, staff and buildings as it seems strategic, though we are very tight with budgetary discipline, and generally raise most of the funds needed before a project is completed. This has enabled us to stay largely unencumbered by debt during most of the church's history.

As the senior pastor, I sit on the management team, the elder board and the board of directors. Although I have a definite influence on the decisions of these governing bodies, I have only one vote, and often temper or change my views based on influence of a plurality of leadership in each of these groups.

We are evangelical and conservative in our theology, yet we are progressive in our methods, as we take risks and try new approaches to reach unchurched people in a secular society.

THE WILLOW CREEK ASSOCIATION

About five years ago we created the Willow Creek Association, initially as a reactionary move. The church had been gaining increasing attention from the national media, and this was resulting in growing interest from church leaders in every corner of the globe.

Many would call and say, "If I could just have five minutes of your time, I'd like to ask you what you all are doing in the area of..."

Forty-five minutes later our staff member finally would finish the conversation, and then have to follow up on requests for printed pieces about our subministries, our philosophy of outreach, our doctrinal positions and so on. It was a good problem to have, but a problem just the same. We started a "Church Relations Department," but when that grew to four full-time staff members, all dedicated to answering increasing numbers of questions from other ministries, we knew we had to find a new approach.

In 1992, we started the Willow Creek Association (WCA) as a separate, self-funding organization, dedicated to serving the needs and requests of like-minded churches around the world. The undersized but dedicated staff immediately began to operate and promote our Church Leadership Conferences, publish our growing line of printed and recorded resource materials and try to serve the needs of our expanding base of member churches.

RELATIONSHIPS WITH LEADING-EDGE PASTORS

Today, just five years later, under the direction of Jim Mellado and his leadership team of 6 and staff of 40, the Willow Creek Association has developed a solid plan to "help churches turn irreligious people into fully devoted followers of Christ." In effect, they are helping churches discover transferable, biblical principles that are working at Willow Creek and applying them in ways that are relevant and appropriate within their own unique culture. The WCA's strategy is to establish and strengthen relationships with leading-edge pastors and church leaders who will pioneer and pave the way for the other churches in their own denominations and localities, who will, in turn, inspire still more churches.

As of this writing, the WCA has grown to a movement of more than 3,000 member churches from more than 70 denominations and 24 countries, and for the last two years it has been expanding at an average of nearly 3 churches a day. We now have a domestic staff of about 40, as well as affiliate WCA organizations in 5 countries: England, Germany, The Netherlands, New Zealand and Australia, and teams of leaders in several other countries are getting ready to sign on.

The WCA and its affiliates host a dozen or more major conferences around the world each year, including two Church Leadership Conferences, the Student Impact Leadership Conference and *The Leadership Summit*, which are held on the campus of Willow Creek. We are also planning new conferences about children's ministry, evangelism, small groups and the arts. Most of them are now running at capacity, and it seems apparent that God is very active in anointing and using these events to encourage, inspire and equip church leaders around the world.

The following is an example of the kind of feedback we receive from attenders that motivates us to continue providing these events:

> We keep on sending leaders to Church Leadership Conferences and *Leadership Summits* and Student Impact Leadership Conferences. And our people keep returning, having had their lives indelibly marked by God's call and His confirmation. It's not a better way to organize and grow churches. It's a movement of God that is traveling around our nation and world.— *Bill Elder, Over the Mountain Community Church, Birmingham, Alabama*

WILLOW CREEK RESOURCES

The WCA also publishes a wide variety of Willow Creek Resources®, including books, drama scripts, sheet music and recordings, videos and curricula, and it has a growing vision for providing the wider church with more and more relevant, proven resources for doing high-impact ministry. In addition, the WCA has a growing portfolio of member benefits and a web site (www.willowcreek.org), where more than 10,000 pages of Willow Creek's weekend service elements, complete back to 1990, have been organized by more than 150 topics (message transcripts, drama sketches, multimedias, music, etc.). Many of these resources are available for downloading.

TANGIBLE RESULTS FOR THE KINGDOM

The result of all these efforts through the WCA? Growing numbers of leaders and churches that are taking risks to reach and disciple unchurched people. We hear accounts daily of how God is working, how people are coming to Christ and how churches are growing. It is also my fervent prayer that at least some of what the Willow Creek Association is doing, both here and abroad, will encourage and inspire you in your efforts to build a prevailing church that will expand the Kingdom in your own corner of the world.

Bill Hybels
Willow Creek Community Church
P.O. Box 3188
Barrington, IL 60011-3188
    OR
67 East Algonquin Road
South Barrington, IL 60010-6143
Phone: 847-765-5000
Fax: 847-765-5046
Web site: http//www.willowcreek.org

• for more information on Willow Creek
Resources, please see page 285

6
THE FELLOWSHIP OF INTERNATIONAL CHURCHES

Bishop Wellington Boone
Duluth, Georgia

Wellington Boone is a best-selling author, pastor, ministry leader and Promise Keepers speaker. His special mission is mobilizing people to pray for a spiritual revival in the inner cities of the United States. Ministries founded by Bishop Boone include the Fellowship of International Churches, New Generation Campus Ministries, Athletes for Jesus, Network of Christian Women and Network of Politically Active Christian Women. He is also a board member of March for Jesus, Evangelical Council of Financial Accountability (ECFA) and Gospel to the Unreached Millions. He currently pastors the First International Church of Atlanta.

I don't know if you have ever had a great family reunion with your very favorite people where everybody was just hanging out and loving one another and eating and playing all day until it was time to fall into bed at night. That is what we have in the Fellowship of International Churches (FOIC).

Some of us had been together for almost 20 years, but by late 1993, we thought it was time to show that we were in fellowship with one another, that we wanted to reach the nations and have people of all nationalities come to our churches, and that we have the vision to "see" the potential for revival in the cities in which we plant churches. So, for example, in Raleigh, North Carolina, our International Church is called "Raleigh I.C." or "Raleigh I see."

At that time, when we organized the Fellowship of International Churches, the elders decided to ordain me as bishop of the movement.

WE ARE SCATTERED, BUT WE ARE CLOSE.

We have scattered now in obedience to the Lord's apostolic calling to start other churches, but we are close in our hearts just the way we used to be when we would come crawling into the 6:00 A.M. prayer meeting every Saturday in Richmond, Virginia. Everybody was close in those days—families brought blankets for the sleepy kids; college students wore T-shirts, their eyes half open; working-class people and professionals came. You could hear Mother Isabel Tindall's penetrating prayers, calling on God, clear from the parking lot!

At that time, almost everybody was African-American. From the beginning, however, God had given us a clear vision for people of all nations coming together in our churches. By His grace, that vision is now being fulfilled.

A passion of our hearts is revival. We have carefully studied the great spiritual revivals and awakenings led by people such as Jonathan Edwards, John Wesley and Charles Finney. We want God to use us right on the front lines to help bring in what we believe will be the greatest spiritual awakening of them all.

OUR ROOTS HAVE HELPED US TO BLOSSOM AND BEAR FRUIT.

Some of us are the descendants of American blacks—slave and free—who were converted and who kept their faith in Christ alive even when forced to sit in the balconies of white churches. Some split up when their churches, that mostly met in barns, became too large, because whites feared another uprising like that started by Nat Turner. God used those restrictions that were meant for evil, however, to accomplish His good purposes. The "pastors" were able to shepherd the sheep more personally because their churches were kept small.

These men of God had to become apostles to accommodate the exponential growth, continuously planting new churches and starting new denominations, primarily within the Baptists, Methodists and

Pentecostals. These churches would become the center of each black community, providing practical needs such as food, literacy and oversight of people's lives in the context of Christianity.

Men such as C. H. Mason, founder of the Church of God in Christ, were models of forgiveness and racial reconciliation. Mason ordained multitudes of white pastors and still embraced them when they later turned their backs on him to form exclusively white denominations, such as the Assemblies of God and others.

In the Fellowship of International Churches, we strongly believe that God has called us to build on the best of the foundations of spiritual awakening, reconciliation and consecrated lives in both black and white churches. We are called (1) to help restore a sense of urgency to unite the Body of Christ to win the multitudes of all races and nations in these last days, and (2) to a commitment to consecration. We do all this because Christ is preparing us to be His Bride, who will rule and reign with Him in the life to come.

IT'S AMAZING THAT I GET PAID
TO PREACH—I LOVE IT SO MUCH!

I started out as a wild inner-city kid who fought other boys in elementary school. Then when my unsaved mother was miraculously healed through the prayers of some consecrated women, she gave her life to the Lord, and I did, too. God's hand kept me when I backslid in high school, then got into drugs in Vietnam and the years following. When I was in my 20s, God broke through to me again in such a dramatic way that I started right out in ministry and I have never wanted to do anything else since. The wonder is that some people actually pay me for preaching! I love it so much.

My future wife, Katheryn, wasn't "seeing me" until I got right with God, even though I had known her and loved her since our high school days in Germany where our fathers were both in the army. After we married, I began looking for godly men who could mentor me. I still do, even as I am serving as a mentor to many others.

I was licensed in the A.M.E. Zion Church and then, sometime in 1975 after we moved to Richmond, Virginia, I was ordained in the Baptist church. One of my surprises was to discover that many of the other preachers I associated with in those early days were not interested in godly living. They would even put me down for trying to be a serious man of God. They told me, "You'll get over it," but I never did. Most of them are now either out of the ministry or dead.

MY FIRST MESSAGES WERE "FIRE AND BRIMSTONE," AND IN SOME WAYS THEY STILL ARE.

When my first two spiritual mentors died, I couldn't find many others who were as intense as I was about the holy life, so I started out on my own and began preaching at public meetings in a hotel in Richmond and speaking on the radio. My message was pure "fire and brimstone," but people still kept coming up to me after I preached in those hotel conference rooms the same way they do now when I preach in stadiums.

In those days, I didn't have enough sense to take offerings. I thought it would be enough just to leave a basket at the door. As a result, we stayed not just poor but "po!" My wife's salary barely carried us, but along with some timely rescue efforts from my father-in-law and from some godly white men who sincerely believed in me we made it. By the grace of God, we never stopped the meetings and reaching new people for Christ.

Through the years, I have developed more financial sense as well as more mercy in my messages, but people say I still "slice them up" with the truth when I preach. They say it cuts through and reaches their hearts, but they love me for it because they want to know God with a new intensity. They can feel the great compassion I have that makes a difference in the lives of people who want the truth (see Jude 22).

WHEN I PREACH OUT OF TOWN, FOIC PEOPLE COME TO HELP MINISTER TO THE CROWDS.

When I preach out of town, I know that a crowd will come to the front of the room and talk to me afterward, so I try to gather some of my disciples from other states to help. Many times they come at their own expense. Often they bring some of their own disciples with them. We usually stay long enough to shut the place down! Frequently the workmen will start tearing down the stage, flicking the lights and even vacuuming while we are still hanging out talking about Jesus. That is all God's doing. He just wants to reach our hearts.

From the time I was saved, I have made disciples the way Paul discipled Onesimus. The disciples didn't all become part of the Fellowship of International Churches, but we are still in fellowship as Christians. Many of them have become awesome men of God who are now training their own disciples, believing that "the things that you have heard from me among many witnesses, commit these to faithful men who will be able to teach others also" (2 Tim. 2:2).

ACCOUNTABILITY TO PEOPLE SHOULD LEAD TO ACCOUNTABILITY TO GOD.

I have always believed everyone around me has potential. I never actually have tried to look at others for where they were, but rather for their potential destiny. I never strive to maintain an attitude of exclusivity, as if I were the main one or as if our Fellowship was "it." I never have wanted people to become dependent on me. Their relationship with God, not with me, is what will carry them through their journey. We always are there for one another, watching each other's lives, but we expect one another as men and women of God to come to a place where we are so close to the heart of God that His purity and holiness keep us from sin.

I know that some church traditions teach that you can never totally stop sinning, so you always need people around you asking about your sin life. I don't find that in the Bible. The Bible doesn't say that the blood of Jesus has no power to obliterate sin. It says His "blood...cleanses us from *all* sin" (1 John 1:7, emphasis added).

I am not tempted to drink or take drugs or fool around with women. Anybody around me can see that, because my life is an open book. I don't want to sin. Sin doesn't attract me. I have the power of an endless life that came through Jesus Christ, and because of my going with Him and taking up His cross daily, sin has no more dominion over me. It is not that temptations don't come—because we live on earth—but the desire to yield to them isn't there anymore. From where does all this originate? It comes only from the fullness of God in my daily life.

IN ETTRICK, VIRGINIA, WE LAID A FOUNDATION FOR HUMILITY AND REACHING THE INNER CITY.

After we held meetings for a while in the hotel and after we had built up to a couple hundred people, in 1981 God told us to leave behind the "multitudes" and to plant a church with "the few" who would follow us to an out-of-the-way place called Ettrick, Virginia. We met in an old church building there, starting with about 12 people. We had no heat in the winter because the furnace burned up our first tank of oil in one week. We couldn't afford to fill up the tank again, so we sang and shared a pioneering church experience in the cold wearing coats, with vapor coming out of our mouths, until we could buy some more oil.

Ettrick was God's location, however, partly because we needed to build the ministry on the foundation of humility and partly because it was right near the campus of Virginia State University. It was one of the schools founded to provide separate education for blacks in the segregated South. That is where we began one of the Bible studies that developed into what we called New Generation Campus Ministries. God gave us a vision for reaching every one of the historically black college campuses with the gospel.

Although we wanted to reach people of all races and nations, we wanted to make sure those young blacks were not neglected. Many of those college students came from the inner cities and might go back there and win those people to Jesus. Most of the black schools didn't have any serious outreaches emphasizing salvation and a holy lifestyle. They all had gospel choirs, though, and a widespread sensitivity to Christianity that you often don't find in the predominantly white schools. Young black men may have a reputation for being criminals, but when we go to them and they hear our hearts, they respond and become serious Christians. Through the years, several young men and women have come into full-time ministry with us at no salary—just faith.

BACK IN RICHMOND, WE BECAME SERIOUS ABOUT SERVING GOD FOR HIS FEET, NOT FOR HIS HANDS.

When we left Ettrick in 1985, we went back to Richmond, Virginia, where we rented a downtown church. Later we moved to a used-car dealership about a mile away. At what we called Manna Christian Fellowship (MCF), we preached at a weekday lunch hour and at a bookstore called Strong Meat. People on drugs, as well as businessmen, would wander in to hear the Word. We had meetings with pastors from other denominations who would join with us to pray for the

> *We were determined to serve God for His feet (what we could do to serve Him) instead of His hands (what He could do to serve us).*

city. They wouldn't let us join their church basketball leagues, though, because our Athletes for Jesus Sports Ministry (AFJ) drew serious players to the church who could beat everybody else's teams!

In 1988, AFJ started weekly Bible studies in all of Richmond's inner-city high schools during sports practices, and eventually it became a national ministry. No serious church/state contentions have surfaced through the years. This is because former pro-basketball players Monty Knight and Rolando Lamb offer a tremendous service to the community by helping the coaches build character into their players, including many of the rebels. Although they accomplish it by preaching Jesus every time they are there, and although kids are saved right there at practice, the coaches leave them alone. Some of the coaches are changed themselves!

By the time we moved to the Richmond suburbs in 1989, we had established a serious core group of members who were accustomed to 5:00 A.M. prayer every weekday (we slept in until 6:00 A.M. on Saturdays). An intercessory prayer team also held three-day prayer and fasting shut-ins every month, and weekly fast days. We were determined to serve God for His *feet* (what we could do to serve Him) instead of His *hands* (what He could do to serve us).

We have always received an incredible amount of offerings to sustain our vision, particularly considering the income level of our people. They have sacrificed a lot so we can keep the heat and lights on and the air conditioning running while we all fulfilled the vision. They had a spiritual hunger for God and a vision that we were supposed to change society.

Before we redecorated our church, we taped world maps to the cinder-block walls and a computer printout that read, "Ask of Me, and I will give You the nations for Your inheritance, and the ends of the earth for Your possession" (Ps. 2:8). Then we put up flags from many nations throughout the sanctuary because we had an eternal vision that simple people who did what God said could reach the world.

At this church location in the predominantly white Varina area of Richmond, known for Ku Klux Klan activity, we started a daycare facility, a summer camp and a Christian elementary school, besides continuing all our other outreaches across the nation. People were often at the church 24 hours a day—praying all night or just passing through to prepare for our conferences and leadership training schools. Lots of church families had members of our low-paid or unpaid staff living with them, usually without charging them a cent. People shared cars and rooms and everything else they owned.

WE HAD TO SEND OUT THE LOCAL FAMILY TO BUILD AN EXTENDED FAMILY OF CHURCHES.

By 1992, I felt I had to break up our church family by encouraging the elders to go to other cities and plant churches. In 1995, my wife and I, along with our youngest son, Justin, also left Richmond at the call of the Lord and moved to Atlanta, Georgia. We left Manna Christian Fellowship in the capable hands of one of our elders and his wife, Marvin and Kate Mason. Our daughter, Nicole, was attending the University of Virginia, and our oldest son, Jason, stayed with my wife's father, who had recently been widowed.

Many people from our other churches have now moved to Atlanta to be with us. We planted one church in Atlanta in 1995, and we are now planting a second one, the First International Church of Atlanta. Although this latest one is still in the core-group stage, the congregation already represents several nations and cultures.

Out of those humble, but intense, beginnings, we have now built a network of churches and ministries in several states, but more importantly we have built a group of people into a family of individuals who think like godly leaders. Through the years, I preached messages to them such as "What One Man Can Do," "Bloodless Martyrdom," "The Crucified Life" and "Slaves of God," and my elders preach the same way. People are hungry for that kind of message today. They are tired of being "christianettes." They want to grow and get serious so God can use them to bring a revival. We believe we can bring revival to the civil government, so another of our serious leaders, Eileen Hunt, heads an organization we started called the Network of Politically Active Christian Women (NPAC).

WE HAVE BUILT INTO OUR MEMBERS A LEADERSHIP MENTALITY BASED ON A FOUNDATION OF PRAYER AND THE WORD.

Because we have built a leadership mentality into our church members through the years, almost all of those who really are serious about God have some kind of personal ministry going, from a Bible study at work to a dance ministry to preaching at a drug rehab center. You can be saved just by calling people's answering machines! Our members are an awesome reservoir of consecrated people working full time to support themselves while they minister in all the free time they can spare. It is one of our dreams to someday help finance more of these consecrated people into full-time ministry. When they are released, they will be some of the key people who will help initiate the next worldwide spiritual awakening.

Whenever we start a church or a ministry, it is built on the foundation of the Word and prayer. Most of us haven't attended seminary, but we love to pray and study the Bible and we read many of the same books the seminaries use. We adhere to the traditional creeds of the

Church, and we fellowship with people from any Christian background. Some of us have degrees and some do not, but we all stand together in humility and love for one another. We all pray together, and we all pray alone. Sometimes we pray all night or for several days together. We try to lead a "fasted lifestyle," fasting for results in God's kingdom. God has allowed me to take several sabbaticals of up to 40 days away from the ministry just to fast and pray.

We have hundreds of people in the leadership core of our churches and ministries, but almost no divorces. In 20 years of ministry, only two people at the elder level have divorced. We don't have to go searching when we need a pastor for a city because we have trained many faithful pastors from among us by personal discipleship and what we call "Worm Training," learning to be a worm who is easily crushed instead of a snake who always strikes back. That is because the grace of God allows us to know Him and reveals to us from His Word how important it is to live a life of humility.

MEETINGS DON'T MEET PEOPLE'S NEEDS— MEETING JESUS DOES.

If you want to start a church, probably a few people will come for weddings and funerals and Sunday-morning meetings, but meetings don't meet people's needs. Meeting Jesus does. To be successful, a church has to create a tidal wave of the reality of Jesus in the lives of the members so that when people meet them, they have met Jesus. You want Jesus to come upon you so strongly that hardly any difference exists between a personal encounter with Jesus and a personal encounter with you. You are changed and you are changing lives. The whole church is called to be like Jesus.

The Church in heaven is multinational and multicultural (see Rev. 7:9), so that is our model for earth. Abraham looked for a city whose "builder and maker is God" (Heb. 11:10). That means we build churches that cross denominational, social, cultural, racial and economic boundaries. We are not in competition with other churches. We do whatever we can to help and support them. We team up with them to win the lost, restore families and bring reconciliation between denominations and races.

The Bible says, "Beloved, now we are children of God; and it has not yet been revealed what we shall be, but we know that when He is revealed, we shall be like Him, for we shall see Him as He is" (1 John 3:2). The clearer Jesus becomes to you the more you become like Him. You will not only be like Him when He appears at the Second Coming, but also when He appears in your heart. People are changed when they meet somebody like Jesus.

WE WANT TO TRAIN PEOPLE TO BE GREAT MEN AND WOMEN OF GOD, WHETHER ANYBODY ELSE SEES THEIR POTENTIAL OR NOT.

Probably what gives me the greatest fulfillment is recognizing and then pushing to another level in God somebody who is motivated to accomplish something great, but is somebody nobody else "sees." That is probably driven by the fact that in the beginning of my ministry a few people recognized that kind of potential in me, in spite of my flaws, and sowed into me their time, money and especially their "I believe in you." God sent His Son just for that purpose—not only to be a sacrifice for our sins, but also to prove His love by providing a sacrifice—before any of us could accomplish anything to please Him, just because He believed in us.

I want people to be serious men or women of God, to seek the Lord for a specific calling—whether it is in planting churches in the cities of this nation and then the world (as pastors and pioneering members), or in what the Puritans called "specialized callings" of serving God in the marketplace. I want them to become everything God wants them to be.

If I were to define the present state of the Fellowship of International Churches, I would have to say that we are in process. We are under construction, both personally and corporately, but I believe we have some sincere Christian men and women whom God has established among us and whom He is going to use to reach the nation. They are pastoring FOIC churches in Florida, Georgia, North Carolina, Tennessee, Texas and Virginia.

Some, like myself, speak to hundreds of thousands of men at Promise Keepers (PK) events. Some, like Garland Hunt of Raleigh

International Church in Raleigh, North Carolina, speak on daily radio. All of us have a heart for the other pastors in our cities, and we participate in citywide networks for prayer and reconciliation. We encourage people everywhere we go to pray for revival in the inner city. We do it all knowing that it can't possibly happen without God, because we know how little we know!

When I spoke at a Promise Keepers stadium event recently, people started telling me what it was like to hear Larry Jackson, pastor of Clinton International Church in Fayetteville, North Carolina, at another PK event. He is one of my spiritual sons from the inner city who is an outworking of the biblical phrase, "The glory of this latter house shall be greater than of the former" (Hag. 2:9, *KJV*). Larry keeps trying to surpass me! The people were saying to each other, "Larry's just like Wellington! It's so awesome that this man produces men who are like him."

We operate on the principle of "touch somebody's life." What the people might not know is that Larry is also training disciples who are just like him, and my other leaders are doing the same. All of us are in competition to be just like Jesus! In our ministry, we invest our lives into individuals. When we have a public platform to speak, we bring along our disciples and expose them to that, to give them a vision for reaching nations and for loving people outside the comfort circle that defines most churches.

CHURCHES HAVE TO GUARD AGAINST THE "PRIDE OF GRACE" BY RECOGNIZING HOW LITTLE THEY REALLY KNOW.

Many churches have what I call a "pride of grace." They secretly think they are better than the people who attend other churches or have other lifestyles that are not like theirs. God wants us to reach beyond our circles to love all kinds of people—black, white, rich, poor, educated, uneducated, saved and unsaved—in varying denominations. Paul wrote in the "love chapter" of 1 Corinthians 13 that "we know in part" (v. 9). I don't know anything about anything without the help of almighty God. "Most people don't know what they don't know," says Monty Knight. He is one of the men who has worked his way up from an inner-city background to become a ruling elder, president of Athletes for Jesus and pastor of one of our churches.

When God sees how ignorant and prideful we are about the puny amount of knowledge we have, I can just picture Him falling out laughing! We have this expression to keep each other straight, "You aren't all that!" We watch out for pride in one another and kick it to the curb.

WIN THEM, TRAIN THEM AND SEND THEM.

Our goal in each of our churches and ministries is to win people to Christ, train them in a godly lifestyle, then send them out to be missionaries to the world.

We have a vision of what God is going to do because we ask God to help us see what He sees. God gave Abraham a vision of what was going to come before it became a reality. God told him, "I will multiply thy seed as the stars of the heaven, and as the sand which is upon the sea shore" (Gen. 22:17, KJV). That was long before Abraham had a son. The Bible says that God "calleth those things which be not as though they were" (Rom. 4:17, KJV).

We see a future where Christians of all races will be unified, praying, sharing resources and helping one another so that the Kingdom can come on earth as it is in heaven. Because we will be together for eternity, we might just as well develop our fellowship now.

You don't have to join our organization for us to love you. It is just there for you if you need it, and if you don't need it, we just want to hang out with you anyway when we have the chance and fellowship the way we will in heaven.

Bishop Wellington Boone
4930 Riverlake Drive
Duluth, GA 30155
Phone: 770-242-2711
Fax: 770-242-2773

Resource List—Books
Breaking Through
Your Wife Is Not Your Momma

Resources may be ordered through:
Wellington Boone Ministries
P.O. Box 16886
Atlanta, GA 30321
Phone: 770-242-2711
Fax: 770-242-2773

7

DOVE CHRISTIAN FELLOWSHIP INTERNATIONAL

Larry Kreider, International Director
Ephrata, Pennsylvania

Larry Kreider currently serves as international director of DOVE Christian Fellowship International, a network of cell-based churches scattered through south central Pennsylvania and various parts of the world. For 15 years he pastored DOVE Christian Fellowship, which grew from one cell to more than 2,000 people involved in cell groups. Churches have been planted in Scotland, Brazil, Kenya, Uganda and New Zealand. He has spent the past decade training Christian leaders nationally and internationally to make disciples by using the cell group concept. He has written several books, including *House to House*, a practical manual for home cell group leaders, which contains spiritual insights for the church of the twenty-first century.

"Are you willing to be involved with the underground church?" The words I heard in my spirit were distinct, even piercing! During the 1970s, I was involved in a youth ministry to the unchurched. One afternoon in 1978, while praying, I was startled when I heard the Lord speak to me through His still, small voice. Yet at first I was baffled by what He was trying to tell me.

My mind raced immediately to the Berlin Wall and the barbed wire fences that then surrounded the borders of many communist nations. I thought of the persecuted church, meeting underground in nations that opposed the gospel. It still did not make sense, yet I knew I had to respond: I had heard the call of God.

"Yes, Lord," I replied, as tears formed in my eyes. "I am willing." I chose to obey, even though I didn't understand what it all meant.

AN UNDERGROUND CHURCH IS LIKE A TREE

In time, I began to understand what the Lord had in mind. An underground church can be compared to a tree: its trunk, branches and leaves are only half of the picture. The unnoticed half, the underground root system, nourishes the whole tree and keeps it healthy. The underground church, I began to realize, was to consist of believers gathered through a structure of small cell groups meeting in homes to pray, evangelize and build relationships with one another. In this way, each believer is made an active and vital part of the Body of Christ.

When every believer is nourished and healthy, the whole church is strong. Just as water and nutrients feed the tree by climbing up through the root system, so the church is nourished and strengthened by what happens in the underground (unseen) realm of church life—believers involved in home cell groups. These cell group relationships are not to be mere appendages of the church; in actuality, they are the church. Meeting together in homes and experiencing relationships in cell group life is just as important as meeting together each week in a larger gathering to worship and to receive teaching from the Word of God.

NEW WINESKINS FOR THE NEW WINE

Although we had tried to involve the new believers to whom we were relating, they simply didn't seem to fit into the established churches in our community. It seemed clear new church structures were needed that were flexible enough to relate to new converts from a variety of backgrounds. That is why Jesus said we need to put new wine into new wineskins.

> "Nor do they put new wine into old wineskins, or else the wineskins break, the wine is spilled, and the wineskins are ruined. But they put new wine into new wineskins, and both are preserved" (Matt. 9:17).

So began our church's adventure into cell groups. We discovered cell groups to be places where people have the opportunity to experience and demonstrate a Christianity built on relationships, not simply on meetings. In the cell groups, people can readily share their lives with each other and reach out by sharing the healing love of Jesus to a broken world. We desired to follow the pattern in the New Testament Church as modeled in the book of Acts as the believers met from house to house.

FROM THE LIVING ROOM TO THE NATIONS

We started a cell group in our house and when our living room was filled to capacity, we gave the responsibility to leaders we had trained and started a second cell in another home. By the time our church officially began in October 1980, approximately 25 of us were meeting in a large living room on Sunday mornings and in three cell groups during the week.

We prayed for two kinds of people to join us: new Christians and laborers. During the first 12 years, these three cell groups had grown and multiplied to more than 2,000 believers meeting in 125 cell groups in south-central Pennsylvania. New churches were planted in Scotland, Brazil, Kenya and New Zealand. Believers met in cell groups in homes during the week and in clusters of cells in geographical areas for celebration meetings each Sunday morning. Here believers received teaching, worshiped together and celebrated what the Lord was doing during the week through the cell groups. Every few months the entire church met together to worship on a Sunday morning in a large gymnasium or in a local park.

Five times we closed down our Sunday celebration meetings for a four-week period and met in home cell groups on Sunday mornings to strengthen the vision for building the church underground. During one of those times, we came back together after a month of meeting solely in cell groups and realized the Lord had added a hundred people to the church!

PRIDE AND CONTROL CREEP IN

Although the church had grown rapidly in a relatively short time span, we had made our share of mistakes. The Lord began to show us the pride and unhealthy control in our lives. We found that the Lord's purpose for cell groups was to *release* and *empower* His people, not to *control* them. We repented before the Lord and before His Church. Our cell-based church had reached a crossroads. We were experiencing the pain of gridlock among some of our leadership. An exodus of some good leaders from our ranks occurred. It was painful, and I almost quit.

The mistakes we made were partly because of my immaturity as a leader and partly because of our not having an outside accountability team to help us when we ran into conflicts in decision making. Perhaps also the Lord in His providence was repositioning some of His players elsewhere in the Body of Christ. The Lord kept taking us back to the original vision He had given, however, calling us to be involved with the "underground church." Today we walk with a spiritual limp, but we are deeply grateful to the Lord for what He taught us during those transition days.

GIVING THE CHURCH AWAY

It became clear that for DOVE (an acronym for "Declaring Our Victory Emmanuel") to accomplish what God originally had in mind, we needed to adjust our church government and be willing to "give the church away." The vision the Lord had given us—"to build a relationship with Jesus, with one another, and reach the world from house to house, city to city and nation to nation"—could not be fulfilled under our existing church structure. We recognized the Lord had called us to be an apostolic movement, but we did not know how it should be structured.

It took more than two years to prepare for this transition. On January 1, 1996, our church became eight autonomous churches, each having its own eldership team. We formed an Apostolic Council to give spiritual oversight to DOVE Christian Fellowship International (DCFI), and I was asked to serve as its international director.

The Apostolic Council gave each church eldership team the option of becoming a part of the DOVE Christian Fellowship International family of churches and ministries or connecting to another part of the Body of Christ. Each of these eight churches expressed a desire to work together with us to plant churches throughout the world and became a part of the DCFI family. The majority of the overseas church plants also desired to become a part of the DCFI family of churches and ministries.

A New, Safe Environment

We have found that apostolic ministry provides a safe environment for each congregation and ministry partnering with DCFI to grow and reproduce itself. This new model emphasizes leading by relationship and influence rather than hands-on management. A senior elder and team (we prefer to call the leader of a congregation a senior elder, rather than senior pastor, simply because that individual may or may

> *We see an "apostolic movement" as a family of churches having a common focus: a mandate from God to labor together to plant and establish churches throughout the world.*

not have the actual anointing of a pastor), has a leadership gift to equip believers to do the work of ministry in cell groups within a congregation. The Apostolic Council members are responsible to spend time in prayer and the ministry of the Word and to provide training, oversight and mentoring to local church leadership. They also are called to give clear vision and direction to the entire movement.

We Are an Apostolic Movement

Unlike an "association of churches" or a denomination that gives ordination and general accountability to church leaders, we see an "apostolic movement" as a family of churches having a common focus: a mandate from God to labor together to plant and establish churches throughout the world. Although some may want to call us a new denomination, we prefer the terminology "apostolic movement." We

do not mind being called a new denomination, but denominationalism—an elitist attitude toward others in the Body of Christ—tends to
separate us rather than to focus on our need for the Lord and for each
other.

We believe that each denomination and movement has a redemptive
purpose from God, and we want to honor our traditional denominations. We want to relate to them positively on an ongoing basis so that
we can serve and learn from each other. We build on the shoulders of
those who have gone before us because they have given us a solid
foundation.

As a cell-based church planting movement, we are intent on training a new generation of church planters and leaders just waiting for a
chance to spread its wings and fly! We are called to mobilize and
empower God's people (individuals, families, cells and congregations)
at the grassroots level to fulfill His purposes. Every cell group should
have a vision to plant new cells. Every church should have a God-
given vision to plant new churches.

PARTNERING

For many years we knew we were called to plant new churches, but a
few years ago the Lord spoke to me, "I have many orphans in my Body,
and I am calling you to adopt some of my orphans." I knew He was
calling us also to open our hearts to cell-based churches that had no
spiritual oversight and apostolic protection. Now, in addition to
church planting and multiplication, the Lord has given us a process of
adopting churches that are called to partner with us. After going
through a one-year engagement process of discernment, churches having similar values and vision are becoming partner churches with the
DCFI family.

Our transition from one church to eight has allowed the old structure to die so we could experience the new: a network of cell-based
churches partnering together. This network of churches started less
than two years ago.

At the time of this writing, nine DOVE congregations of cell groups
are working together in south-central Pennsylvania and have plans for
two new church plants within the next six months. Presently, more
than a half dozen cell-based congregations are in the process of either

entering the engagement period or partnering with the DCFI family from other parts of the United States. Also in the partnering process are churches ready to begin an engagement period in Canada, a network of DCFI cell churches in New Zealand, three congregations in the engagement period in France, four congregations in East Africa (Kenya and Uganda) and two new cell groups in Northern Scotland. The Lord has taken us on an amazing ride during the past 19 months.

Our desire is to have congregations of cell groups clustered together in the same area so leaders can meet easily as regional presbyteries for prayer and mutual encouragement and to find ways to be more effective in building His kingdom together. Senior elders of DOVE churches in Pennsylvania have the blessing of meeting together each month for prayer and mutual encouragement. An Apostolic Council member also meets individually every month with each senior elder.

Each DCFI partner church is governed by a team of elders and consists of believers committed to one another in cell groups. Each cell and each local church has its own identity, but is interdependent with the rest of the DCFI family.

NETWORKING

We believe another important aspect to Kingdom building is networking with other churches and ministries outside the DCFI family. In this way, we can share resources with one other. No single church or family of churches has it all! We welcome the exchange of Christian leaders between the DCFI apostolic movement and others in the Body of Christ as we learn from the rest of God's family and share what the Lord has given us. DCFI partner church leaders are encouraged to pray regularly with other pastors in their regions. DOVE leaders in Nairobi, Kenya; Warkworth, New Zealand; and in south central Pennsylvania all participate in pastors' gatherings in their regions.

God has given us a wonderful support team at DCFI. This team consists of the Apostolic Council, a team of Fivefold Translocal Ministers, a Stewardship Council that handles the administration of financial details and legalities, and various ministries that are committed to provide resources to the leadership and believers in DCFI partner churches and serve the greater Body of Christ.

These various ministries offer leadership training and ministry development on many levels, many of which are listed at the end of this chapter. An important 24-hour Prayer Ministry includes a team of "prayer generals" who recruit, train and encourage a team of "prayer warriors" responsible to cover segments of time each week while praying for the entire DCFI family 24 hours a day.

THE INTERNATIONAL LEADERSHIP CONFERENCE

The Apostolic Council and leadership from DCFI partner churches throughout the world meet together each March for our annual DCFI International Leadership Conference at a conference center on the east coast. They meet for the purpose of mutual encouragement, leadership training, relationship building and to receive a common vision from the Lord. We believe the Lord has called us to work together as a team to have a shared vision, shared values, a shared procedure and to build together by relationship.

> *A major aspect of cell ministry is preparing and training future spiritual fathers and mothers....The philosophy here is to train them to give them away!*

For the DCFI family of churches and ministries to be effective in laboring together, we have written down our procedure in a DCFI Leadership Handbook. This handbook is available by contacting the DCFI Office (see the resource list at the end of the chapter).

TRAINING AND RELEASING BELIEVERS

An important philosophy of ministry at DCFI is to release each believer and local leadership to provide a delegation of authority and responsibility to all believers. Unless elders can release responsibility and authority to the cell leaders at a cell group level, this principle will not work. In this way, the Lord releases every believer to be a minister.

Every church leader is encouraged to maintain security in the Lord and to take the risk of empowering and releasing cell leaders to minister to others. They do this by giving water baptisms, serving communion, praying for the sick, providing premarital counseling and discipling new believers. A major aspect of cell ministry is preparing and training future spiritual fathers and mothers. For many of these cell leaders will be future elders and church planters. They are experiencing "on the job training."

The philosophy here is to train them to give them away! We expect the believers in our cell groups and churches to have their own families soon: the new cell groups and new churches they plant.

AVOIDING A PAIN IN THE NECK!

We find in the Scriptures that God appoints leaders who are called to lead through servanthood. We believe God is organizing teams of elders and teams of apostolic leaders who will pray and work together, and each team needs clear headship.

We use the analogy of a head and shoulders regarding church leadership. The head of every team needs to be properly attached to the shoulders (the others on the team) through God-ordained relationships of trust and affirmation. If the head moves too far from the shoulders (by not honoring and communicating with the team) or if the head is forced down (by the team not honoring and affirming the head), the body will experience a pain in the neck! If the head is appropriately attached to the shoulders through relationship, trust, servanthood, prayer and proper communication, and the shoulders support and affirm the head, the oil of the Holy Spirit will run down from the head to the shoulders to the body. As these leaders dwell together in the unity of Christ, God will command a blessing as indicated in Psalm 133.

We encourage leadership teams on all levels to strive to receive the mind of the Lord through prayer and consensus whenever possible. If for some reason a team of elders cannot reach complete agreement about every decision, however, they should clearly recognize the senior elder as the head, who has the grace to discern what the Lord is saying through the entire eldership team. The senior elder has final authority, but not absolute authority.

If a conflict remains, the Apostolic Council provides an outside court of appeal for the eldership team. Although the final decisions affecting the local church are made by the elders, the wisdom of God is often manifest in God's people in the church. We encourage church leaders to draw from this wisdom before making decisions. We find these leadership principles modeled by the Early Church at the Jerusalem Council in Acts 15 and throughout the Bible.

ACCOUNTABILITY

Every leadership person needs to be an active part of a cell group and be involved in the life of the local congregation. In this way, accountability is built into every level of the DCFI movement. The Apostolic Council receives oversight from a team of recognized spiritual advisors: spiritual leaders from outside the DCFI family who provide advice, counsel and accountability. In cases of irreconcilable disputes, disorderly conduct, apostasy, moral failure or other faults on the part of the International Director or a member of the Apostolic Council, the recognized spiritual advisors will work closely with the Apostolic Council members to bring mediation to the conflict or discipline and restoration as needed.

MINISTERIAL LICENSING AND ORDINATION

We view ministerial licensing and ordination as an affirmation of a leader's call to a lifetime of ministry, which gives the person the right to perform the duties of the office and any other ministerial functions within the scope and practices of DCFI. The Apostolic Council holds the authority to license and ordain and is spiritually responsible for all licensed and ordained persons and their spiritual training. In most cases, we prefer a person to be involved in active ministry for at least two years before ordination. We also encourage a person to have completed our six-month Leadership School, either on location or by video correspondence. We ordain both men and women.

WOMEN'S ROLES IN CHURCH GOVERNMENT

Because DCFI is called by the Lord to focus on the Great Commission of our Lord, we are of the conviction that we cannot become sidetracked by the many differing understandings about a woman's role in church government that often divides us and causes us to lose our focus. We believe there is no question biblically or historically that women can and should be involved in ministering to the Body of Christ. We affirm the need for women's perspective in ministry and church life. DCFI has licensed and ordained both men and women in ministry.

> **According to Ephesians 4:11,12, the five ministry gifts of the apostle, prophet, evangelist, pastor and teacher are called by the Lord to equip the saints to minister and encourage the Body of Christ.**

If a senior elder and the elders of a DCFI partner church believe a woman is called to serve in an eldership position, and they can affirm her with faith and a clear conscience according to their understanding of Scripture, then we believe she should be appointed to serve. If, on the other hand, the elders of the local church believe only men should be appointed to eldership in their local church, then only men will be appointed to eldership in that local church. We affirm both understandings. Some DCFI partner churches have both men and women serving as elders, and others have only men serving in eldership.

FIVEFOLD TRANSLOCAL MINISTRY

According to Ephesians 4:11,12, the five ministry gifts of the apostle, prophet, evangelist, pastor and teacher are called by the Lord to equip the saints to minister and encourage the Body of Christ. Within the DCFI family, fivefold ministers who have proven ministries and are recommended by their eldership as having a larger sphere of ministry than their own cell and congregation are recognized and affirmed by the Apostolic Council to serve translocally. These translocal ministers are often invited by other cell groups and congregations for ministry. We are presently trusting God for a strategy to have these fivefold translocal ministers supported financially as He restores their ministry to the church.

DCFI MISSIONS OUTREACHES

During the past 17 years, DOVE has sent hundreds of short- and long-term missionaries to the nations. Each long-term missionary is "embraced" by a cell group, a congregation and by individuals from DCFI partner churches. A team of people join a missionary's support team by giving financially and praying for the missionary. Cells who "embrace" a missionary or missionary family pray for them, write to them and serve the missionary practically while on furlough or during times of crisis.

The DCFI Missions Resource Center endeavors to serve all DOVE missionaries who are sent out from DCFI partner churches regardless of their chosen "field." Some missionaries are directly involved in the DCFI church-planting "field," others may serve instead with the "YWAM field" or some other missions agency. We believe we are called to build the Kingdom, not just our own network of churches.

FINANCE AND ADMINISTRATION

A Stewardship Council prayerfully fulfills the legal and financial policies of DCFI and its operations according to the vision, direction and purpose of the Apostolic Council. Each July a weekend summit meeting is held, at which time the Apostolic Council and other DCFI leadership share a written vision with the Stewardship Council for the next calendar year. During the next four months, the Stewardship Council serves the Apostolic Council by helping to set the yearly budget by December 1 for the following year. After the Apostolic Council approves the budget, the Stewardship Council holds the Apostolic Council accountable to stay within the budget.

Members of DCFI partner churches are encouraged to give tithes and offerings to support the vision, mission, leadership and ministry of their particular church. We believe in giving tithes and offerings to honor and provide for those who give us spiritual oversight. In the same way, partner churches also give a tithe (a tenth of the tithes and undesignated offerings) and offerings to support the greater vision of DCFI. As church members and local partner churches tithe and give offerings, finances are released to support the entire mission of the DCFI family. Partner churches are self-supporting and responsible for their own balanced budget. If a partner church purchases its own building, the building is owned by the partner church, not DCFI.

Accountability and faith for finances permeates all levels of DCFI. The Lord may provide for those of us who are apostolic leaders through a base salary, honoraria, gifts, a support team, "tentmaking," supernatural provision or through other creative means.

LOOKING TO THE HARVEST

Like our early beginnings, we are again sensing that the harvest is upon us. The Lord, like a great magnet, is drawing people into His kingdom. Because new wineskins eventually get old, many who have been believers for years are becoming dissatisfied with life as it is in their present church structures. God's people are again thirsting for new wine and wineskins. The Lord is renewing and refreshing and reviving thousands of His people around the world. He is also requiring us to provide new wineskins for the new wine, as He brings in His harvest.

We believe as we continue to commune with the Lord and obey His voice, build together as a family of churches and reach the lost in our generation, a need will exist for thousands of new houses (new churches) and new rooms (new cell groups). Every generation is different and has different needs and preferences. We are committed to empower, release and support the next generation among us as it fulfills its call in God. Just as Elisha received a double portion of Elijah's anointing, so we want to have our spiritual children far exceeding us in their depth of spiritual experience and church leadership. Believers will be called to various areas of leadership: some to cell group leadership, others to local church leadership, others to fivefold ministry and others will serve in apostolic leadership.

Our long-term goal is to establish many apostolic councils in various regions of the world. Already a new apostolic leadership team consisting of African leaders is responsible for oversight of DCFI churches in Africa. Eventually, we believe the leadership for the DCFI movement will be a true DCFI International Apostolic Council, whose members will include apostolic leaders from many nations. This International Apostolic Council will be responsible for providing spiritual oversight and mentoring apostolic leaders and apostolic councils located around the world.

The DCFI family is called to keep actively involved in what the Lord is doing in the world and to participate in the present expressions of His anointing. We desire to empower, train and release God's people at the grassroots level to fulfill His purposes. It happened two thousand years ago in the book of Acts. Let's obey our God and experience the book of Acts again!

Larry Kreider
DOVE Christian Fellowship
1924 West Main Street
Ephrata, PA 17522
Phone: 717-738-3751
Fax: 717-738-0656

Resource List—Books
House to House
Biblical Foundation Series
Teaching With Confidence
The Tithe: A Test in Trust

Resources may be ordered through:
DOVE Christian Fellowship
International/House to House
Publications
1924 West Main Street
Ephrata, PA 17522
Phone: 717-738-3751 or 1-800-846-5892
Fax: 717-738-0656
E-mail: dcfi@redrose.net
Web site: http//www.dcfi.org

8

EMBASSY CHRISTIAN CENTER

Pastor Roberts Liardon
Irvine, California

Roberts Liardon is president of Roberts Liardon Ministries and founder and senior pastor of Embassy Christian Center in Irvine, California. He is also founder of Spirit Life Bible College and Life Ministerial Association in Irvine. A best-selling author and historian, he has preached in more than 80 nations, and has an extensive ministry in Europe, Asia and Africa. His books have been translated into more than 27 languages and have been circulated throughout the world. As a historian, Roberts possesses a wealth of knowledge regarding the great leaders of three Christian movements—Pentecostal, Divine Healing and Charismatic. He has established ongoing research through founding the Reformers and Revivalists Historical Museum in California.

Embassy Christian Center and Spirit Life Bible College had many years of spiritual preparation behind them before they began. This church and Bible school didn't just happen. It wasn't just a good idea I had one day and began to implement the next day. Embassy Christian Center and Spirit Life Bible College emerged from a clear mandate from God that was given to me while I was yet a young boy.

Aside from having a genealogy of circuit-riding preachers and pastors, I was raised by a grandmother and mother who taught me how to go after God. It is true that godly generational calls are often passed down to those who seek the Lord and who obey His Word.

A VISION FROM THE LORD

Because I was the first child born to an Oral Roberts University student, I was named after the founder, Oral Roberts, and I was later dedicated to God by him. At the age of 12, I received a vision from the Lord. He asked me if I would preach for Him while I was still young. So at age 12, I began pioneering my ministry.

When I was 15, I began Roberts Liardon Ministries. In 1983, at the age of 17, I was teaching in an international Bible School. Then I was invited to serve as a guest professor of Church History at Oral Roberts University in 1985.

Roberts Liardon Ministries became international when I was 20 years old. Now in my 30s, I travel more than 180,000 air miles a year, and I preach more than 400 times a year—or 8 to 10 times a week. I have ministered in 88 nations, and we now have started three international offices. At this writing, I have authored more than two dozen books, which have been translated into 35 languages.

A PRAYING HOME

I was raised in a home that stopped and prayed before we considered anything else. My mother built spiritual tenacity into me; my grandmother ignited spiritual hunger as I watched her life and listened to the stories of her ministry.

My grandmother, Gladoylene "Gram" Moore, and her husband, LeBasker, were dynamic Pentecostal preachers in North Carolina. My grandfather also began preaching when he was 12; my grandmother shortly after she turned 17. When the two met, they became recognized as a strong couple of the Word and the Spirit. Giving their lives for God, they pioneered and established churches throughout the eastern section of North America.

THE CALL TO
SOUTHERN CALIFORNIA

In the 1940s, while the family was in prayer, my grandparents had a supernatural experience. My grandfather received a vision and at the same time my grandmother received a prophetic word. The Lord clearly told them to go to Southern California and to establish a strong church there.

Although my grandfather knew that God had spoken to them, he wouldn't agree to move his family so far from the life they had known. Gram was ready and willing, but my grandfather couldn't bring himself to take the step. Operating under a divine time limit, my grandparents therefore never moved to Southern California.

My grandfather died when I was a baby, but I believe his calling was added to my own. As I have said, I knew from my youth that God had called me to establish an international Bible school and church. Personally, though, I thought the timing would probably come when I was an old gray-haired man. I thought I might spend my life ministering in Europe, living in a centralized metropolitan city having a small office staff.

Almost 50 years after God spoke to my grandparents, I was ministering in Israel. During a group prayer, God told me it was time to pioneer the Bible school and the church. At the time I had forgotten about my grandparents failing to reach Southern California. So when the stirring of my heart leaned toward that area, I carefully tested it. Realizing it was indeed the will of God, I determined to continue my international ministry, at the same time building the Bible School and the church in Southern California. During this time, I remembered the call upon my family.

As you can see, establishing this Bible school and church didn't happen instantly. This call to Southern California has gone through two generations of my family before we came to the area and established our spiritual roots. I had my own plans, and I had a successful international ministry. After many years, however, God still held to His plan. He wanted an established, international Bible school and church in Southern California.

THE LOCAL CHURCH IS CENTRAL

If you have studied church history for more than factual information, you may have discovered that past revivals might have had an immediate effect, but the revivals didn't last if they failed to birth or pioneer churches.

John Wesley and George Whitefield were examples of that truth.

Whitefield was a fiery evangelist, able to draw thousands to Jesus Christ by his piercing words. He was one of the first evangelists to cross the Atlantic many times, and was significant in pioneering revivals in America and Europe.

> George Whitefield said, "My brother [John] Wesley acted wisely. The souls that were awakened under his ministry he joined in societies, and thus preserved the fruit of his labor. This I neglected, and my people are a rope of sand."

However, when speaking of his ministry and that of John Wesley's, Whitefield said, "My brother Wesley acted wisely. The souls that were awakened under his ministry he joined in societies, and thus preserved the fruit of his labor. This I neglected, and my people are a rope of sand."[1]

Although both had a strong spiritual kinship, their methods were different. How? Wesley did more than preach. He organized churches in the midst of revival. Thus, the Methodists were born.

The local church is the only institution that has the spiritual strength and authority to change a community. Evangelism is good, but the local church is what ultimately secures the territory for Christ.

I believe that God has brought a fresh enhancement for this particular hour. In our generation, that fresh spiritual enhancement will again have its emphasis in the local church. In other words, spiritual occurrences and insights will begin within the local church, spread throughout the community and world, then return to their foundational source, the local church. Everything will revolve around, through and by the local church, one way or another. I believe in the future, that the dominant world leaders of Christianity will be the pastors.

God is organizing these kinds of churches to spiritually influence their given territories. Because of this authority, some call these territorial churches "apostolic" because the first foundations of God will again be built within a territory.

The godly leadership that leads these territorial churches has been divinely placed and graced by the Spirit of God. These leaders will restore many truths that have been misplaced or neglected for hundreds of years. Under the godly strength of these leaders and through the eagerness of the Church, the Kingdom of light will shine on entire cities, communities and nations. Evil atmospheres will change, cultural and racial conflicts will be subdued and social ills will fade.

EMBASSY'S PLACE IN THIS GENERATION

We believe that Embassy Christian Center (ECC) is one of the many churches God is preparing for this role. The vision of ECC is "To raise a new generation who will aggressively invade the nations with the spirit of revival and restoration." We do not pretend to know all the answers, nor do we think we have even scratched the surface of all

> *We are ever reaching for two high goals: One, to produce strong fruit that remains; second, to constantly respond to the inner witness of what God is saying for today.*

God has planned for us. We know that we have a long way to go, but we have begun. In great fervency and joy, we are ever reaching for two high goals: One, to produce strong fruit that remains; second, to constantly respond to the inner witness of what God is saying for today.

Our church chose the name "Embassy" because in the secular world, an embassy is a place where ambassadors live. We are in the process of establishing ECC as a strong international home church, teaching our people to spiritually govern the nations of the world. We do not believe in a mere "church on the corner." Instead, we strive to meet the needs of the whole community, and to reproduce ourselves in belief, character and outlook. I believe that the authority of the Church in our times will not just be in its numbers; it will also be found in the sending power of the Church. To date, ECC has started 43 churches and has placed missionaries in four of the seven continents of the world.

"Action" is a key word for today's churches. I strongly teach our people to place function over titles. I believe titles are secondary to the call of God. Nations do not change because of a title. The world can only change and come under the authority of God if the people are operating with anointing, present truth and spiritual discernment. A person who has the heart of God will have action and fruit to show it.

Everyone at ECC is offered an equal opportunity to fulfill his or her God-appointed destiny. We do not embrace cultural dominance or doctrines; nor do we accept racial exaltation within the framework of ECC. We also believe that proven, seasoned women should be as honored as men in the fivefold spiritual offices. After a strong season of counseling, we also accept some who have been divorced to fulfill their place in ministry.

Our goal is to be a vital, New Testament church in character, principle, action and belief. To achieve that goal, Embassy Christian Center (ECC) and Spirit Life Bible College (SLBC) are built on five basic principles.

EMBASSY'S FIVE BASIC PRINCIPLES

1. Prayer
The Bible calls the church "a house of prayer" (Matt. 21:13; Mark 11:17). I believe that if a church is not known for the power of its prayer, then it is not truly the house of the Lord.

The way people pray determines what kind of work God can do for them, through them and to them. In our services, we pray with the voice of authority. One of our foundational Scripture references for answered prayer is James 5:16: the "fervent prayer of a righteous man avails much."

We think it is unnecessary to pray loudly to attract God's attention. The word "fervent," however, implies "heat, zeal." Prayer without righteous heat is like a lady ironing clothes—ironing board and iron—but no heat on the iron. She can iron all day, but only the heat will remove the wrinkles. The same is true with prayer. You can pray all day, but if no fervency or righteous heat ignites your prayer, the answer will never come.

James 5:16 also refers to the righteous jealousy of God toward an enemy. In other words, strong, fervent prayer comes from knowing who you are in Christ. When Jesus prayed, His prayers were strong and focused. When people pray fervently, their souls, emotions, minds and bodies must stand at attention to their spirits. The spirit is always focused, and sometimes, fervent prayer is loud. Whether a whisper or a shout, nothing is lethargic about fervent prayer.

Prayer of this nature will banish inhibitions, break any shame and expect the answer. In fact, one of our philosophies is to drive out any shame attached to the Christian life. We believe if your life is one of prayer, then you will not be ashamed to do the works of God.

Our definition of prayer includes every kind of prayer, not just the binding and loosing prayers. We also embrace the prayer value of

> **Preaching is proclamation and demonstration. Teaching is the divine explanation of why a spiritual principle operates as it does.**

what today is called "warfare prayer," accompanied by groanings, travailing and diversities of tongues, both corporately and privately. We teach our members to pray fluently in tongues and in their native languages, to pray freely in their homes, in prayer meetings and in public services.

We believe that everyone should be a prayer warrior. Everyone is an intercessor. We do not believe in an elite, spiritual office of intercessor. We do not allow people, no matter how seasoned they are in prayer, to obtain the title of intercessor. We do not believe in, nor do we have, intercessory prayer *groups*. These groups only eliminate others from the responsibility of praying. *Everyone* has the mandate to pray. From infant to elder, we teach our people the varieties of prayer and expect them to live accordingly.

2. Preaching and Teaching

Preaching and teaching are different from each other, but both are required to have a healthy church. Preaching is proclamation and demonstration. Teaching is the divine explanation of why a spiritual principle operates as it does. Both are imperative so the people can grow, develop and overcome life's situations according to the Word.

I preach *and* teach, and I bring in a variety of the fivefold gifts (apostle, teacher, pastor, evangelist, prophet). SLBC fluently trains its students to understand all five gifts—not just the pastor, teacher and evangelist—and even presents the ministry of helps as a vital gift and function in the present-day Church. In fact, SLBC has been noted as a strong leader in the understanding and ability to instruct students about the prophetic and apostolic operations. I personally teach a class about prophetic ministries and another about apostolic ministries. That same understanding of spiritual gifts flows over into our church members.

In one aspect we are different from many churches today. Usually churches allow a limited number of guest speakers to share in their ministries. If they also sponsor a Bible school, the students may hear the guest speaker the day after he or she ministers at the church.

Not so at ECC and SLBC. Our church and Bible school are intentionally combined to be a church family. In Bible school chapel, guests come to minister in their specialized training. Then in special evening meetings open to the public, they deliver stringent messages. The school and church both receive the training and maturity they need systematically and in equal proportions. Part of that training comes through observing the variety of proven callings and anointings upon the seasoned men and women of God who visit us.

If a central theme runs through the veins of revivalists and reformers it is this: With God, there is no such thing as "generic." According to 1 Corinthians 12:4,5, all ministers, though they may fall into the category of evangelist, prophet, apostle, pastor or teacher, have different anointings and giftings. They each have a different focus on ministry emerging from personal experiences. As a result, they typically address situations from their own viewpoint and effectively minister by it.

My pulpit is not open to just anyone. I always try to bring in those who know more than I know, or who have had a variety of experiences I have never had. Why would the people need a repeat of me? Those who are allowed to preach in the school or church must have a recognized anointing and a word to deposit into the hearts of my people.

My mind and heart are confident in the guests I select. I give them freedom to do everything they can to maximize their anointing. When they leave, I stand with them. I will not undermine them or backlash what they did under the anointing. Because I have prayed and checked their credentials before they came, I have never had to publicly correct anyone in my pulpit, or make up for anything said. I believe it is important for our people to have their eyes opened to see the width and depth of individuality within each calling and across the richness of the Body of Christ. I am only one part of the vast variety of giftings and insights God has given to His Church.

3. Praise and Worship

Just as I believe everyone is called to pray, so I also believe everyone should praise and worship the Lord. Preference of song and style should never dictate corporate or personal worship. Everyone has a personal preference. By forsaking personal preferences, we teach our people to override their emotions and worship or praise from their wills.

Praise and worship are designed to draw people into the presence of the Lord, not to entertain them. In entertainment, the people watch and clap because they enjoy it. In worship, the people get lost in God and participate.

So I watch over the praise and worship songs, styles and flows of anointings. I make sure that whatever our worship team does, the congregation can follow easily. One of the areas I particularly watch is the flow of anointing. We may feel led to sing one song 10 times, but then I watch to see that the next song continues to lead the people further into the presence of God.

The worship team can make or break the flow of anointing by its choice and placement of songs. It is very important to be sensitive to the Spirit. If we are flowing in the right direction, but then the next song totally throws us into another direction, I might stop the entire service. I explain what happened, and the worship team goes back to the right song. If the songs and styles do not build upon each other, immediately after the service I meet and confer with my worship leaders. We find the problem and correct it.

The song of the Lord, the psalmist and the minstrel all have strong places in our church. The song of the Lord is a musical prophecy from God or a divine utterance in song. It can come through anyone, but if the psalmist or minstrel has a prophetic thrust with a song, the results are dramatic.

The psalmist is a singer who has a dedicated calling to music. The person's number one goal is to be sensitive to the direction of the Spirit, creating an atmosphere for the gifts of God. Through song, the psalmist leads the people into His presence. Minstrels are musicians who have dedicated themselves in the same manner.

People cannot stand and play an instrument or sing in our church just because they like to do it or because they are highly skillful. They must understand that to minister before the congregation of the Lord, they need to yield their gifts and talents solely to His purpose and use.

Our ultimate goal for praise and worship is for the people to praise with all their being. Our praise is enthusiastic and expressive. We are eager to find that intimate, high place of worship with the corporate Body. In that place, the congregation enters together, yet everyone has an individual experience. To reach this high goal, everyone is involved. The congregation must come willing and expectant; the minstrels must be creative and the psalmist sensitive to lead in the right direction.

4. Fellowship

I believe that God has a social nature. He loves to fellowship with people. We also have that nature. We want to fellowship with God and with other people. I believe godly fellowship can help close the revolving door of the church. If people come to church just to sit and receive, never establishing relationships within the church Body, they are unable to establish their roots. These people end up roaming from church to church or falling away.

Fellowship is an important aspect of the church. I believe, though, that fellowship doesn't have to be deep, spiritual relationships. It is vital to feature fun activities that are lighthearted and entertaining. In the book of Acts, the believers fellowshipped and communed day to day from house to house.

Everything has its place. We sponsor special dinners, functions, tours and even birthday parties. We provide married, single and youth activities. Each year, we try to take our SLBC alumni on a short ocean cruise. Life with God is more than the pulpit or the church services. When it is time for encouragement or correction, the right fellowship can provide it. When it is time for fun and activities, the church should produce the most enjoyable people on earth.

5. Evangelism and Missions

I teach that everyone is an evangelist and a missionary. Our people are constantly taught that the earth is the Lord's and that they are free to be His ambassadors wherever they go. The Great Commission doesn't say, "Go ye that are called to stand behind the pulpit"; it says, "Go ye." I believe this is not a Scripture verse you can take or leave; it is the last commandment Jesus gave to His Church. So it is vital for people to redirect portions of their money and time toward missions.

In 1995, while seeking the Lord for direction, I received a radical mandate. He said, "All members of ECC will be taking a missions trip in 1995." When the Lord speaks, it is law at ECC and SLBC. Immediately, the people were required to sign up for a missions trip. They were given various options—from two weeks to a weekend, from overseas missions to local missions. If the members didn't sign up, they were called and given the option to remain a member. If they needed help, ECC assisted in various ways, including placement on a trip.

As 1995 ended, 26 highly successful mission trips were taken in 14 states and 4 nations. More than 400 people—many included families—launched into a missions trip. As a result, the people exploded with a desire to evangelize. Hundreds of testimonies poured into the church. After a local missions trip to Mexico, a single parent who had two small children moved to that area to evangelize!

This spiritual fervor birthed the Missions Program of ECC. Because the people showed corporate obedience, we received a corporate blessing—our new building that houses our church, Bible School, bookstore, various ministries and corporate offices was obtained!

Currently, we send out a different missions team each month, including international teams. Our new members and potential members are instructed that within the first 18 months of membership, a missions trip is required. I believe to be a modern-day book of Acts church, the people must be known as bold believers, led by the Spirit and fed by faith—not fear.

Our method for effective evangelism is: "By any means possible." Locally, we pray and develop strategies for ways to show God in our community. We go to the streets and evangelize through drama, preaching, singing and witnessing. We use the means of television, radio, books, tracts—even matchbooks.

I heard of a man who witnessed through a printed message on

matchbooks. I used to laugh about it. One day, however, I realized that a matchbook contains about 20 matches. Each time a person lifted the cover to strike a match, he or she was witnessed to. It was a great concept; so now we use it and other approaches like it. We knock on doors to pray for people in their homes. We hang door knockers telling of what Jesus has provided for them. We evangelize during Gay Pride festivals, on beaches, in hospitals or nursing homes. It is our goal to reach whatever moves on the streets of Southern California!

One of our programs, called "Project Joseph," feeds families in Orange County. Our people and other contributors provide the food or the money for it. Recently this outreach provided food for 1,000 people. In keeping with the book of Acts where people had all things in common, this food ministry isn't only for the community; it is also available for our people. Everyone in our church who has a need is strongly encouraged to visit Project Joseph and take whatever food is needed—no questions asked. I believe it is important to take care of your people *and* your community.

We have all been excited about the last-day harvest of souls. Until the Church understands *how* to go into all the world, however, it will never understand how to harvest it. Every believer is called to go into the world and meet the needs of humanity through Christ. Some will stay; some can go for only a week or a month. It is the going that fulfills the Great Commission, though, revealing the end-time Church and harvest. Unless the people are taught how to go, they won't understand how to harvest their communities, nations or world for Jesus Christ.

TRAINING LEADERS FOR MINISTRY

Our Bible school's name—Spirit Life Bible College—is based on its emphasis. That is, teaching students to live in the Spirit and partake of life's reality according to heaven's mandate. Although knowledge can be acquired in many educational institutions, SLBC creates an atmosphere for people to receive knowledge *and* to experience the life of God.

As of 1998, SLBC plans to be a nationally accredited Bible school. I believe in strong academic excellence, but not at the expense of the flow of the Spirit. I strongly believe in teaching Spirit life while at the same time grounding students in the Word of God. The Word and the Spirit will always agree. Therefore, I have advised the accrediting agency that I would withdraw from the full accreditation process if at any time the vision or call of the school was threatened.

SLBC offers two years of in-depth training. The first year, students are treated as new Christians—no matter who they are or the location of their hometown. The year is dedicated to a foundation of prayer, faith, sound doctrine and principles that bring character and unity.

The second year takes students into practical ministry. By now, the calling of the students are revealed and their hunger grows toward their destinies. Each year we adjust the curriculum to meet the spiritual thrust of the class.

Every race and age from 18 to 80 is in attendance at SLBC. One year, 28 nationalities were represented in the student body.

Though the students have accomplished great works, overall, I became dissatisfied. In seeking the Lord, I realized that students came to receive from their instructors, but the instructors couldn't be involved with the students for the sheer number of them. So as of 1997, we are only accepting 70 students in each new class. This way the instructors and I can corporately *and* personally be involved in the students' growth.

BORN TO MAKE A DIFFERENCE

I believe that each person in this generation was born to make a difference for the kingdom of God. To be a cutting-edge believer, we must know how to bring the power of God into our circumstances. The Word of God and His commands must be upheld at all costs.

Having that understanding, ECC will continue to have a twofold purpose. One, that the church Body will always accommodate God's heart and desire. Church is not a social club where carnality runs rampant and pet peeves are exalted. Second, by accommodating the heart and desire of God, the people will be blessed in all areas of their lives. It is our high goal to be obedient and bless the heart of God. I believe it is the only voice that will be heard by the multitudes in these exciting days.

Note
1. Basil Walker, *John Wesley* (Minneapolis: Bethany House Publishers, 1943), p. 97.

Roberts Liardon
Roberts Liardon Ministries
17601 Fitch
Irvine, CA 92614
Phone: 714-833-3555
Fax: 714-833-9555

Resource List—Books
God's Generals
Sharpen Your Discernment
I Saw Heaven
Breaking Controlling Powers
How to Survive an Attack

Resources may be ordered through:
Roberts Liardon Ministries
P.O. Box 30710
Laguna Hills, CA 92654-0710

9

MORNING STAR INTERNATIONAL

Rice Broocks, President
Brentwood, Tennessee

Rice Broocks is the president and cofounder of Morning Star International, a ministry focused on church planting, campus ministry and world missions. Rice is a graduate of Reformed Theological Seminary in Jackson, Mississippi, a Presbyterian seminary. Currently, Morning Star International is working in 15 nations of the world. Other affiliated ministries of Morning Star include the following: Champions for Christ, a ministry dedicated to reaching college and professional athletes; Victory Campus Ministries, a ministry in making disciples on the university campuses of the world; and Victory Leadership Institute, a two-year leadership training school.

The Florida State football program is not where people expect to find potential missionaries. The young minister was asked to speak to the team chapel service, and most expected him to give the normal pep talk: go out and "win one for the Lord." Instead, he challenged the team to give all to Christ, repent of their sin and become disciples. "If you are serious, truly serious, I want you to stand to your feet." Nine men stood.

One of these men was Franco Gennaro. Franco was a scrappy defensive back who made the team as a walk-on. By no means the star of the team, Franco nevertheless was a young man who was convinced that anything worth doing was worth doing 100 percent. During the next few months, he threw his life into Bible study, prayer and an all-out

assault on winning the campus. Within a few years, Franco was planting churches throughout Latin America.

Sutan and Morgante were brothers who came to study in America
from Indonesia. Their hopes were to earn their degrees and return
home to start successful careers. Because of the international student
outreach by a local church, they were not only converted to Christ,
but also discipled, and given a vision to go back and change their
nation. Upon graduation, they returned to Jakarta and helped pioneer
a church that has now planted 11 other churches.

These stories capture the heartbeat of our ministry as well as a vital
strategy.

CHANGE THE CAMPUS, CHANGE THE WORLD

It is no coincidence that the cofounders of Morning Star International,
Phil Bonasso, Steve Murrell and I, were converted to Christ during our
student years. During this critical time, someone reached out to us by
presenting a message of commitment to Christ as His disciple. We were
told, "If you would do the most with your life, find out what God is
doing in your generation and throw yourself into it." This became our
battle cry.

For Steve Murrell, it was a Presbyterian youth pastor, Ron
Musselman, fresh out of seminary. Almost daily, he would come to
Steve's high school, reaching out to the students. Though Steve recalls
being this young pastor's "chief persecutor," he eventually yielded his
life to Christ through Ron's persistence. In fact, by the end of his high
school years, hundreds of Steve's classmates were won to Christ and
many entered into full-time ministry. Steve refers to this harvest as
"Mr. Musselman's Opus."

For Phil, it was a conversion through a prayer group during his
junior year in high school. His father was an officer in the army and a
West Point graduate, and two brothers would go to West Point and the
Air Force Academy, so leadership was in his veins. Yet, while a student,
a deep awakening came as he realized that empty religion would not
satisfy his heart, but only a radical commitment to Christ as Lord. As
the student body president, he began reaching out to his classmates
and teachers, realizing that God's hand was on his life for ministry.

For me, it was a combination of several fellow classmates. My first encounter with God came because a young man cared enough to call my bluff and invite me to a Christian meeting. Just seeing people study the Bible and pray had a huge effect on me. The second and most devastating witness was from a young student named Greg Anthony (now a Presbyterian pastor). His confidence in God was contagious. I wanted to be exactly like him.

WINNING THE FAMILY

As a result of Greg Anthony's witness, I got the courage to face my family—a family that already thought my new Christianity was another "fleeting fad." My brother was a borderline atheist. Having earned a master's degree in psychology and finishing his third year of law school at Southern Methodist University in Dallas, Texas, he was determined to get me out of the "born again thing." My father was an oil company executive traveling the world and climbing the corporate ladder. Though not a Christian, he was a man of tremendous character and resolve, but to him I was more or less an embarrassment.

Reach a student, reach the family.

My conversion, however, put us on a collision course. This collision came one evening when my brother dropped by to show me "all the contradictions in the Bible." By the end of the evening, I had not only seen my brother repent of his unbelief, but I also immediately baptized him in a local swimming pool!

His conversion shook my father, who couldn't dismiss my brother as a "flake." At 57 years old, my father became a Christian. This pattern has been repeated again and again. Reach a student, reach the family. Upon graduation, my desire was to reach other students so that their families might be changed as mine was.

Our history together as the founders of Morning Star began in college—Steve and I were roommates. During this time, God began to form a bond between two total opposites (Steve was the more quiet one). Eventually we jointly pioneered a church in Manila, Philippines, that has now planted more than 30 churches in five countries.

Phil and I met while he was still in college at Auburn University in Auburn, Alabama. Our first recollection of each other was in a football huddle and my telling him to "run long," and I would get the ball for him. Phil says, "It's been like that ever since." We then worked together to pioneer a ministry at the University of Southern California in Los Angeles, which has produced more than 75 full-time leaders as well as birthed many other churches.

All this occurred during the late 1970s and 1980s. During this time, we were a part of the same ministry organization, but that ended in 1989. Many people had a significant influence on our lives during this time. My first pastor, Walter Walker, was an incredible man of faithfulness and commitment. For Steve and me both, he laid a strong foundation in the Word of God. For all three of us, Bob Weiner was a key figure as well. Bob's passion for world evangelism as well as for student ministry were key ingredients in preparing us for our calling.

THE "MIRACLE IN MANILA"

During the '90s, our lives—Phil's, Steve's and mine—would be woven together into what is now known as Morning Star International. We have come to call this watershed moment the "Miracle in Manila." In March 1994, Steve, Phil and I sat in Steve's living room, asking God to show us how we could work together in the area of world missions. We compared our common vision, our desire to reach students and train leaders as well as to plant churches around the world. Each of us underscored the critical core values we possessed in making disciples, not decisions; building character, not crowds; and making certain churches were established that would have a vital strategy for clearly the most wide-open harvest field in history: the youth of the world.

What stood out even more to us than ever before was the relational and foundational ties that existed between them and me. The fact that I had helped both of them plant churches gave us a relational link that was critical in ensuring a sense of family and not just an organizational bond. All those years spent building trust and faith in each other now began to make sense. It was as if the Lord Himself came into the room and put us together in a new way. We all sensed God lay His Hand upon us as a team: a threefold cord. Our commission from Him was clear: Church Planting, Campus Ministry, World Missions.

Today (1998), Morning Star International comprises approximately 90 churches in 16 countries. Each of these churches, though widely diverse, possesses the same pattern for accomplishing this mission: Make disciples, train leaders. Although some may call their movements such names as "networks" or "associations of ministries," we refer to ourselves as a family of churches and ministries. The Morning Star family not only includes local churches, but other vital arms as well, such as:

- Victory Campus Ministries (VCM) is a worldwide campus outreach sponsoring campus groups that are local-church based. Having a campus ministry that is distinct from the churches, yet covered by them, allows us to keep a clear focus on student ministry, while encouraging other strategies as well. VCM is staffed by leaders who spend almost all their time on campus. The national offices are located in Los Angeles, California.

- Champions for Christ (CFC) is an outreach to college and professional athletes. This ministry is led by Greg and Helen Ball, who not only serve in this arena, but also help lead the worldwide outreach of the Morning Star churches. CFC also has chapters using full-time staff who devote their attention to reaching athletes. The National Offices are located in Austin, Texas.

- Victory Leadership Institute (VLI) is a two-year institute dedicated to providing advanced discipleship for every Christian as well as a second year of study for potential full-time Christian pastors, leaders and missionaries. My training at Reformed Theological Seminary in Jackson, Mississippi, reinforced a desire to establish an Institute that could give students a solid theological grounding in the historic Christian faith as well as training men and women to minister in the power of the Holy Spirit. Currently VLI headquarters are located in Manila, Philippines, and branches in Nashville, Tennessee; Raleigh-Durham, North Carolina; Los Angeles, California; Ukraine; Jakarta, Indonesia; and San Jose, Costa Rica. Our vision is eventually to establish a training institute in every Morning Star church.

- Victory Publishing is the publishing arm of our ministry. Discipleship books, cell group material and other key resources are available to assist the local churches. Steve Murrell, in Manila, leads this department and also is the editor of our monthly magazine, *The Victory Fire*.

WHAT HAS GOD CALLED US TO DO?

As Morning Star International has developed, seven crucial ministries have surfaced, which guide our direction:

1. *Evangelizing the lost.* Our primary mission is to reach the lost. Each local church must possess a strategy to accomplish this task. In promising to make His disciples "fishers of men," Jesus put the Church's focus on evangelism. Before there can be any reformation in society there must be regeneration in the people.
2. *Making disciples.* When a person is saved, that person must be taught and mentored. Foundations of repentance and faith must be properly laid. They need to be water baptized as well as released into the power of the Holy Spirit. All this is vital. Most of this will not happen without a deliberate plan (i.e., without people helping these new believers). Our goal is to build "disciple-making" churches that emphasize one-on-one and small-group ministry.
3. *Training leaders.* Discipleship is the first step toward leadership. Leaders are those who disciple others. Paul called them "faithful men who will be able to teach others" (2 Tim. 2:2). Without this vital step, there cannot be real leadership development within the Church. Leaders, like disciples, must be trained intentionally. In training leaders, our emphasis is on developing homegrown leaders, not transplants.
4. *Building relationally.* In Acts 13:2, the Holy Spirit said, "Separate to Me Barnabas and Saul for the work to which I have called them." We see this as an example of God joining people together for His greater purposes. In Ephesians 4:16 it says, "The whole body, joined and knit together by what

every joint supplies." God joins you together rather than you joining something. Yet, though you are joined by God, the relationship must be nurtured and properly protected or it can be severed (as in the case of Paul and Barnabas). Much time and energy is spent building the bonds of friendship between the leaders of our movement.

5. *Targeting youth.* As a father, my primary concern is for the spiritual health of my four children. In the past 20 years of ministry, by far the most frequent prayer request we receive is for someone's children or grandchildren. The attack today against the youth culture has been as deliberately planned as was the attack against the children during the time of the birth of both Moses and Jesus. Just as the enemy knew there was the promise of deliverance through these lives, so the promise that in the last days "I will pour out my Spirit on your sons and daughters" (see Acts 2:17) has unleashed a demonic retaliation in an attempt to stop it. Besides this, studies have shown that the majority of people who are saved are saved before the age of 25. It is our contention that the most energy should be spent on those who are most open to the gospel. This doesn't limit our ministry to just youth, because this approach actually gives us tremendous inroads to reach their unsaved families.

6. *Planting churches.* Church planting has been called the most effective form of evangelism. Local churches also provide the spiritual family for new believers to be nurtured and trained. They are the Lord's strategy to reveal His wisdom to a community or nation and are given the promise by Christ Himself that the gates of hell will not prevail against them. Our calling is not just to further evangelism or win students, but also to establish churches where the Word of God is given preeminence and the work of the Holy Spirit is honored.

7. *Establishing world missions.* More than 2 billion people have never heard the name of Jesus Christ. The major blocks of humanity that are Buddhist, Hindu or Islamic remain for the most part unevangelized. Our commission is to penetrate these areas with the gospel. Considering the more than 400,000 international students that are studying in American

universities, God, it seems, has helped us get started by bringing these nations to us. In many other nations the growth in the number of international students is unprecedented. As we reach out and befriend the foreigner in our midst, we are reaching future church planters who will return to reach these unreached people groups.

WHERE ARE WE GOING?

Our mission is to plant churches in every nation. These churches primarily will be planted in cities consisting of large campus populations. Although we target the youth, we don't want to limit the influence of these churches, but we attempt to equip them to reach a wide spectrum of society. Our primary task is to continue to expand our training arm, Victory Leadership Institute, in order to have the staff necessary to meet the vast opportunities that exist worldwide. As Jesus said, "'The harvest truly is plentiful, but the laborers are few'" (Matt. 9:37). Because VLI is a fully equipped training school, our short-term goal is to release at least 100 new leaders each year into the ministry.

At the present time we have several churches that serve as "apostolic centers." These centers are churches that have not only birthed other churches, but also serve as a spiritual covering for others. Our apostolic centers are located in the United States in cities such as Nashville, Los Angeles and Raleigh-Durham; in other nations such as Manila (Philippines), Jakarta (Indonesia) and San Jose (Costa Rica). Our goal is to establish such apostolic centers in 100 nations in the next decade. Because our churches in these major cities have a strong outreach to the campus community, our hope is to be able to make a significant difference in the media, the arts, business, government as well as education, and to have revival and awakening come to the nations!

THE INTERNATIONAL LEADERSHIP TEAM

The governing board of Morning Star International is referred to as the International Apostolic Team. This team functions as a presbytery of elders in overseeing the churches and ministries throughout the world. Various national and regional teams also perform this oversight under the auspices of the International Team. For instance, a Philippine apostolic team serves the churches in that nation, and an Asian apostolic team assists all the churches in that region. An apostolic team serves in North America in that function, as do similar ones in Latin America and Europe. Ephesians 4:11 describes this function, which some have called the "fivefold ministry"(referring to the offices of apostle, prophet, evangelist, pastor and teacher), and its job to equip the saints for the work of the ministry. It is understood that regular input from these fivefold ministries is vital to the life of the church.

Under the covering of the apostolic team, each local church is governed by a presbytery of elders or leaders led by a senior pastor. These leadership teams decide the specific strategy and direction for their congregations. The extra-local government primarily focuses on overseeing five areas:

1. *Birthing and receiving new churches.* Churches are started in many ways using a wide variety of strategies; however, this process is overseen by the national leadership team. Should an existing church seek to become a part of our fellowship, the national board decides this as well.

2. *Maintaining doctrinal purity.* The parameters of orthodoxy have been set forth in Holy Scripture. Paul wrote, "Hold fast the pattern of sound words,...that good thing which was committed to you" (2 Tim. 1:13,14). Doctrines such as the deity of Christ, the Trinity and the authority of Scripture must be upheld with full conviction. The historic statements of faith such as the Apostles' Creed, Nicene Creed and Chalcedon Creed are recognized as crucial definitions of Christianity. Although liberty is allowed for each individual and church in areas such as eschatology and soteriology, it is vital to guard against "strange doctrines." Such error can manifest in works-oriented salvation, or its opposite, antinomianism. It also is prevalent in an atmosphere where subjective experience and prophetic revelation go unchecked.

3. *Developing leadership.* The process of developing leaders is a vital part of the job description of the apostolic team. Working hand in hand with the leaders of the local churches, the goal of training workers for the harvest is at the forefront of everything we do. Some of the particular ways in which

this is accomplished will be discussed in the next few pages.

4. *Conducting ordination.* We recognize two kinds of ordination. First, the ordination of local church elders. It is the responsibility of the national team to fulfill the task of providing elders in every church. Those who are candidates for eldership must comply with the requirements set forth in 1 Timothy 3 and Titus 1. These candidates are nominated by the senior pastor and local elders and are confirmed by laying on of hands by the local presbytery along with a representative from the apostolic team.

Second, the ordination of men and women into the gospel ministry. Besides fulfilling the biblical requirements for eldership mentioned, the recognition of the calling, the demonstration of proven character and the evidence of fruitfulness is examined. The first step in this process is the status of licensed minister. After a period of time, the board will lay hands upon the person for ordination.

5. *Mediating church conflicts.* Should the unfortunate occasion arise in which leaders or congregations find themselves in unresolvable disagreements, the extra-local team will help in the attempt to resolve the situation. This underscores the need for healthy personal relationships to exist between the local leaders and the apostolic team members. Organizational authority, as contrasted to relational authority, can mean very little in the midst of emotionally charged situations.

ACCOUNTABILITY AND TEAM BUILDING

Obviously, our teams work together because enormous amounts of time and energy have been invested in building relationships across the board. Through these personal relationships, genuine accountability takes place.

Each year at the regional conferences, the local elders and the extra-local team members are able to "hang out" and get to know each other. The members of the congregations also come together during this time in a "camp meeting" atmosphere to build the family ties and the vision of the movement even stronger. It is our quest to have every member of the local congregations own the vision. A yearly retreat is also held for all the pastors in each region of the world. This time is devoted to ministering directly to their specific needs.

A highlight each year are the International Conferences held for all the members of the Morning Star movement. In Asia, it is called "Asian Invasion." This conference is held in Manila and draws more than 3,000 potential leaders from throughout Asia to trumpet the call to reach the world.

In North America, the Morning Star International Conference is held in Los Angeles; more than 1,500 attend this gathering. In South and Central America, the same gatherings of people come from around the region. They are held in Lima, Peru; and San Jose, Costa Rica. These conferences attract more than 1,000 people. During these conferences, church-planting teams are sent out, friendships are formed and finances are released for the harvest.

In Manila, reaching the 10/40 Window is the primary focus. Currently, churches have been planted in Bangladesh, Russia, China and the United Arab Emirates as a direct result of the effect of this conference. The list of future church plants where leadership teams have already formed includes Korea, Vietnam, Taiwan, Hong Kong, Burma and Australia.

VIEWS OF LEADERSHIP AND LEADERSHIP TRAINING

The primary way leaders are enlisted is through the ministry of the local church. In this setting, the character of each individual is formed and best observed; and in this atmosphere, the gifts and callings also can be developed properly. As well, discipleship is the first step on the road to leadership. In many cases, ministry skills are cultivated through the vehicle of small groups or cells. Thus, most of the churches have some kind of cell strategy in place.

In Asia, for instance, cells are the primary method for outreach and leadership development. Each cell structure begins through evangelism or outreach. The cell consists of a leader as well as an intern or assistant. From the beginning, it is understood that the intern is a leader in training who will one day soon take part of the group and start another cell. In monthly cell-ministry training days, intensive instruction is given to all cell leaders and interns. Those who have borne fruit through cell ministry become the best candidates to pastor churches or take on greater responsibility.

As was mentioned, our training arm, Victory Leadership Institute, is also a vital part of our training strategy. For the first year academic courses are taught, such as Theology, Church History, Old and New Testament Survey, as well as practical ministry courses such as Discipleship and Evangelism, and Cell Ministry. The second-year curriculum is intended for those who are called into full-time ministry. The areas of emphasis are Pastoral Ministry and Theology, Campus Ministry, and Church Planting and Missions.

> *The critical nature of prayer is vital to any successful ministry. In our ministry, it cannot be separated from anything we do.*

All leaders of Morning Star are encouraged to attend VLI. Although it is not a requirement for ordination at this time, understanding the principles of ministry taught at VLI are definitely a prerequisite.

PRAYER AND POWER MINISTRIES

The critical nature of prayer is vital to any successful ministry. In our ministry, it cannot be separated from anything we do. The first Thursday of every month we sponsor a worldwide Morning Star day of prayer and fasting for our churches and ministries. Our prayer coordinator in Los Angeles receives faxes and E-mails, and then sends out a summary of all the requests deemed appropriate for the whole movement to consider for prayer. Prayer teams in most local churches also cover the leadership and the local work. So much has been written about prayer and intercession lately that we have noticed a noteworthy prayer revival in our midst. We have come to see the visible connection between much prayer and increased results in ministry.

This is especially true when it comes to signs and wonders. Many of the breakthroughs around the world have been the result of a notable miracle or healing after corporate prayer. In one case, a highly visible NFL quarterback who is a part of our ministry suffered what was said to be a season-ending injury. People around the world began to intercede for this young man's healing. On the eve of the surgery, the doctor proclaimed that it was now unnecessary to operate. The end result is that his teammates continue to come to Christ because of his testimony.

There is no way that Muslim, Hindu and Buddhist nations will be penetrated without prayer as well as signs and wonders. In China, one of the members of the International Apostolic Team, Ron Lewis, was ministering in a covert setting to a group of Chinese students. As they met in a stuffy upper room, Ron was teaching about the gift of the Holy Spirit. As he spoke, a strong wind unexpectedly began to blow through the room. Just as in Acts 2, they were all filled with the Holy Spirit and began to speak in other tongues. This group became the foundation for a new church in this very difficult place.

We believe that God has given us a tremendous gift in Jim Laffoon. Jim operates in the office of the prophet and brings tremendous inspiration and balance to our midst. Through his leadership, our movement is challenged to believe for greater results and efforts in the areas of prayer, prophecy and signs and wonders.

FINANCIAL PRINCIPLES

Every movement needs adequate resources to grow and advance. Recognizing this, each member church and ministry sends a partial tithe of 5 percent of its own tithes and offerings to the International Apostolic Team. This money is distributed to the various apostolic offices for salaries and basic office expenses. As might be expected, this does not meet all the financial needs for the extra-local ministry or for the funds for planting new churches. Thus, through our world and regional conferences, we invite all members of the ministry to become monthly partners of the ministry. In this way, every person has a sense of ownership when it comes to the worldwide vision.

IN CONCLUSION

In attempting to give the necessary facts about our ministry, it becomes difficult to avoid using phrases that cannot be adequately explained in this short space. For instance, the very terms "apostle" or "apostolic" have been used without the necessary definitions of what is meant by the term. It is a deep concern that the focus of our attention isn't on the term "apostle," but on the dimension of ministry it represents.

None of us at Morning Star think we are in the same league as the original 12 apostles or that anything we say is equal to Holy Scripture. In the past, some charismatic ministries have been criticized for their use of terms such as "prophetic" or "revelation," suggesting that these terms imply the information given through these means are infallible utterances.

We firmly believe that Holy Scripture is above everything we do as the objective judge. All of us combined still "know in part and we prophesy in part" (1 Cor. 13:9). Our passion at Morning Star is to combine the strengths of charismatic ministry with the framework of sound historical theology.

As one of my favorite professors once said, "We Presbyterians build a great fireplace, but many times we can't seem to get a fire started." My reply was that we charismatics build a fire all right, but we have this tendency to burn things down! Obviously, we need both.

Another term that begs definition is the term "discipleship." In some circles when it is used, images of "heavy-handedness" come to mind. It must be clearly stated that what is meant by the term is not people having other people tell them what to do and attempt to run their lives. For us, discipleship means to mentor people in the foundations of the Christian faith; to encourage them and pray for them so that they may follow Christ more effectively. The goal in discipleship is to release people, not to become their personal "guru."

As usual, if the enemy can't get the Church to ignore a vital truth, it seems his alternative is to get it to abuse it. Restoring the vital truth of biblical discipleship is critical, however, if we are to ever make any advances in reaching the world more effectively.

Finally, we always seem to go back to Psalm 127:1, "Unless the Lord builds the house, they labor in vain who build it." We want to build in such a way that what is done will last more than one generation. It is our hope that God would be glorified through what we do, and that He would allow it to be transferred to our sons and daughters in the Lord. Most of all, even as the book of Revelation speaks of Christ as "the Bright and Morning Star" (22:16), in naming our ministry Morning Star, we pray that His honor and His glory will continue to be our focus.

Rice Broocks
Morning Star International
P.O. Box 1787
Brentwood, TN 37024-1787
Phone: 615-371-8479
Fax: 615-371-8433

Resource List

Books
Discipleship—Following the Road
that Leads to Life
Change the Campus Change the World

Audiotape Series
The Making of a Disciple

Videotape Series
Making a Decision that Lasts Forever

Resources may be ordered through:
Morning Star International
P.O. Box 1787
Brentwood, TN 37024-1787

10

CHRISTIAN INTERNATIONAL MINISTRIES NETWORK

Bishop Bill Hamon
Santa Rosa Beach, Florida

Dr. Hamon is cofounder with his wife, Evelyn, of Christian International Ministries, CI School of Theology, CI Network of Churches, CI Family Church, CI Network of Churches and CI Family Worship Center in Indiana. Dr. Hamon's 40-plus years of ministry experience provide a balanced biblical approach to the restoration of the office of the prophet, in which he has functioned for the last 40 years. He founded and currently serves as Bishop of Christian International Ministries, home to an undergraduate and graduate School of Theology. CI's School of Theology has served more than 7,500 students in the past 26 years. He holds bachelor of theology, master of theology and doctor of divinity degrees, and is respected by church leaders around the world as a senior leader of the prophetic company God is establishing in these last days.

To introduce myself, let me say that I began my public ministry in 1954 at age 19. Two years later I married Evelyn Hixon, and we now have 3 married children and 11 grandchildren. All our children, Tim and Karen Hamon, Tom and Jane Hamon, and Glenn and Sherilyn Miller, are ordained ministers with Christian International (CI). They are 3 of the 18 couples who serve on the CI Board of Governors. Tim serves as the president of CI School of Theology (CIST) and the CI Learning Network (CILN). Tom and Jane are copastors of CI

Family Church (CIFC) and the International Training Center (CI-ITC). Sherilyn and Glenn travel full time as prophets in the Body of Christ. Glenn also serves as District Representative to all CI churches and ministers on the west coast of the United States.

A VARIED MINISTRY

During my 43 years of prophetic ministry to the Body of Christ, I have functioned in many kinds of ministries: six years as a pastor, three years in evangelistic work and five years as a teacher in a Bible college. I founded Christian International School of Theology and served as its president for more than 25 years. Christian International's School of the Holy Spirit was founded in 1979. CI Conferences and Seminars followed soon after in 1983.

We established Christian International Family Church in 1985 and Christian International Network of Prophetic Ministries in 1987. Scores of ministers and churches had come into our network by early 1990. We also established the CI Business Network in 1989, Christian International Network of Churches in 1992, the CI Prayer Counseling and Training Ministry in 1994 and the CI Residential Ministry Training college in 1996.

In addition to national conferences and ministry engagements, I have written five books: *The Eternal Church, Prophets and Personal Prophecy, Prophets and the Prophetic Movement, Prophets: Pitfalls and Principles,* and most recently, *Prophets, Apostles and the Coming Moves of God.*

CHRISTIAN INTERNATIONAL AS A
RESOURCE CENTER FOR THE CHURCH

Christian International is a resource center to the prophets and apostles in the Body of Christ, providing books and instructional manuals for teaching, training, activating, mentoring and maturing those called to the fivefold ministry. We are committed to having all fivefold ministers fully released and unified in their ministries to the church of Jesus Christ. We, of course, train evangelists, pastors and teachers, but our greater anointing is for calling forth and establishing prophets and apostles.

We have conducted hundreds of conferences at our CI headquarters in Florida and around the world. We hold an annual International Gathering of Prophets and Apostles every October. Our eleventh IGPA Conference was held in 1997. More than 25,000 saints and 6,000 ministry leaders have been trained to recognize and to operate in their supernatural gifts of the Holy Spirit through the CI *Manual for Ministering Spiritual Gifts*. Other special seminars are conducted each year to establish Christians in prophetic ministries, praise, dance-arts-drama-mime, warfare praise, prophetic counseling and the role of prophets and apostles to the nations.

OUR NETWORK OF CHURCHES

I am bishop over the CI Network of churches (about 200) and ministers (about 500). We have twice as many ministers as churches because we ordain both husbands and wives. About 50 of our ministers are in full-time traveling ministries. The others are staff and faculty at CI Campus in Santa Rosa Beach, Florida.

Christian International School of Theology has functioned as a distance education college for 30 years. We have enrolled 8,000 students in 60 nations and more than 900 graduates are ministering throughout the Body of Christ around the world. Hundreds of CI extension colleges have been established in local churches.

CI's international headquarters, the School of Theology campus and the Family Church are located on 67 acres north and south of 5200 E. Hwy. 98, Santa Rosa Beach, Florida. Other administrative centers are located in Versailles, Indiana; Ontario, Canada; Sunderland, England; Sano Shi, Japan; Durban and Johannesburg, South Africa; and West Bengal, India.

OUR PHILOSOPHY OF MINISTRY

Our commission from Christ is to help bring full restoration and recognition of prophets and apostles back into the church until they have the same recognition, acceptance and placement as the evangelists, pastors and teachers have had for hundreds of years. We have been given the revelation and divine anointing to produce the teaching materials and equip fivefold ministers with the wisdom and ability to teach, train, activate, mentor and mature the saints in their gifts and callings.

Jesus is involved in the restoration of the fullness of His Church. Each of us at CI feels compelled to look beyond our personal and local ministry goals to catch a glimpse of Christ's vision for His whole Church and for the nations of the world.

CHRISTIAN INTERNATIONAL MINISTRIES NETWORK

Christian International Ministries Network (CIMN) has been birthed in response to what we have sensed to be an order from King Jesus. Our desire is to help usher in apostles and prophets as foundational ministries in the church, while training and activating all fivefold ministries and facilitating the full restoration of biblical truth and practice. In Ephesians 4:8-11, we read that Jesus gave fivefold ministers as gifts to the church. "It was he who gave some to be apostles, some to be prophets, some to be evangelists, and some to be pastors and teachers" (v. 11, *NIV*). We call this the "fivefold ministry." We view these ministries as ascension gifts of Christ for the government of the Church.

These five ministries are dear to the heart of God. They are keys to His plan. The apostles and prophets are central to building the foundation of the Church.

> [You are] built on the foundation of the apostles and prophets, Jesus Christ Himself being the chief cornerstone (Eph. 2:20).

In talking about these ministry gifts, Paul goes on in Ephesians 4:12,13 to indicate that the purpose of these gifts is "for the equipping of the saints for the work of ministry, for the edifying of the body of Christ, till we all come to the unity of the faith, and of the knowledge of the Son of God, to a perfect man, to the measure of the stature of the fullness of Christ."

God is currently bringing forth a large company of fivefold ministers who will help prepare the way for Christ's second coming. These men and women of destiny are to be voices to the Church and to the nations. They are calling forth apostles and prophets of power who will join them in helping to bring the Church to unity and maturity.

Many things must yet come into order. Jesus wants to return, but according to His Word, He is being held in heaven until the "times of restoration of all things" have been fulfilled (Acts 3:21). God has given certain requirements and mandates regarding Christ's second coming. As the people of God, we must do our part to "grow up in all things into Him who is the head—Christ" (Eph. 4:15), and become a people "not having spot or wrinkle or any such thing" (5:27), but rather a Church holy and blameless before Him.

NETWORKING FOR ACCOUNTABILITY AND OVERSIGHT

God has been speaking to me, both in my spirit and through other prophets, during the last five years about accepting increased responsibility to train and oversee those called to prophetic and apostolic ministry. Apostles and prophets must have their fingers accurately on the pulse of what God is doing and they must be able to righteously demonstrate His power and plan. Christian International Network of Churches was birthed from this desire to not only see ministers trained and activated, but also to provide a place of accountability and oversight.

Just as Samuel and Elijah headed schools of the prophets scattered throughout Israel, so I believe God continues the work of "fathering" and schooling His people into ministry through similar means. God uses individuals, their messages and their ministries to help propagate new truth. The same principle seems to be at work in His desire to restore and establish the offices of all fivefold ministries within the Church.

OUR VISION FOR THE FUTURE

VISION STATEMENT: To bring about full restoration of the corporate body of Christ by proclaiming present truth for the purpose of establishing dynamic, growing local churches, building on the restored foundational ministries of the apostles and prophets.

The National Symposium on the Postdenominational Church, convened by Dr. C. Peter Wagner at Fuller Seminary, May 21-23, 1996, was a historical occasion in God's annals of church history. I believe it was prophetically orchestrated by the Holy Spirit to fulfill God's purpose of bringing His Church to its ultimate destiny. The consensus of the panelists was that there are still apostles and prophets in the Church. The emerging apostolic movement will revolutionize much of the twenty-first-century Church.

This New Apostolic Reformation will initially bring revolutionary changes on the scale of the Protestant Reformation of the sixteenth century. The New Apostolic Movement will accelerate the final restorational work of the Holy Spirit, most likely causing it to be accomplished in one generation.

The Protestant Reformation started the Church on its process of the restoration of all truths, life experiences and ministries that were present in the Early Church, and this work of restoration is now continuing.

> **The New Apostolic Reformation is making church leaders and pastors more committed to establishing an army of equipped saints than gathering an audience of paying spectators and fans.**

The members of Christ's corporate Body are being taught, trained, activated and matured in ministering through the spiritual gifts God has given them. Millions of souls are yet to be harvested and incorporated into the Body of Christ. Jesus purchased, produced and is perfecting His Church that He might present it to Himself as a glorious bride. The New Apostolic Reformation is bringing about the removal of many man-made traditions within the Church, such as distinctions between laity and clergy, spiritual and secular, and members and ministers.

REDEFINING "PASTOR"

I believe that the position now called the "pastor" of a church will be significantly redefined. Those who fill that position will begin to function more like the coach of a sports team rather than the owner. The coach knows that his calling is to teach, train and equip all players so that they can reach their highest potential. He discovers what position each team member is best qualified to play. He develops the skills of each player, but at the same time unifies them to play as one team. Their goal is not just to have fun, but to enjoy fulfilling their individual roles while striving to be winners over all the opposition.

The owner is more concerned about the team winning to bring in more paying participants. He is concerned about meeting the payroll, making a profit and building bigger stadiums. Too many of today's pastors function more like a team owner than a coach. Owners are interested in a bigger audience. The coach is interested in a greater team. The New Apostolic Reformation is making church leaders and pastors more committed to establishing an army of equipped saints than gathering an audience of paying spectators and fans.

DEMONSTRATING THE POWER OF GOD

The New Apostolic Reformation is allowing believers to manifest the supernatural grace, gifts and power of God. The one-man show is coming to an end. A few great public demonstrators of God's power will soon transition into multitudes of common believers demonstrating God's power. The world will no longer exclaim, "What a mighty man!" but, "What a mighty Church!" God will get all the glory through His Church.

The church leaders will be those ministers who have progressed from "called to be" to "being commissioned" to their ministry. The gift of apostle is being fully restored during the Apostolic Reformation, but apostles will not be the only leaders.

I believe that apostolic ministry has a broader meaning than just those called to be apostles. Apostolic ministry will include miraculous ministries manifesting signs, wonders and miracles through both ministers and church members.

THE NATURE OF APOSTOLIC NETWORKS

We are seeing a new emphasis on prophetic and apostolic heads of ministerial fellowships and denominations networking together. Networking does not infer that all groups should come under the headship of one great apostolic leader. Jesus is the only Apostle of apostles. Networking (a working net) is illustrated by a good fishnet. Each network, ministerial group or large church is like one of the knots that ties the lines together. Those who have the vision, grace and wisdom to network with other networks will then become the great fishing net God will use to draw in multitudes of souls.

The common meeting ground and corporate vision for apostles and prophets is the task of reaping the great harvest and proclaiming Jesus as Lord over all the earth. The Great Commission is central. Those who continue to be more interested in indoctrinating people into their own religious Christian beliefs than in winning new people to Jesus Christ will not be particularly interested in networking. Many Christian groups today, though, do desire to establish God's kingdom more than their own. The Holy Spirit is drawing those of like vision together to form networking relationships that go a long way to fulfill God's eternal purpose for the Body of Christ and for planet Earth.

Every God-ordained network within the Body of Christ has its part to play in fulfilling the overall vision of Jesus Christ, the Head of the Body. Some networks may have more of a hand ministry, others the eye, some the ear, feet, heart, etc. Each major member (network) of the Body has its own contribution to make for the functioning of the whole.

Those who know what part of the Body they are and what their part is in fulfilling the vision of the head will not be competitive, jealous, envious or critical of the others. For in the Body, the eye cannot say to the ear, or the mouth to the hand—I have no need of you. We need each other. One network or denomination can never be the whole Body of Christ. All true believers are members of the one universal many-membered corporate Body of Christ under one sovereign headship of Jesus Christ our Lord. We all have only one Church and one kingdom to build—Christ's Church and God's kingdom.

Therefore, we who are called to be and are now apostles need to concentrate on serving and ministering to the saints, upholding and building them into the building God wants them to be. Remember, the apostles and prophets are not the roof and pinnacle on top of the building, but rather the foundation at the bottom of the building. We are not to lord it over the saints and other ministers, but to remain the apostle-prophet servants who undergird the Church.

THE CHRISTIAN INTERNATIONAL NETWORK

The overall direction of CI Ministries Network is guided by Bishop Bill and Evelyn Hamon and a Governing Board. The Governing Board functions as the head and heart of CI. This board is responsible to keep the vision pure and provide headship direction. It includes strong prophetic and apostolic persons of integrity and national recognition who are fully committed and related to the vision of CI. Most members of the board pastor a growing church and function with their spouse as husband/wife ministry teams.

Christian International Ministries Network (CIMN) is the parent organization that networks all the other ministries of CI into one unified ministry to the Body of Christ. Christian International is our common denominator. The related ministries include CI Family Church, CI Family Worship Center, CI Network of Churches (CINC), CI School of Theology, and CI Business Network, CI Prayer Counseling, and CI's Residential Ministry Training College.

ACCOUNTABILITY SYSTEMS

From our perspective, a "network" describes a group of ministers, churches and other special ministries who are interrelated together to link their vision, resources, products and people in one unified purpose. A name and organized structure are established to provide levels of leadership responsibility to fulfill the vision, purpose and ministry of the network as a whole.

Networking ministries and churches retain their autonomy, but are also required to be accountable within the network structure. The bishop and the Governing Board provide mutual accountability. District representatives and regional coordinators minister personally to those in their regions.

Ordained CI ministers maintain accountable relationships with the national and regional network centers. Areas of accountability are described under what I call the "10 Ms": Manhood, Ministry, Message, Maturity, Marriage, Methods, Manners, Money, Morality and Motives.

Whenever CI ministers travel, they provide the hosting minister a one-page form to rate the CI minister against these 10 criteria and then send it directly to the national office. Similarly, CI local churches have a complementary evaluation form they provide to the traveling minister, who will submit an evaluation of the particular church.

LEADERSHIP AND LEADERSHIP TRAINING

CINC requires the standard biblical criteria for ordination plus some things that may be unique to our network. Christian International has sensed a strong commission from Christ Jesus to establish team min-

> **We are attempting to bring the wife from a subservient position of standing behind her husband to standing alongside him as a colaborer in the ministry.**

istries; therefore, at the time of ordination, both the man and the woman are ordained. We are attempting to bring the wife from a subservient position of standing *behind* her husband to standing *alongside* him as a colaborer in the ministry.

We prophetically commission both husband and wife to the fivefold ministry. Many of those whom we ordain have been in ministry for some time and have received many prophecies and ministry proofs concerning their fivefold calling of apostle, prophet, evangelist, pastor or teacher. If the spouse is not sure of his or her ministry call, we ask God to reveal that calling and then we prophetically declare and germinate that seed of ministry that previously had been dormant within him or her.

CI does not ordain men or women without the support and involvement of the spouse. CI does, however, ordain unmarried men and women who are called to a fivefold ministry. All who are ordained with CINC receive apostolic and prophetic revelation, impartation, activation and commissioning as hands are laid on them by Bishop Hamon and an anointed presbytery.

A prophetic presbytery is held at each ordination. CI does not believe that ordination is ever to be merely a formal religious ritual. Ordination of fivefold ministries with the laying on of hands is to be on the order of 1 Timothy 4:14, which speaks of "the laying on of the hands of the presbytery" *(KJV)*. Supernatural anointing is ministered through this laying on of hands accompanied by divinely inspired prophetic utterances for impartation, revelation, activation and the fullness of the Holy Spirit.

OUTREACH: DOMESTIC AND INTERNATIONAL

Christian International believes in sending prophets and apostles to the nations rather than using the more traditional missionary model. Prophets and apostles who go to the nations of the world will be some of the main instruments God uses to reap the great end-time harvest. The primary anointing of the prophet is not manifested through mass evangelism or church-planting missions. We view that as the particular function of the evangelist.

Prophets and apostles are divinely sent to give God's revelation and prophetic word for a given nation. How that nation responds to God's Word will have much to do with its status as a goat or sheep nation. God will continue increasing His ministry of separating sheep nations from goat nations. CI prophetic teams have now gone to more than 50 nations, and in many of them God's prophetic word was spoken directly to the head of that nation.

The vision of CI is to train and activate fivefold ministers and saints nationally and internationally. In the past few years we have been successful in training and activating thousands of ministers and saints around the world. Our goal is to set up headquarters on every continent from which ministry and training for the nations can be launched, as well as to provide legal covering for our churches and ministers. CI now stands at the threshold of realizing its vision for the nations, as headquarters are being established on four continents.

PRAYER AND POWER MINISTRIES

CI has a strong commitment to intercession. We have received a great deal of teaching and impartation from Cindy Jacobs and the Generals of Intercession. We pay a full-time staff member to be our intercession coordinator. The intercession coordinator's only responsibility is to pray, teach others to pray and to direct and organize corporate prayer for the ministry.

CI's primary emphasis has been in activating and teaching about the revelation and vocal gifts. However, we regularly see miracles in services throughout the network. As we have embraced the apostolic calling, we have begun to experience a new faith to manifest more of God's miraculous power.

FINANCIAL PRINCIPLES

CI teaches strongly in the faith message of sowing and reaping. We believe that where your treasure is, so will your heart be. We also believe in the tithing principle. All CI ministers are committed to tithe into the organization in the same way their congregations tithe to them and their local church. CI also tithes from all its income to various other ministries and outreach opportunities.

CI operates financially primarily on the contributions of individuals and of networking churches. We also generate income from sales of books, tapes and other materials and from seminar and conference registration fees.

CONCLUSION

We believe we have come a long way in Christian International, but we also know we have a long way to go to fulfill the ultimate purpose of God for our movement. We are deeply grateful to God for establishing networks similar to ours within the New Apostolic Reformation and also within some of the traditional denominations with whom we can establish relationships and from whom we can continue to learn.

For Information Contact:
Christian International Ministries
Network
Phone: 850-231-2600
Fax: 850-231-1485
E-mail: cinpm@arc.net

• *for additional information and resources, see page 286*

11

VICTORY CHRISTIAN CENTER AND VICTORY FELLOWSHIP OF MINISTRIES

Pastor Billy Joe Daugherty
Tulsa, Oklahoma

Billy Joe Daugherty is founder and pastor of Victory Christian Center, which has a membership of 10,044 in Tulsa, Oklahoma. He is also founder of Victory Christian School, Victory Bible Institute and Victory World Missions Training Center. Pastor Daugherty is an Oral Roberts University graduate, where he earned a master's degree, and has attended Rhema Bible Training Center and Christ for the Nations. He serves as vice chairman of Oral Roberts University Board of Regents, is on the board of Pentecostal / Charismatic Churches of North America and is the executive director of International Charismatic Bible Ministries.

My wife and I grew up in southern Arkansas and attended a United Methodist Church. In the fourth grade, I began reading through the Bible and reading Billy Graham's *Decision* magazine to which my mother subscribed.

At a lay-witness mission in the Asbury United Methodist Church of Magnolia, Arkansas, I heard a young man talk about a personal relationship with Jesus. It awakened me to the reality that there was more to Christianity than I had been experiencing. That spring of 1970, I was given Bill Bright's Campus Crusade tract, "The Four Spiritual Laws." For the first time I clearly understood God's plan of salvation: (1) God loved me; (2) Sin had separated me from God; (3) Jesus died for my sins; and (4) I must believe and confess Jesus as my personal Lord and Savior.

That spring in speech class we were required to make a seven-minute extemporaneous speech consisting of four points. The idea came to me to speak about "How to Be Saved." The funny thing was, I had not yet surrendered my life to the Lord. The Lord, however, had the last laugh because I had to memorize all the verses in the plan of salvation.

PRAYING THE PRAYER OF FAITH

In May of that year, a Southern Baptist friend, Jim Davis, talked to me at my kitchen table about my spiritual condition. He asked me if I knew I was saved. Then he led me in a prayer of faith to ask forgiveness of my sins and make Jesus the Lord of my life. The moment I prayed that prayer, I knew that I was a born-again new creation in Christ. Everything in me became brand new.

My wife, Sharon, was the United Methodist preacher's daughter. We both attended Southern Arkansas University and then transferred to Oral Roberts University (O.R.U.) in 1972. On the beautiful O.R.U. Campus in Tulsa, Oklahoma, I began to learn more about abundant life, seed faith, the whole person and the baptism of the Holy Spirit. My wife and I were involved in the summer as youth directors and during the school year in campus outreaches.

Upon graduation from O.R.U. in 1974, we became youth pastors at Sheridan Christian Center in Tulsa. That summer, Kenneth Hagin held a camp meeting in the church and announced the start of Rhema Bible Training Center in the fall. I was able to get in on the classes and seminars for the first year and a half. From that time on, we began to take God at His word in every area of our lives and to live by faith.

In January 1976 we began a traveling ministry, speaking in churches, camps and various meetings until September 1978. During that time frame we were exposed to world missions while attending Christ For The Nations' summer school in Dallas, Texas. We also worked with Christian Retreats in Minnesota and Florida, and with Blue Mountain Christian Retreat in Pennsylvania. These places brought us in contact with a variety of leading ministries in the United States.

SHERIDAN CHRISTIAN CENTER

In the fall of 1978, we returned to Tulsa and began attending our second year of Rhema. We were then voted in as pastors of Sheridan Christian Center, taking the leadership of the church in January 1979. Rhema had moved out of the church to Broken Arrow after its first two years. By the time we started pastoring, the church's attendance was running from 300 to 400 on Sundays and a midweek attendance of 25 or less.

Back in 1974, while Kenneth Copeland was teaching a Rhema seminar in that same church, I had a vision of myself standing behind the pulpit. Then I heard the voice of God say, *You will be the next pastor of this church.* Brother Copeland stopped his teaching at that point, and began to prophesy: "This church will burst out of its walls and touch the whole world." For more than four years I had lived with this prophetic word and vision. Therefore, as we began pastoring that church in 1979, we fully expected great things to happen. In two years we grew to about 2,000 people attending six Sunday services.

Victory Christian School and Victory Bible Institute (VBI) started in the fall of 1979. We also started home groups at that time. We applied to the city to build a larger auditorium, but we were turned down because of limited parking in that neighborhood. The night of the city's decision, I received a word from the Lord about a new location— an Auto Mart about four miles down the road.

BIRTHING VICTORY CHRISTIAN CENTER

The Auto Mart was a car dealership and consisted of 66,000 square feet of building space on 10 acres. As the board reflected on the new location, they felt the need to keep the existing church site, but they also realized the need to establish a new church to receive the growth. I was asked to pastor both the new church and also the original one, but I sensed this was not what God wanted. The direction I received was to go with the new church, which we called Victory Christian Center, and to trust God to enlist someone else to lead Sheridan.

We started Easter Sunday 1981, having 1,600 people attend the morning service. That fall, 735 students enrolled in the Christian school and our Sunday attendance climbed to more than 3,000 by

September. We moved into a tent on the parking lot for four months to try to handle the growth. The cold and rainy weather of November forced us back into an overcrowded, remodeled maintenance building auditorium.

That December we faced major financial challenges as a result of having assumed a note on the building for $3.3 million, including our remodeling costs. In the darkest hour of our despair, we decided to give our tent to a missions ministry, Jim Zirkle in Guatemala. That same month at a VBI Christmas banquet, I saw an open vision of our church meeting in the Oral Roberts University Mabee Center—a 10,500-seat multipurpose facility.

A series of miracles took place in supernatural contacts with Oral Roberts, and by August 1982 Victory was conducting Sunday morning services in the Mabee Center on a lease basis. That same year, the Lord gave me a vision of our present church in a field just across the street from O.R.U. In January 1986, we bought a portion of that land and built Phase I of Victory from 1987 to 1989.

From 1,600 people on the first Sunday of Victory Christian Center, the church has grown to 10,016 as of August 1997. The staff consists of 241 people working in the church and schools of Victory.

VICTORY FELLOWSHIP OF MINISTRIES

Victory Fellowship of Ministries (VFM) was started in 1979 to provide a place and time for the ministers who were traveling out of our church to come together with the staff ministers. In the beginning, only four or five people met. After each passing year, more traveling ministries, pastors, teachers, evangelists and missionaries began to identify with VFM. We had no intention of organizing an office or support system for these particular ministers. As the years have passed, however, these ministries have come to look to Victory for help and support. It has caused us to change our thinking and revamp Victory Fellowship of Ministries into more of a service organization.

We sponsor an annual meeting that provides an opportunity for workshop participation in all areas, and specific ministry of inspiration and guidance for those in the ministry. In addition, now throughout the year, a director travels to many of the churches and meets regularly through the week with ministries that travel through Tulsa. The director also regularly spends time on the phone to counsel various members. Several traveling ministries now also help us greatly by visiting the churches and mission bases of VFM.

VFM is established in regional zones, and has regional directors located in those areas. Our goal is to have a regional representative present in every state. At present, some areas are served better than others. The regional representatives are available when someone has a need. They also make an effort to contact those in their areas and provide some form of ministry in a conference or meeting together during the year. Whenever the office in Tulsa receives a contact of crisis or major problem in a particular church or with a minister, the regional representative or closest VFM member in that area is contacted to go and assist in whatever way possible.

At the present time, we have organized VFM basically for fellowship or assistance. We are not trying to hold the members to a strict code or accountability system. To explain this, we are not daily, weekly or

> **Victory Christian Center focuses on a fivefold philosophy of ministry: worship, prayer, the Word of God, fellowship and evangelism.**

monthly monitoring all the activities of these churches or ministers. As we hear or learn of problems and needs, obviously we address those needs. We believe we were not meant to be a denomination or to establish a denominational hierarchy system to police the activities of our ministers.

The primary objective has been to support our ministers and to assist them when they do need help. Obviously, all kinds of needs, problems and difficulties have arisen and we have done what we could to support them through those trying times.

New churches and individuals are able to enroll in VFM through an application and review process. We look for someone to recommend each new person. All new members look for existing members to sponsor them and have them recommend them into VFM. A few of the churches are into church planting. This has not been a big focus at this point because most of the churches that are a part of VFM are just newly planted churches within the last 10 years.

WHERE WE ARE TODAY

Victory Christian Center is an interdenominational, interracial and international church that focuses on a fivefold philosophy of ministry:

1. Worship
Our highest calling is to love the Lord our God with all our hearts, souls and minds (see Matt. 22:37). We are called to worship Him in spirit and in truth (see John 4:24).

2. Prayer
We are called to pray God's will be done in our lives, our family, church, city and nation (see Matt. 6:10). Our fellowship is with the Father, Son and Holy Spirit (see 2 Cor. 13:14; 1 John 1:3).

3. The Word of God
We are called to proclaim the truth of God's Word that sets people free (see John 8:31,32). Jesus said to make disciples by teaching others to observe all that He commanded (see Matt. 28:20).

4. Fellowship
We are called to love one another as Christ has loved us (see 1 John 4:7-11). Love is the bond of perfection that holds the Body together (see Eph. 4:16). The first believers were faithful, not only in worship, prayer and the Word, but also in fellowship (see Acts 2:42-47).

5. Evangelism
Jesus said after the Holy Spirit had come upon us we would be witnesses in Jerusalem, Judea, Samaria and the uttermost parts of the earth (see Acts 1:8). Evangelism begins right where we are, but it takes us into missions around the world (see Mark 16:15).

We have experienced God's blessing in pursuing this fivefold vision. Each element strengthens and balances the others. To leave off any area limits the church in growth and maturity. The five areas are broad and all-encompassing in that we are liberated to pursue a variety of different approaches in fulfilling the vision.

CELL GROUPS

At the heart of Victory is our small group or cell group ministry. Mobilizing people in ministry became a focus for us in 1979. As I read Ephesians 4:11,12 concerning the calling of the ministry gifts, I received the revelation personally that my job was not only to minister to people, but also to equip others to minister.

> And He Himself gave some to be apostles, some prophets, some evangelists, and some pastors and teachers, for the equipping of the saints for the work of ministry, for the edifying of the body of Christ.

Saints are believers who need to be equipped for the work of the ministry. God's goal for each Christian is to bring forth much fruit (see John 15:16). This means outlets or opportunities must be established for believers to release their ministry potential. Cell groups are the number-one place for us to focus our members into ministry.

SCHOOLS

The ministry began Victory Christian School to train students from kindergarten through high school. More than 1,075 boys and girls attend the fully accredited school. About 40 varied churches are represented by the student body, which also receives several international students each year.

Victory Bible Institute is a Bible college established to train adults in morning and evening classes. More than 600 people attend classes each year from September through May. The addition of the VBI Correspondence School has made the classes available to people outside Tulsa. Victory Bible Institutes are also being established in several other nations.

Victory began by having a vision of a multifaceted ministry. At the heart is a family church geared to minister to all ages. The Christian school, Bible Institute and Missions Training Center each add a special ingredient to a local congregation. The outreaches of missions, radio, television and literature distribution have helped to create a soul-winning atmosphere in the congregation. Every day the people of Victory are aware of the church's evangelistic focus and their part in personally loving people into God's kingdom.

VICTORY WORLD MISSIONS TRAINING CENTER

Victory World Missions Training Center (VWMTC) began in 1983 for the purpose of training missionaries for the field. At this time, we have 152 graduates of VWMTC working in 45 countries and 34 others in various realms of ministry.

My wife and I travel to the mission field fairly regularly. In 1997, I traveled to Jamaica, Nepal, South Africa, Romania, Korea and Spain. In past years, we have made one overseas trip a month. New missionaries are sent out from Victory primarily to work with organizations already in place. We have found that a great need exists for additional training right on the mission field underneath a successful missions ministry.

Very seldom do people go and start a brand new work as soon as they leave our Missions Training Center. The church does not fully support any of the missionaries. We encourage each person going out as a missionary to raise personal funds from a broad base of support and to go when ready and prepared.

I am part of a committee that reviews applications for Victory Fellowship of Ministries and for missionaries who are supported by Victory Christian Center. All of us have an opportunity to speak about the issue of our approval of support for those new ministries and missionaries. We ask our missionaries to send regular monthly reports or letters that will communicate what is happening in their lives. We believe it is not only good for us to be aware of what they are doing, but also for others who are regularly supporting them.

Each year an annual missions meeting is held during the Ministers' Conference, which enables missionaries to come together. In addition, special meetings are held on the field, allowing missionaries to come together to strengthen each other.

WHY WE EXIST

Jesus said that He would build His Church and the gates of hell would not prevail against it. He loves variety, and Victory has a varied flavor. The church is evangelical in its basic beliefs and statement of faith. It is charismatic and full gospel in the sense of embracing the truths of the gifts of the Spirit, divine healing, signs, wonders, miracles and the word of faith. The praise and worship is a jubilant celebration combined with reverential awe of the holiness and majesty of God Almighty. All colors, nationalities and denominations are welcome in the church. The constant focus on evangelism and missions keeps the heartbeat of God at the center of Victory.

Our belief is that people are more important than buildings. Meeting the needs of people is our heart cry.

We meet in two locations on Sundays. Two of the Sunday morning services are held in the O.R.U. Mabee Center, a sports complex capable of seating 10,500 people. Two Sunday morning services are held in our Activity Center, across the street from O.R.U., capable of seating 2,500 people. We feature special youth and children's services in another building in close proximity.

Our belief is that people are more important than buildings. We have moved many times from one building to another to accommodate people. At times, feelings of attachment to a building or location have been strong, but the majority of the congregation has realized our focus must be on *meeting the needs of people.*

Meeting the needs of people is our heart cry. Every person needs to be saved and filled with God's Spirit. Forgiveness, provision, comfort, strength and healing are all basic human needs. We are called to proclaim the gospel of Jesus Christ to see these needs met by the power of God. We can't save anyone, but Jesus can. As we lift Jesus up through teaching and preaching, He draws people to Himself and needs begin to be met.

The miracle power of God is an absolute necessity in Victory. Our whole ministry would collapse without God's supernatural intervention. We stand openly and publicly for miracles, signs and wonders. Every time someone is saved, it is a miracle. Each healing of a sickness or disease is a sign and a wonder. Deliverances from drugs, alcohol, perversion, addictions, witchcraft and crime are all testimonies that God is alive.

We expect God to confirm His Word through accompanying signs (see Mark 16:20). This is not an arrogant demand, but rather a simple trust in God's mercy. We cannot alleviate the misery and torment in people by our own power. We need God to do it. In every service, each cell group and all the outreaches are asking God for His help to meet the thousands of needs we encounter.

We exist to meet the needs of people and thereby glorify our God and Father and our Lord Jesus Christ. If some part of the ministry ceases to meet the needs of people, we discontinue it. If opportunities are presented to us that don't meet the deepest needs of people, then we decline the offers.

CELL SYSTEM

The church focuses on cell groups to accomplish the ministry of Jesus by mobilizing every member of the Body to do the work of the ministry. Not everyone has responded to become involved, but enough people have stepped into the vision to have a major effect.

We do the same five things in cells that we embrace as the vision of Victory. Worship, prayer, the Word, fellowship and evangelism are all emphasized in the cells. Evangelism is the one that needs the most emphasis. It is natural for Christians to enjoy doing the first four, but it takes effort to reach out to the unsaved. Special outreaches are planned by cells to focus on soul winning. Weekly the members are encouraged to bring the unsaved to their cells.

Cell multiplication is emphasized in all our cells. Leaders look for potential leaders to assist them as apprentices. The process of training, mentoring and equipping happens right in the cell. At the appropriate time, new groups are launched by those who have faithfully prepared to lead them.

Many kinds of cells are formed to reach the various interest groups. Family, singles, children, youth, international and business are just a few areas of cells. We allow people to identify with groups they choose rather than assign them to a group.

PRAYER

The power behind the scenes is praying continually in the cells. Special prayer cells meet daily at 5:00 A.M., 6:00 A.M., 7:00 A.M., 12:00 noon and in the evenings. All our members are challenged and taught to begin each day in early morning prayer. Massive prayer is coordinated in relation to special needs or events. Teams focus on crisis situations in the church. Hundreds of phone calls for prayer are answered by the Victory prayer team each week.

DEBT FREE

Victory decided in 1981 to get out of debt and go along on a cash basis. All the present buildings (more than 325,000 square feet) and land (70 acres) were acquired by paying in cash and by the grace of God. Our policy is not to borrow, but to give out of our need, expecting God to multiply our seed and supply more than enough.

THE FUTURE

Our plans are to continue growing in every facet of the ministry—church, school, Bible Institute, radio, television, tapes, books and missions. We are working to put missionaries in every nation. Most of all, our plan is to lift up Jesus and obey His command.

Billy Joe Daugherty
Victory Christian Center
7700 South Lewis Ave.
Tulsa, OK 74136-7700
Phone: 918-491-7770
Fax: 918-491-7795

Resource List—Books
Led by the Spirit
Principles of Prayer
Killing the Giant of Ministry Debt
You Can Be Healed
Building Stronger Marriages and
Families

Resources may be ordered through:
Victory Christian Center Bookstore
7700 South Lewis Ave.
Tulsa, OK 74136-7700

12

MINISTERS FELLOWSHIP INTERNATIONAL

Pastor Dick Iverson
Portland, Oregon

Dick Iverson is the chairman of Ministers Fellowship International (M.F.I.), a growing group of pastors and leaders from around the world. He is the founding pastor of Bible Temple, a large charismatic church in Portland, Oregon, where he and his wife, Edie, pastored for more than 40 years. In 1995, he transitioned out of the senior pastor role so he could devote most of his time to M.F.I. Although still serving in Bible Temple, his main function is that of apostolic ministry to pastors and church leaders.

My background has always been in classical Pentecostalism. I was saved in an Assembly of God church as a child, baptized in the Holy Spirit in a Foursquare church and baptized in water in a Pentecostal Church of God congregation. As a teenager here in Portland, Oregon, my pastor was T. L. Osborne. My parents were not pastors, but were wonderful deacons and they were the kind of people from which great churches are built.

In 1948, when I was 18 years old, William Branham came to Portland and greatly affected my pastor as well as me by teaching about the ministry of signs and wonders. Pastor Osborne was so moved that he shut himself in a room and fasted and prayed. He heard from God and began his worldwide healing ministry that continues to the present day. I traveled with him for a short time before launching out into my own healing ministry at the ripe age of 19.

THE BIRTH OF BIBLE TEMPLE

In 1951, after returning home from a series of evangelistic meetings in the West Indies, my parents were asked to pastor a small church in Portland, Oregon. Because I had been ministering as an evangelist, they asked if I would copastor with them, which I agreed to do.

During the next 10 years of ministry in Portland with my parents, a little church was established. That church is now called Bible Temple, and has become the mother church of hundreds of churches and leaders around the world.

We struggled in the early days of Bible Temple. For nearly 15 years we saw very little growth. Then God began to work on my heart and mind concerning certain Bible truths. I became increasingly convinced that we were to build on biblical principles rather than church tradition.

BUILDING ON THE BIBLICAL PATTERN

In 1965, God began to give us a vision of the New Testament church. He began to open the Scriptures to us and help us understand the importance of the local church built on the Bible's pattern. At that time, a new river of praise and worship came into the congregation in a dynamic way. For the first time in 15 years we began to grow, both spiritually and numerically.

At the insistence of our own young people, we started Portland Bible College in 1967. That soon became the chief instrument God has used to spread New Testament church principles through our movement around the world. Thousands of young people have now attended Portland Bible College, and many of them have gone on to leadership positions through their ministry gifts.

Bible Temple itself also experienced rapid growth in the late 1960s and the 1970s. By 1972, we were averaging around 800 people in the Sunday morning service. Yet I was still *the* leader of the congregation. I soon began to realize something was wrong. Since 1965 we had believed in the ministries of the apostle, prophet, evangelist, pastor and teacher, but we had no understanding of "team ministry." I was the one the people came to because I was *the* shepherd.

I had good men ministering around me, but I did not know how to give them any of my honor and responsibility. I had been taught traditionally that there could be only one leader. I had a lot of people working *for* me, but not *with* me, and I believed I was losing ground in the church. I was becoming a stranger in my own church. Though God was moving powerfully and we were growing rapidly, I did not have the ability to keep up with the growth.

THE NEED FOR TEAM MINISTRY

One day the Lord spoke to me and asked if I wanted to pastor a *crowd* or a *family*. Being a family man who had four children, I told the Lord I did not want to pastor a crowd. I had seen that pattern in my evangelistic days and it was not fulfilling. I needed a family.

Then the Lord told me I needed to have a better understanding of the biblical pattern for church government if I was going to succeed. So I began to search the Scriptures diligently to find out how the Lord had governed the New Testament church. To my amazement, it seemed to be very plain. The Lord had used team ministry to oversee His Church.

This was a revolutionary thought to me. We have followed team ministry principles now for more than three decades and as a result, I have found great joy in pastoring Bible Temple. We simply refer to "the eldership."

WHO ARE THE ELDERS?

Who are the elders? They are the overseers, the parents of the church. Do they have various functions? Yes, according to the Scriptures. Some are pastoral, some are teachers, some are evangelists, some are prophetic and some are apostolic. They are to govern the local church together, however, as a team.

After discovering this, I appointed 10 elders, organized the congregation into 10 districts and gave each elder pastoral responsibility for one of the districts.

Bible Temple has been ruled by a team of elders since 1973. During that time, we have never known even one year that we didn't have growth, that we weren't involved in church planting, missions and enlisting new leaders. It is not an accident that these things have happened. They have been the clear results of following the mandates of Scripture.

One man was never given rule of the church, nor was the deacon board to rule the church, nor were the people as a democracy. The elders were to oversee the house of God with a "first among equals," a chief elder or senior pastor or "set-man" or whatever term you wish to use.

APOSTOLIC MINISTRIES ARE SURFACING

From this experience, we have come to further understand and apply the ministry gifts, and especially now the apostolic ministry. We have always been strong in the prophetic ministry, but now God is establishing apostolic leaders to care for the congregation of the Lord.

MINISTERS FELLOWSHIP INTERNATIONAL

Through the years, Bible Temple has sent out more than 30 church-planting teams. As a result of this, and almost before we knew it, we found ourselves involved in a relational network that extended around

> *For us, apostolic ministry describes the whole task of pastoring pastors. It describes a relational covering and network for like-minded church leaders.*

the globe. In the early 1980s, we began to convene annual Outreach Church meetings. Soon, other new, nondenominational churches who had heard of our meetings asked to attend. We even found ourselves "adopting" some of those churches. Finally, at our 1985 annual meeting we agreed to launch what we were to call the "Ministers Fellowship International (M.F.I.)." We spent 1986 organizing M.F.I. and officially launched it in 1987. Ministers Fellowship International has grown between 10 and 20 percent every year and now provides apostolic covering for almost 1,000 pastors and elders.

For us, apostolic ministry describes the whole task of pastoring pastors. It describes a relational covering and network for like-minded church leaders. Ministers Fellowship International provides that for us.

M.F.I. is basically the fruit of Bible Temple and Portland Bible College, though it has expanded far beyond the original vision of planting churches away from Bible Temple. Our conviction is that every local church should be self-governing, self-supporting and self-propagating. Our goal was to form an apostolic fellowship without the structure and restrictions of a "denomination."

THE APOSTOLIC LEADERSHIP TEAM

We immediately faced the challenge of forming a fellowship in a way that would avoid denominationalism and sectarianism. Our desire was to have a committed fellowship of ministers, without seeking to control local churches. We wanted relationships and accountability, but not translocal governance. To accomplish our goal, we formed an Apostolic Leadership Team of 19 leaders appointing me as the founder and chairman.

This leadership team gives oversight to the whole fellowship as a team. We see it as an application of the biblical local church team ministry on a broader scale. Each individual apostolic team member also has a defined leadership function covering many aspects of the fellowship.

The Apostolic Leadership Team meets twice a year, for several days, to seek the vision from the Lord and to set appropriate policy. Out of the larger team we have formed a smaller Administrative Team. Its members meet every two months to take care of the "nuts and bolts" of fellowship administration, and they report to the Apostolic Leadership Team for their blessing and approval. Within the Administrative Team an Executive Committee functions to handle the ongoing, day-by-day operation of M.F.I. This committee is made up of the vice-chairman, the administrator and me.

REGIONALIZING M.F.I.

We now have organized the M.F.I. North American constituency into 10 regions. Each region has a Regional Representative and annual regional conferences. Several international pastors have also joined M.F.I. They are now in fellowship with us in North America. As the interest has grown in a nation, we have then established a regional fellowship and conference in that part of the world. For example, we have been holding a European Regional, gathering several leaders in Europe. As that conference grows, it will spread into national conferences. Already "Ministers Fellowship of East Africa" and "Ministers Fellowship of Australia" have been formed and they are growing rapidly.

Our fellowship is different from many in that it is not a fellowship of churches or parachurch ministries or ministers. It is actually a fellowship of local church pastors and elders who have chosen to identify themselves with other pastors and to submit themselves to apostolic covering.

AVOIDING DENOMINATIONALISM

We have built several features into M.F.I. from the beginning that we believed would enable us to avoid denominationalism. We are committed to doing whatever we have to do to maintain our fellowship as a network and to avoid any kind of controlling hierarchy. We don't

> *The three positive ingredients that strongly bind us together at M.F.I. are relationships, integrity and doctrinal compatibility.*

oppose denominations or those who are in them. We thank God for what He has done and for what He continues to do for the kingdom through denominations. However, we share among ourselves a personal conviction that a central headquarters will not dictate policy for local churches. Every church is to be autonomous, and yet the pastors also can enjoy the security of meaningful accountability and checks and balances in their leadership.

The three things that, in our view, have historically caused fellowships to become denominations are:

1. *Credentialing.* We believe that the local church, not a translocal institution, is to provide its leaders with ministerial credentials. Thus, our fellowship does not ordain ministers or issue ministerial credentials.

2. *Ownership of buildings.* We do not own any local church's buildings. We believe every local church should have its own corporation and own its own buildings. If we help any fellowshiping pastor financially, no strings are attached.

3. *Central missions board.* We encourage every church to be a missionary supporting church and to voluntarily cooperate with other churches in sending missionaries and in other projects.

On the other hand, the three positive ingredients that strongly bind us together at M.F.I. are:

1. *Relationships.* We do not want just a list of names. We want people gathering who are committed to each other, who relate to each other and who really love and care for each other. No one becomes a part of M.F.I. without some such relationship.

2. *Integrity.* We certainly can't go far in fulfilling the will of God if we can't trust one another.

3. *Doctrinal compatibility.* We must be moving in the same basic direction doctrinally if we are going to really walk together in fellowship and unity. This doesn't require uniformity on every single "jot and tittle" of doctrine and scriptural interpretation, but it does call for a general unity and doctrinal compatibility.

AFFILIATING WITH M.F.I.

What follows is the process by which a local church pastor may identify with M.F.I.:

First, the pastor must have a "sponsor." The sponsor is another senior pastor who is already a member of M.F.I. The sponsor is to have a personal relationship with the pastor who is applying. The sponsor therefore verifies his or her character, gifting and ministry.

Second, the pastor must fill out a lengthy questionnaire covering many aspects of personal life—domestic, practical and doctrinal. This helps us determine the extent to which we are genuinely compatible and able to walk together. It also gives the pastor who is applying a specific sense of who M.F.I. really is.

Third, we ask the pastor to attend a regional or annual conference so he or she can get to know us as a fellowship and begin to feel at home with the larger family of leaders.

Fourth, members of the Apostolic Leadership Team interview the pastor to discuss the questionnaire. This starts us with some areas of specific communication in our new relationship.

Fifth, the Apostolic Leadership Team then takes the information gathered and discusses it together to arrive at a consensus whether the pastor truly is walking with us and sharing a common vision and purpose.

Sixth, the pastor is introduced at the annual conference, openly received by the other members and given a certificate of membership in Ministers Fellowship International.

As you can see by this process, it takes time to become a member. We often say that it is hard to become a member of M.F.I., but it is easy to leave. All pastors need to do is notify the leadership that they no longer want to walk with us and they are free to do whatever they desire. I thank the Lord for such liberty because, for more than a decade, very few have walked away. This is because our fellowship is based strictly on relationships, and if relationships don't hold us together, nothing will.

FINANCES IN M.F.I.

Everything requires some financing, though finances are not the purpose of our fellowship. To maintain an office and sponsor conferences and activities, finances are needed.

Our finances are brought in on a sliding scale. The larger the church, the more a pastor contributes monthly; the smaller the church, the less. All elders, mobile ministries and international pastors pay a flat contribution each year.

THE POWER OF APOSTOLIC LEADERSHIP

The apostolic leadership given by our Apostolic Leadership Team is quite simple in nature and yet powerful in performance. All are to have a father's heart to care for the churches God has put under our influence. Each Apostolic Leadership Team member has a responsibility to one of the regions, of which there are 10, to relate to the Regional Representative and the pastors of that area.

If a church has problems, the first to be on the scene is the sponsoring church. Often this is the mother church that has originally sent the pastor. We do not want to separate any natural ties God has put there. If the sponsoring church needs help with the struggling church, however, then they may ask the Apostolic Leadership Team, and we will go with them to work on the problem.

One of the things required for us to come into a church is that we are invited into the church, either by the eldership team or by the senior pastor or by both. We will not come into a church on our own initiative to superimpose our will.

We have found that most local church problems stem from the leadership, not the congregation. It is the same as a family. If Mom and Dad stay together in unity, the problems in the family can usually be worked out. The most serious problems in the home occur because Mom and Dad, husband and wife, become divided.

If an eldership were to invite us because of a problem they were having with the pastor, it would have to be a moral problem, embezzlement, substance abuse or doctrinal heresy. If such were the case, then we would come in, along with the sponsor, to find out what was happening. Or it could be by the invitation of the senior pastor who was sensing a revolt among his eldership and who needed help. In either case, we would come by invitation only.

GUIDELINES FOR APOSTOLIC AUTHORITY

I believe apostolic authority has often been misread in the Scriptures. Because of our strong conviction that the local church is to be self-governing and self-propagating, we do not believe in translocal authority over the churches. That is why we call ourselves a ministers *fellowship*.

If the pastor of a church in our fellowship has trouble and cannot get help from the sponsor, then we are available to come in and try to resolve the problem. Because we maintain a close relationship with the leaders, it is very easy to speak into their lives. This has been the key to the success of Ministers Fellowship International.

I will leave you with what I believe the Bible teaches concerning an apostle's responsibility.

First of all, the apostle is not a dictator or a pope. He does not control the local church. In 2 Corinthians 1:24, Paul declared he was a helper of their joy and that he did not have dominion over their faith.

I look at my apostolic responsibility to be similar to the way I speak into my married children's lives. I would be very honest and speak into their lives. I also know, however, that they could, at any time, tell me, "Thanks, but no thanks. We're going to do it our way." There's nothing more I can or would want to do. Through it all, you hope it doesn't harm your relationship, and it shouldn't. We do not believe the apostle is the pope of the church, although his authority and influence are very strong.

M.F.I. DISTINCTIVES

M.F.I. came together based on certain distinctives that have been proven over decades, and that continue to be used today to establish viable churches. Let me bring to your attention 12 distinctives that we do not consider to be archaic words, but that we hold as vital foundations for biblical churches.

1. *Davidic praise and worship.* We believe that the pattern for New Testament worship is to be found in the Davidic order of worship described in the psalms and birthed in the Tabernacle of David in the Old Testament. Within this belief is the concept that we as believers are to be spiritual priests who offer spiritual sacrifices to God. One of the primary sacrifices is the "fruit of our lips" or our audible worship given to God (Heb. 13:15). Davidic worship is demonstrative worship characterized by the biblical expressions of clapping, shouting, singing, dancing, lifting hands, bowing and kneeling.

2. *Prophecy and the laying on of hands.* We believe that prophecy and the ministry of the prophet are to be fully operational in the Church today. If the Church is going to be filled with vision and under the full direction of Jesus, the prophetic voice must be heard. We do not accept that this and other ministries were to be confined to an "apostolic age," but that they are to be fully activated until the physical return of Christ.

3. *Prayer and intercession.* We believe that both personal and

corporate prayer are absolutely essential if the Church is to succeed. The New Testament church was birthed in prayer, it continued steadfast in prayer and bathed all its activities and ministries in prayer. When the Bible labels the Church or the House of God, the label it gives it is "a house of prayer for all nations" (Isa. 56:7). If that is the name God has chosen for His house, prayer should be a major focus of all our churches. Prayer will be a pipeline through which the Spirit can move.

4. *Local church*. We believe that the local church is the aspect of the Church that God is focusing on building in these days. Although we all recognize and understand that the larger Body of Christ encompasses all believers, all the plans and purposes of God are going to be demonstrated and fulfilled on the local scene. Every believer must find himself or herself in right relationship to God and to a specific local church to find a place of ministry and fruitfulness. It is essential that rather than criticizing the Church, we do everything we can to make the Church of Jesus Christ glorious. The Church is God's instrument to extend His purposes on earth today. It is the instrument of the Kingdom.

5. *Eldership government*. We believe that God has a plan and pattern for government in the local church. It is the same form of government God has used in every institution He has established. We refer to this as team ministry or an "eldership" form of government headed by a senior pastor or chief elder. This is a form of government that involves equality and headship modeled in the Godhead, established in the natural family, set up by God in Israel, used in the synagogue and ordained for the Church in the New Testament (see Acts 14:23; Titus 1:5; Heb. 13:17). The elders are to the church what parents are to a family. They are the spiritual parents of the local assembly and are responsible before God to establish and equip the members of the church to be able to function in the God-ordained callings.

6. *Restoration of the Church*. We believe that the Church that began with great power and anointing, fully functioning as God's instrument on earth, went through a period of serious spiritual and doctrinal decline through the Middle Ages.

Since Martin Luther's time, God has been in the process of restoring the Church to its former glory and power. As we get nearer to Christ's return, we can expect this process of restoration to become complete and we can expect the Church to rise up and be what God has designed for it to be (see Isa. 60:1-5). The Church is the final instrument in the hands of the Lord to extend His kingdom on earth. Some other program will not replace the Church or people to finish the Commission laid upon it by Jesus Himself.

7. *Restoration of the family.* We believe that at the same time God is restoring His Church, He is also restoring the natural family to its proper place and function (see Jer. 31:1). One of the things God is doing is turning the hearts of the fathers to the children and the hearts of the children to the fathers (see Mal. 4:6). God is in the process of healing marriages, strengthening parents and teaching men and women more about their God-given roles. He is doing this because He wants to use a godly seed in this generation to rise up and destroy the works of the wicked one. Such a prodigy will need to be parented by those who understand God's purpose and have kingdom priorities established in their lives.

8. *House-to-house ministry.* We believe that the Early Church focused on two equally important expressions of its assembly life. A corporate gathering was vital for equipping the saints and for corporate expressions of prayer and worship. In addition, a ministry was taking place from house to house for the sake of fellowship, relationship, nurture and evangelism (see Acts 5:42). If the Church today is going to be successful in its ministry to the world and to itself, both expressions must be cultivated to the fullest extent.

9. *The Kingdom and the Church.* We believe that the extension of the kingdom of God is the function and ministry of the Church. The Church, which is composed of both Jew and Gentile, is God's instrument on earth to establish God's rule and His reign. The Church is the instrument, the Kingdom is the message. If the Church is going to fulfill its God-given calling, it must reclaim its primary function of bringing the lost to Christ and extending the borders of God's kingdom until the

glory of the Lord covers the earth as the waters cover the sea.

10. *The fivefold ministry.* We believe that the ministries listed in Ephesians 4:11 are to be fully functioning right up till the return of Christ. This includes apostles and prophets, not just pastors, teachers and evangelists. All these ministries are needed if the Body of Christ is going to be properly equipped and the Church is going to be properly built up.

11. *The gifts of the Spirit.* We believe that the gifts of the Spirit enumerated in 1 Corinthians 12:7-11 are not only for today, but also should be desired, sought after and evidenced in every church. If there was ever a time these gifts were needed, it is today. We do not believe that these gifts were intended only for the embryonic Church of the first 100 years. They are to be a part of the Church right up till the return of Christ for His perfected bride.

12. *Unity and diversity.* We believe that every local church should be inclusive and actively seek to include all peoples of all races, ethnic origins and social and economic standings. The Church of Jesus Christ is a multiethnic group that has within it the seeds for demolishing the scourge of racial prejudice. God's purpose is to make all people into one for the glory of God.

Dick Iverson
Ministers Fellowship International
9200 NE Fremont
Portland, OR 97220
Phone: 503-252-4634
Fax: 503-252-2210

Resource List—Books
Team Ministry
Building Churches That Last
Maintaining Balance
Present Day Truths
The Holy Spirit Today

Resources may be ordered through:
Bible Temple Publishing
Phone: 1-800-777-6057

13

HOPE CHAPEL

Pastor Ralph Moore
Kaneohe, Hawaii

Ralph Moore is the founding pastor of Hope Chapel in Hermosa Beach, California, and also Hope Chapel in Kaneohe, Hawaii, where he is senior pastor. Beginning with just 12 people in 1971, his ministry now spans more than 100 churches in Hawaii, the United States mainland, Japan and the South Pacific, involving more than 20,000 people. Pastor Moore travels extensively through the United States and Japan, teaching pastors and church leaders the biblical models for spreading the gospel and church planting.

The prize faded quickly from my mind's eye. I knew I would never get my Sunday School perfect attendance badge as we stood outside that New England-style church building. My father's anger was directed at the pastor as they heatedly argued about whether the Bible was or was not the Word of God. My dad, a non-Christian at the time, held out for inspiration. The pastor did not. Even as a five-year-old, I could see that I wasn't coming back to this place.

Weeks later, Dad took me "forward" at a Youth for Christ rally. After the argument with the pastor, he had spent several weeks convincing himself that the Bible really was God's Word. In the process, he surrendered his heart to Jesus. So we joined that altar call to make it official. The following morning we attended the Portland, Oregon, Foursquare church.

My mother then accepted the Lord just before a major crisis hit our fledgling Christian home. My sister contracted polio! Our fear-stricken parents arranged prolonged family prayers. Amazed, we watched God heal my sister, leaving only a mild shrinkage in one leg. Within a few short months, I had been imprinted with the validity of the Scriptures and the power of God to answer major prayers. Somehow that Sunday School attendance award had faded in significance.

CALLED TO THE MINISTRY AT AGE SIX

Our newfound enthusiasm for the Lord did have what I at first regarded as a significant downside. My parents began discussing the possibility of entering full-time ministry. Their discussions frightened me with the possibility of moving away from friends and familiar surroundings. Sometime later, my dad made a comment about "one of my boys becoming a pastor." I first reacted in rage: it would never be me! From that moment on, however, I knew in my heart I was called into ministry. I was only six years old, but I held out against that calling for the next 13 years.

I grew up in that church and in the Portland Area Youth for Christ. The church's style would be called "seeker sensitive" in today's terms. Our pastor was Dr. Nathaniel Van Cleave. He later served as a District Supervisor, and, when I went into the ministry, he appointed me to my first church. At a district meeting, he later introduced me to the ministry of Chuck Smith, and that one night with Chuck Smith radically changed both my preaching style and my approach to ministry.

FROM "SEEKER SENSITIVE" TO BIBLE PREACHING

The 60-seat church building we inherited in Manhattan Beach, California, had been closed for several months. To accommodate more people, I turned the morning service into an adult teaching ministry, much like Chuck Smith was doing at Calvary Chapel, and held multiple services. Children's Sunday School was conducted concurrent with the multiple services. I switched from the "seeker sensitive" preaching style I had learned in my first church to straight Bible teaching so we could offer solid food to the entire congregation. We would trust the members to evangelize as salt-in-the-earth Christians.

My wife, Ruby, and I soon discovered that the Word and the power of God can cross cultures effectively. We found our very straight selves pastoring a small church of hippies, bikers, former drug dealers and even a topless dancer. I thought maybe the Lord had sent the wrong pastor. The Jesus Movement was in full swing at the time, and we thought we were hanging on to a white-knuckle amusement park ride.

Our earliest discipleship tactics were born of personal relationships. One of my friends was a carpenter, named Richard Agozino. We read the biography of Dawson Trotman and decided to prayerwalk in Palos Verdes, California, every Monday morning. God mentored us through each other. Rich taught five Bible studies each week in addition to maintaining his family and a full-time job.

One of those study groups decided to become a church and called him as their pastor. I opposed the idea at first because Richard had never attended seminary and I knew that our denomination, The International Church of the Foursquare Gospel, would "never go for it." I was wrong. The denomination was already in the process of creating a lay pastor's license. So we decided to go for it, our first daughter church. Though the new church elected to remain independent of the denomination, we found ourselves in uncharted territory. We soon began planting churches as a normal function of our congregational life.

CHURCHES AND MINISTRIES

The first Hope Chapel began in 1971, in Manhattan Beach, California. After five years, we moved to the present location, a former bowling alley in nearby Hermosa Beach. The congregation had grown from 12 people to just more than 2,000 when I announced my departure.

When Aaron Suzuki and I moved our families and a small team to Hawaii in 1983, we were the thirtieth church plant stemming from that one congregation. Today, that church, led by Zac Nazarian, supports a membership of more than 3,000 people. Zac continued the tradition of church planting and had great success. The church is a fountain of growth, responsible for the birth of more than 100 daughter and granddaughter congregations, including those we have planted.

Hope Chapel Kaneohe began life as 70 people worshiping under a tree at Oahu's Kailua Beach Park. No buildings were available, so we did the next best thing. Today, the congregation assembles as a group of 1,700 worshipers spread over six weekend services in a public school cafeteria. Built around cell groups, or "MiniChurches," our geography includes most of the island of Oahu. MiniChurches beget pastoral leadership. As a result, this church now has more than 40

> *My conclusion is that the secret to church-planting success is relentless commitment to the task.*

daughter and granddaughter congregations in Hawaii, the United States mainland and the Pacific.

COMMITMENT TO THE TASK IS KEY

After witnessing the birth of 70 new churches, my conclusion is that the secret to church-planting success is relentless commitment to the task. Our model is simple and easy to duplicate. More important, we manage to keep the vision alive and reproduce it in many of our daughter churches. Our greatest sense of success comes from those few bright spots when we can point to four generations of churches flowing from the original assembly.

Jack Hayford once prophesied that the Lord would raise our church as "a coconut tree planted high on a hill." This tree would naturally drop coconuts that would grow into other trees, repeating the process. Those words, spoken after the birth of the first daughter church, have proven true many times over.

Outside ministries are pretty much limited to those that support our vision for planting churches. We sponsor a couple of daily radio broadcasts in Hawaii. A publishing ministry called Straight Street Publications produces seminars and published resources for pastors interested in church planting and cell-based ministry. Much of our missions effort focuses on planting churches to reach the rising generation in Japan.

TEACHING A PHILOSOPHY OF MINISTRY

Hope Chapel exists to turn ordinary people into faithful, productive followers of Jesus Christ. After a close look, you might say we have gone to seed on Ephesians 4:10-13. Our goal is for every leader to grow two or three others into effective leadership. Little is done to attract new people through programs. Evangelism belongs to the membership. Leaders build strong members who bring people to Jesus.

We anchor our philosophy through teaching from the pulpit. The MiniChurches reinforce the philosophy centering on personal application of the weekend teaching. The MiniChurch system further reinforces our convictions through its recruiting and training structure. Current leaders recruit and train potential new ones from the bottom of the pyramid.

We aim for 100 percent congregational involvement in ministry. In reality, we hit a little over 80 percent. Each year, we measure results by recognizing involvement, department by department. Those who served during the year receive a "Team Hope" T-shirt at an annual outdoor music festival. The shirt separates the doers from the sitters. The ratio between current attendance and the number of shirts given away is our most important statistic.

VISION AND VISION CASTING

For me, vision comes through an intersection of four factors: (1) spending time with lay leaders; (2) reading secular news and best-selling authors; (3) listening to God through prayer and the Word; (4) shaping ideas in consensus with my immediate (and very young) staff. Vision casting passes from the pulpit and down the leadership pyramid of the church.

Our current vision involves Generation X and the soon-to-be adult Millennial Generation. We presently have more Xers than any other generation in our congregation. Our plan is to raise them into leadership and start a new generation of churches in Hawaii. The common assumption is that most churches exist for baby boomers, and many Gen Xers believe they haven't really been invited to the party.

HOPE CHAPEL OPERATING PRINCIPLES

Just before I left California, my friends made a lot of jokes about whether the "Vatican" was moving to Kaneohe. Or did the move only entail the "Pope of Hope"? I didn't appreciate the humor, but was aware that we had built a "movement within a movement." The real question was whether we should leave our denomination, The Foursquare Church, and start a new one.

We believed that we would probably start churches at a faster rate if we left the denomination. We also felt tremendous loyalty to the denomination. This was not loyalty to an institution, but to friends and mentors. I didn't and still don't agree with many details of denominational policy. One hundred percent agreement, however, isn't necessary to maintain an alliance. We chose to stay because a denominational relationship is much like a marriage. You stay in it because of love and commitment.

In his book *Reinventing American Protestantism* (University of California Press), Donald Miller observes that we would probably be a lot larger movement had we left the security and confinement of our denomination. I am sure his observation is correct. Fruit is measured by more than direct church starts, though. Remaining in the denomination affords us the opportunity to be partners in their church-planting efforts. We might not start as many churches as if we went independent, but we can inspire the birth of a lot more churches.

As it turns out, our affinity for our denomination accomplished that and more. Because I remain in favor with my own church family, I am often trusted in other denominational circles. There, I preach a gospel of planting churches, discipleship in small groups and intergenerational ministry. The Foursquare Church provided a wonderful place to invest my life.

I lead through consensus. Comfort with consensus also allows us freedom as a movement within a movement. When we plant a church, it will join our denomination by the choice of the membership. If a church chooses to operate outside the denomination, I respect the choice. We have even pioneered churches within other denominations. The Foursquare Church allows us the freedom to invest monies and leadership in these churches. Once our daughter churches are up and running, I have no direct power over them.

Of course, I and other key leaders have considerable influence over these churches. That influence, however, is rooted in the strength of our ideas and the anointing of the Holy Spirit rather than a system of authority. We are very comfortable with the flexibility and freedom born of this arrangement. Everything we do, either denominationally or with independent congregations, is rooted in the strength of personal relationships.

ACCOUNTABILITY AND TEAM BUILDING

Within our local congregation, I am sandwiched between a church board and my staff. During meetings, I chair that board. Outside the meetings, I submit to the decisions arrived at by the board. The board is the keeper of values; the staff are equippers for ministry. My job is to provide vision and communication between the two groups. Board members serve two-year overlapping terms.

Our board decides through a kind of "forced" consensus. We are never afraid of a good fight, but won't move on anything until all agree. We don't vote. Either the issue works out or it doesn't. Any board member can veto the input of all the rest. This renders us individually responsible for the life or death of every idea. We must remain open to work things through to a Spirit-directed conclusion. Personal ambition wilts under the responsibility. Our escape ladder is the option for an individual to say, "I don't agree, but I am willing to trust the Holy Spirit working in all the others." This is an admission of fallibility and individual limitation.

Through the years, I have swallowed pride with those words more than anyone else. The first time was when the others wanted to form a building fund with just 25 dollars. We had no land or buildings in sight. I thought both were necessary before we could do any fundraising. I gave in to the others and one man (outside the group) donated 5 thousand dollars the first week. Consensus is beautiful.

The staff operates under my leadership, but we arrive at decisions much like the council. Someone submits an idea. We then talk it into practicality or throw it out for lack of consensus. This is a team effort and the newest members often bring the freshest ideas.

All staff-level departments operate as circles of MiniChurches. Each pastor is *primarily* responsible to raise and equip MiniChurch leaders. Any program comes from the opinions and felt needs of people in those MiniChurches. Pastors and leaders gather bimonthly for training and planning. Again, consensus rules.

We enjoy association with our denominational family. This

involves adhering to a simple policy manual, tithing our general offerings, supporting missions programs, attending conventions and seminars, and generally fitting in. The relationship is a mutually beneficial partnership. We are never obligated to have denominational officials speak in our pulpit, but we often invite those who have a message we think we need.

We start churches wherever we find opportunity, fitting the pastor into the denominational structure whenever possible. We send our students to their Bible colleges, but also freely plant churches and have leaders trained at a local church level. Our denomination functions more like a family than an institution.

LEADERSHIP TRAINING AND LAUNCHING

The defining characteristic of any leader is having followers. Unfortunately, many people are identified as leaders when in reality they are just good students. I have always felt guilty for the people we have sent off to seminary or Bible college who couldn't even fulfill their own expectations in the local church. As a result, we have evolved a system built around on-the-job apprenticeship training. We postpone seminary until a person is accomplished in ministry.

For us, *doing* ministry is the gateway to greater ministry. Professional training is an effective enhancer of ministry, but a poor gateway. Most of our pastors got started pushing a broom, folding chairs, serving on a committee, etc. Faithful service begets promotion and those faithful in small things become rulers over larger things.

We never train people until *after* they place their hand on the plow. We don't recruit through training opportunities. They have to do the ministry in order to attend training sessions. Ministry entry points are easy to create. A non-Christian can set up chairs or take them down. New converts can hand out bulletins or participate in a prayer team. Anyone who has a pure heart and a clean record can hand out cookies as a helper in Children's Church.

When someone takes the first step into ministry, we offer training to them in three forms: (1) on-the-job experience; (2) a mentor who develops them spiritually as well as in skill development; (3) inclusion in a group setting where training takes the form of reading and discussing favored books. Our leaders are always in training. I lead my staff in a two-hour weekly discipleship training around books I choose. They, in turn, pass the favor (and the same books) on to their disciples in a pyramid of learning. After 14 years, our longer-tenured leaders have read and assimilated more than 60 books.

We encourage professional training after people are hired to our paid staff or start a church. That can happen only if they have planted three MiniChurches and have shown that others are willing to follow them. They must also display a loving heart toward the church and its leadership. We believe we ourselves can train them adequately enough to bring them to this point.

In our denomination, we are allowed to issue a lay pastor's license to those who qualify. Ordination comes later, after two years of paid ministry. Only about 5 percent of those we have placed into pastoral ministry have ever dropped out. Our supposition is that a person will excel in ministry (have many followers) through spiritual gifts and faithfulness. Seminary training is left to do what it does best: educate and enhance the abilities of someone who has *proven* leadership gifts.

OUTREACH METHODOLOGIES

We believe in *personal* evangelism. Our plan is to start a church that includes interested Christians and God-fearers. After that, we rely on our members for evangelism. Domestically, this is a straightforward process. Overseas, we seek to meet real needs in the country. In Asia, we place workers as English teachers. In Pacific Island nations, one man starts television stations, and his imported employees are free to start churches as their business schedules permit.

Personal evangelism links to the church service. We strive to be user friendly to non-Christians, but we *don't* let the market drive the message. Weekend services still carry the meat and potatoes because that is when we touch the highest percentage of our membership. It is also when we directly touch the largest number of unchurched people. We *do* let the unchurched drive the packaging of the message, however. In terms of music, decor and communication style, cultural anthropology is alive and well in our church, and our guests usually feel comfortable when they first visit.

CONVERTS, NOT TRANSFERS

We work hard to remain a church of *converts* rather than *transfers*. I once read a George Barna publication demonstrating how megachurches were killing small congregations through transfer growth. It suggested that small churches evangelize, one to one, but never accomplish great programs. The trade-off was that large churches are those that learned to program at the expense of personal evangelism. We determined never to do that.

We annually survey our internal congregational demographics. One area we measure is the ratio of converts to transfers. Two years ago, transfer growth accounted for 71 percent of our congregation. After

> **Answers to prayer do two things: (1) incite people to more prayer; (2) give people something to discuss with their friends. Our people gossip about God.**

helping launch another church and after a year of tremendous blessing, our overall numbers went up. More important to us, however, are that last year's survey showed only 51 percent of our people are the result of transfer growth. I think one factor in our success is our belief that evangelism is a process of learning to follow Jesus rather than being an instantaneous event. Our people contentedly move others to Jesus, one inch at a time.

PRAYER AND POWER MINISTRIES

We place heavy emphasis on prayer in evangelism and church life. You will seldom hear terms such as "power evangelism," though. MiniChurches are essentially prayer meetings. The people hold their lives up to the Scripture as it was taught during the weekend. Afterward, they praise God for His sufficiency or pray about the deficits in their own lives. Those prayers are often answered spectacularly. We really believe "that if two of you agree on earth concerning anything that they ask, it will be done for them by My Father in heaven" (Matt. 18:19).

Answers to prayer do two things: (1) incite people to more prayer; (2) give people something to discuss with their friends. Our people *gossip* about God. Prayer and evangelism join hands in everyday conversation.

I teach people to pray with their non-Christian friends whenever they get the opportunity. Sometimes they will not pray one-on-one with their friend, but they will ask their friend's permission to pray when they later meet in their own prayer time or at MiniChurch. In either case, the person being prayed for won't be present, but knows prayer is being offered. This takes pressure off shy Christians who might not feel up to praying for their friend on the spot. It does leave their friend "holding God accountable" for the answer to prayer. When the miracle occurs, the unsaved person is usually very open to whatever else God has to offer.

TITHING IS EXPECTED

Our church is not wealthy. We are located in a middle-income community. Our commitment is to minister to the cross section of our town. Redemption and lift can affect any church, and after a time some pastors might be inclined to fall into the error of tailoring their message to those who are better off financially. We discourage that possibility by intentionally providing support to the poorer people in the community. True, we have wealthy people in the congregation, but most of them view their roles as enablers of ministry to the rest.

We teach tithing and emphasize that the church itself tithes to the denomination. Prayers over offerings are led by a wide assortment of our members. When called upon to pray, we ask them to share a testimony of God's grace in their lives. The testimonies are often about finances, but always about some supernatural provision. This is a great encouragement for people to trust God with their whole lives as they commit their finances to Him.

BUILDING A BUDGET

Financial planning is built around a unified budget. We begin by surveying every department about their vision, then their calendar for the coming year. After building a dream calendar, they cost it onto a spreadsheet. Totaling the spreadsheets usually highlights how much we need to cut back to make the expenses fit projected income. At this point, we announce the difference and ask leaders to prayerfully cut whatever they are willing to surrender. A couple of rounds of this usually generates a workable budget. If we come to an impasse, department heads gather until they can prioritize and reach consensus.

In 14 years, we have only operated with a red-ink budget one time. We do not project shortfalls and cry to our people. We won't operate by faith, if "faith" means asking people to support poor financial planning.

The church council is not involved in the budget-casting process. They simply hold the staff accountable to build a workable budget; they don't set it for them. Afterward, they simply keep us responsible to the budget we planned. We do update the budget freely during the year, spending money pretty freely where opportunity presents itself.

We take few special offerings. Most of these are for missions, for planting a church or for disaster relief. We have almost never asked for an extra offering to provide ministry or hardware for *our own* church. Instead, we train people to tithe and we expect the leadership team to work within the boundaries of God's provision through the tithe.

Our church is currently involved in a building process. We obtained rights to ocean-view property 10 years ago. It was the largest vacant parcel in our community. Government bureaucracies ate up 9 years, but we are finally in the construction phase. During that decade, we have gone to the congregation in five 2-year fund-raising efforts. We always encouraged the people to pray and then left an open-ended goal. Whatever the Lord laid on individual hearts would tally to the corporate goal. Nearly every dollar ever pledged has been received.

CONCLUDING THOUGHTS

Our belief in Peter Wagner's statement, "The most effective evangelistic methodology under heaven is planting new churches," strongly colors our ministry. Our commitment to new churches mandates a continual pruning of our congregational membership and of our leadership personnel. Paradoxically, and just as Jesus said it would, this apparent weakness has strengthened our attempts at effective outreach.

Not possessing our own facility has further molded us. Fourteen years in a public school has its benefits. We use public facilities throughout Oahu island. Having access to only a small school cafeteria forced us to plant new churches just to house new converts.

Dependency on public facilities has also shaped our ability to relate to the community at large. Early on, we got into community service out of a selfish need for continued access to public buildings. We now teach people to read, help welfare moms transition into the work force, and run a large organization dedicated to raising money in support of public schools. By serving the community, we have learned that people are hungry for love and for the gospel. We strongly intend to stay in public service after we move to our own building.

Community service also casts new light on our political views. People we once viewed as enemies of the cross are now serving Jesus because we met them in the public arena. Rather than lobbying against sectors of the non-Christian community, we are making friends with them and watching God deliver people from their sins. To us, the modern world doesn't look much different from the first century. Jesus is still Lord. He builds His Church, and the gates of hell don't prevail against it.

Ralph Moore
Hope Chapel Foursquare Church
46-001 Kamehameha Highway #111
Kaneohe, Hawaii 96744-3724
Phone: 808-235-5814
Fax: 808-247-2070
E-mail: hope@aloha.net
Web site: http//www.planet-
hawaii.com/hopekaneohe

Resource List

Books
Let Go of the Ring
Choices
Financial Freedom

Audiocassettes
*Discovering MiniChurch: Small Groups
That Work*
Discovering Advanced Church Planting
Labor for the Harvest (3 of 7)

Resources may be ordered through:
Straight Street Publishing
P.O. Box 240041
Honolulu, HI 96824-0041

14

GRACE KOREAN CHURCH AND MISSIONS

Dr. David [Kwang Shin] Kim
Anaheim, California

Reverend David (Kwang Shin) Kim was born in Pusan, Korea. He earned a bachelor of arts degree in English Literature in 1961 from Seoul National University. He received a master of divinity degree from Talbot Theological Seminary in 1982, and a doctor of divinity degree from Biola University in 1994. Through Reverend Kim's leadership, Grace Korean Church of Anaheim was founded in 1982, starting with 35 members. One of the founding principles was a commitment to world evangelism, allocating half of the church's budget to support world missions. In addition to serving as senior pastor, Reverend Kim is director of the Grace World Mission Department, sponsoring about 144 missionaries in approximately 38 countries. He is head professor of the Grace Mission University, where he is also chairman and board director.

I pray with all my heart that this may be a humble report to all coworkers of the Lord Jesus, of His work in the mission field.

INTRODUCTION

I would first like to introduce myself and then to share about the mission work of our Grace Korean Church.

I met Jesus Christ on August 20, 1977. Until then, I had been a typical atheist. My encounter with Christ completely changed my life. I attended Talbot Seminary at Biola University in La Mirada, California, so I could serve the Lord by sharing the gospel of Christ. Just before I graduated in 1982, I started Grace Korean Church with three families. From the start, we decided to set aside 50 percent of the church income exclusively for mission work.

A Church for Missions

Our church now has a Sunday attendance of approximately 2,500 members, including children. We have sent out and we financially support 154 missionaries to 38 different countries.

We began mission work to the former Soviet Union in 1990, and to this date, we have opened 670 churches there. We established a seminary in Moscow, three Christian schools and three medical centers, as well as a school of agriculture on the island of Sakhalin and a farm of roughly 300 acres in the city of Volgograd.

In mainland China, God has also worked mightily. We have done mission work there for 12 years now and we have opened more than 1,800 house churches. Most of the churches are registered with the government.

In East Africa, we established a seminary in Nairobi, Kenya, and started more than 500 churches.

However, God's most amazing works are just now taking place in Vietnam. Vietnam, under its Communist regime, prohibits foreigners to do any mission work inside the country. Even so, the Lord has incredibly worked through our Grace Church missionary to start 280 churches in that nation.

Our local church budget supports all this worldwide mission work. In 1996, our church members gave $6.5 million in tithes and offerings, and we spent approximately $5 million of that on mission work.

Our involvement in missions has produced many unforgettable incidents. One of them happened in July 1990 at our first crusade in Yuzno Sakhalin, the capital city of Sakhalin.

Opening the Door to Russia

At that time, the Communist Party still ruled Russia. I had been praying for the chance to share Jesus Christ with the Koreans living in the former Soviet Union. After a year of prayer, the Lord arranged meetings in five cities having large Korean populations: Yuzno Sakhalin in Sakhalin, Habarovsk; Tashkent in Uzbekistan; Almaty in Kazakhstan; and Moscow.

I took with me a church choir of 25 high school and college students trained to perform Korean folk songs, dances and Christian hymns.

The choir presented the Korean folk songs and dances, and I explained the story behind each of them to introduce Korean history and culture. I did not want to incite their strong anti-Christianity sentiment. Then, when the choir went on to present Christian hymns, I could naturally introduce the background of each hymn, and I could share the gospel naturally and indirectly.

At the end of the choir's presentation, I then thought I should preach the gospel directly to the congregation for about 20 minutes. I suspected that when I started to preach, they would probably throw things at me and run me out of the theater. Nevertheless, if even one Christian was there, or a person whose parents were Christians, they might later try to visit us secretly at the hotel. I hoped to make that person our contact point so we could then send our missionaries to that particular city.

On the evening of the performance in Yuzno Sakhalin, more than 1,000 people packed the theater and more than 300 others were turned away because there was no more space.

Our choir presented its musical numbers with excitement. Finally, I stood on the stage ready to share the gospel. You can imagine the tension we felt. All the choir members were praying very hard behind the curtain that I would not be hurt. As I preached, nobody moved. When I asked if anybody wanted to receive Jesus Christ as Savior, I was amazed to see more than half the audience stand up. Many of them cried when I led them in prayer. I was powerfully reminded of what the Lord said in John 4:35:

"Do you not say, 'There are still four months and then comes the harvest?' Behold, I say to you, lift up your eyes and look at the fields, for they are already white for harvest!"

How We Became Involved in Missions

When I attended seminary, I earnestly wanted to discover the Lord's ultimate purpose for establishing His Church on this earth. As His servant and pastor of a church, I thought I should lead the church in that direction. I concluded that all church activities can be divided

> **Upward activities are directed toward God,...inward activities are intended for church members,...outward activities are those activities that reach the people outside the church.**

into three major categories: upward, inward and outward activities. *Upward activities* are directed toward God, such as worship, prayer and praise. *Inward activities* are intended for church members, such as Bible study and fellowship. *Outward activities* are those activities that reach the people outside the church, such as evangelism and missions.

As we were ready to begin our church, a thought came to my mind: What if our Lord had wanted to have His Church in heaven instead of on earth? In heaven, we would have no problems with upward and inward activities, but outward activities would be impossible because there would be no unbelievers. It became very clear to me that these outward activities in reaching unbelievers are the ultimate purpose of God's Church on earth.

Our Lord Jesus knew that He would die, resurrect from the dead and ascend to the heavenly kingdom. After He had ascended, how would people who were born years later understand the heart of God, who loves us so much and wants so much to save us? That is why Jesus Christ wanted to establish His Church on earth.

I am not saying that worship and fellowship of the church members are less important. I am saying that the outward activities to reach unbelievers are the ultimate purpose of the Church. The first step toward this end, however, must be the upward activities. We cannot have a right relationship with God without successful worship. Without a right relationship with God, there cannot be real fellowship among Christians. When we love one another in the church, our Lord will take our love and lead our mission work. Only then can that church truly carry on His work for missions. This has been our philosophy of ministry at Grace Korean Church.

HOW TO GET A CHURCH INVOLVED IN MISSION WORK

To get a church involved in missions, I believe there are four prerequisites for pastors: (1) a firm determination to initiate mission work; (2) a correct understanding of mission work; (3) incessant prayer; and (4) a continuous drive to maintain and establish church growth for mission work.

In 1989, I started praying for the people of Russia. I didn't know why, but every night as I knelt down to pray for the people in the Soviet Union, I could not stop crying. Tears and deep sobs would well up from the bottom of my heart.

Five years prior to this, in 1984, a church member brought a college girl to our church. She came to the United States from Korea when she was young and was then a freshman at UC Irvine. At this point in her life, she felt hopeless. She didn't want to associate with other people and she constantly thought of committing suicide. I explained the gospel to her and she eagerly accepted Jesus Christ as her Savior.

She began to attend our Bible study, and whenever she could, she came to church to pray. After several months, she came to see me. She said, "Pastor, I don't know what to do. While I was praying, the Lord Jesus Christ told me to change my major to Russian. What should I do?"

At that time in 1984, the Russian language was of no practical use in America. I didn't know what to say. So I answered her, "Well, if you are very sure you heard the voice of Jesus Christ, you should obey." So she switched her major to Russian.

She finished her studies at UC Irvine, and in 1988 she went to Leningrad (now St. Petersburg) University for four months of language training. After that, she also visited many parts of the Soviet Union as a professional interpreter.

Then in 1990 the Lord Jesus opened the door to the Soviet Union for us to have a type of crusade in five major cities. If we had not had a Russian interpreter at our church, how could we have held the crusades? Even if we tried to find a native Russian interpreter, if she was not a Christian, she would not effectively interpret the gospel message. The Lord, however, had already prepared a Christian translator for Russian right in our own church.

So even though I started praying for missions in Russia in 1989, the Lord had already starting answering my prayers five years earlier.

If we are determined to obey God's Great Commission to fulfill our role in carrying the gospel to the world, the Lord will open the doors for the church to do so.

TRAINING LEADERS ON THE MISSION FIELD

I do not have any particular expertise in the theory of leadership training. I am a very ordinary pastor of a local church that happens to be deeply involved in mission work. I will simply share the best way we have found to train leaders on the mission field.

When we considered training leaders in the mission field, we analyzed and studied 10 areas: goals, principles, training areas, curriculum, professors, students, regulations, facilities, finance and follow-up.

For the sake of space, I will share only in the areas of goals, principles, students and follow-up.

GOALS

Goals differ depending on the present situation in that mission field.

If the mission field is well established in Christian evangelization, then our goal is to train pastors. If not, as in the former Soviet Union, then we train pastors, but we also focus more on equipping laypeople to be Christian witnesses to the locals about Jesus Christ. If both of these criteria are met in a particular mission area, then we focus on training the missionaries there to send them to other places.

For example, we first began mission work in mainland China in 1985. We first concentrated our mission efforts in three northeastern provinces having a large Korean population. We shared the good news of Jesus Christ and opened house churches. We focused on training Christian leaders to share Jesus Christ with other natives. Currently, if you go to any Korean community in these areas, you will hardly find a village without a house church. We are still training leaders to be more equipped in taking the gospel cross-culturally to the Chinese people throughout mainland China.

PRINCIPLES

First principle: *Contextualization.* We must adjust all curricula, the training period and the contents for teaching to be appropriate for the culture of that particular mission field. If we transplant the training programs or curricula from the outside to the mission field, we will produce little fruit. Missiologists call this contextualization.

Second principle: *Love.* We know that without love, the kind of Christianity we share will drift away from God's Word. I have learned through our ministry that only those who have been loved with the love described in the Bible can in turn love the Lord and their neighbors as Jesus commanded.

Third principle: *Discipline.* To train the leaders effectively, we apply all our regulations with strictness. For example, in Russia, to show love, we provide everything free: meals, room, textbooks, uniforms, tuition and even a small monthly allowance. If a student is late for a devotion time or lecture more than two times, though, we send that person back home. Usually, about 15-20 students out of 130 will be sent home before graduating.

STUDENTS

In the mission field, there are usually not many willing students, and not many Christians in general. In a way, therefore, we have to manufacture our students rather than recruit them.

In the case of the former Soviet Union, instead of opening a church and holding Bible classes there, we set up a church but opened a Bible school at a different location. The reason behind this was as follows:

The Russian Orthodox Church has profoundly influenced the Russian people for more than a thousand years. They teach that Protestantism is a heresy, so Russians naturally hesitate in getting involved with a Protestant church.

When we simply advertised that we were teaching the Bible, however, many people eagerly attended because they believed nothing was wrong with learning more about the Bible. We held classes three nights a week and at the beginning of each class we shared the gospel. Once the students accepted Jesus Christ as their Savior, they felt unhindered in coming to our church. After the initial Bible study, many continued with the advanced Bible studies at our church.

Upon completion of the advanced classes, if they decided to enter full-time ministry, our missionaries prayerfully selected candidates to attend seminary. At the seminary, they would again screen the candidates before a final acceptance.

FOLLOW-UP

Once the native seminary students graduate, they are sent to their mother church where the missionaries and pastors train them for several months. When they are ready, they are sent to open a new church. Every month, the local pastors will gather at the missions center for a two-day seminar. For our mission purposes, we divided the former Soviet Union into three areas: eastern, central and western.

The church also sends associate pastors to each area every three months for a three-day seminar. About once or twice a year, all the pastors and graduates gather for a four-day seminar that I lead personally.

THE MOSCOW SEMINARY

Keeping these principles in mind, I would like to share how we train students at the Moscow seminary as a more in-depth example.

We established the Moscow seminary in March 1992, enrolling 155 students. The program lasted five months, but now has lengthened to one year.

All students live in the dormitory and wake up every morning at five o'clock. By 5:30, they are to be at chapel for an hour of individual prayer. After this, they have an hour for quiet time, during which they are not supposed to talk, but to read and meditate on God's Word. Then they gather into small groups for one and one half hours to share what God revealed to them. Then at nine they eat breakfast. Every day, the students memorize one Bible verse.

To help them share love and teach them the servanthood of leadership, a group of 15 to 20 students will go to the dining hall before the others to set up the tables and welcome the rest of their peers by singing, and then serving them food.

While sitting at breakfast, the students recite that day's Bible verse and review all the memory verses for that week. After breakfast, they have two 90-minute lectures, then lunch, and two more 90-minute lectures, for a total of six hours of lecture daily from Monday through Friday. Then they have two hours of free time before dinner.

After dinner, they have two hours of devotion. During the first part of the semester, the professors lead the devotion, and in the latter part of the semester, the students lead. After devotion time, the students maintain silence to review what they learned that day and meditate on Christ.

At 11:00 P.M., all the lights are turned off. If any students want to study or pray more after this time, they have to do it in the hallway where the lights are still on.

Every Sunday after worship, the students go out in groups of 10 for street witnessing. They go anywhere they see a crowd and start singing to draw attention. Before they go out, they assign three students to preach. One student will share the gospel and challenge people to accept Christ. When the people have dispersed, the students begin the process again. It encourages the students to be bold witnesses for Christ and also allows them time to practice delivering sermons.

Upon completion of class work, the students are sent out on a two-month mission trip. Groups of five are dropped off in remote areas of Siberia, where, for the next two months, they will visit a small village and help the villagers reap the harvest or do other chores. The female students may help take care of the village children or share Bible stories. At night, they gather with the villagers to sing and tell them about Jesus. Once several families have come to the Lord, they organize a house church and choose and train a leader among them. We usually supply the leader with enough sermon materials and supplies for three months, and then the nearest mission center comes to work with them.

Once a house church is established, the students move on to the next village. In this way, we now have many house churches in remote areas of Russia, besides our 670 established churches.

At the end of their mission trip, the students return to the seminary to share testimonies and celebrate graduation. They then return to their own churches to receive resident training from the missionaries there. When they are ready, the missionary sends them out to plant new churches. We currently have 1,107 graduates and 147 students at the seminary. On average, about 65 percent of the graduates enter full-time ministry as pastors.

Among the churches established by our seminary graduates, some have more than 1,800 adults in Sunday attendance and many others

> **To keep the missions fire burning, three things are necessary: the right attitude, being involved and tasting the fruit.**

have 500 to 1,000 members. The average attendance ranges from 100 to 300 and all are mission-minded churches.

KEEPING THE MISSIONS FIRE BURNING

To get your church involved in missions is one thing, but to keep the members involved with fervor is quite another matter. How can a pastor keep the fire for missions burning in the hearts of his members? I have learned that three things are necessary.

Missions Begins with Attitude

First of all, the church members must have the right attitude toward mission work and missionaries. If they don't have the right understanding, sooner or later they will be disappointed. I constantly teach our church members that mission work is not a choice but it is mandatory; that mission work is not the result of church growth but the cause of it; that involvement in mission work is a way to show our love for our Lord Jesus Christ; that mission work is a way to receive blessings from God; and that mission work is a way to receive rewards at the judgment seat of Jesus Christ.

To encourage church members to better understand their relationship with the missionaries they send, I constantly stress that they are not helping the missionaries, but the missionaries are helping them.

Missionaries are like the generals on the battle field, while the home church is the base of supplies. This opens the way for the home church to fully support its missionaries.

Getting Involved
The second thing I teach my church members is that they themselves should be involved in missions.

If church members are not involved in the mission field directly, their support will often wither into mere mannerisms, without any real heart or zeal for missions. Ultimately, they will stop any involvement. So I do four things to encourage involvement of all church members.

First, I insist that they visit the mission field. We usually arrange events on the mission field and we strongly urge church members to participate. When we sponsor seminars on the mission field, about 40 to 60 church members will usually go with us to serve the participants. When we organized the Grace Festival 1994 in Russia, more than 10,000 delegates attended from churches started by our graduates all throughout the former Soviet Union. From the mother church in the United States, about 600 members volunteered their vacation times and money to show the love of Christ by preparing meals and serving the attendees.

As a result of these efforts, more than two-thirds of all members of Grace Korean church have visited the mission field at least once.

Second, I assign selected mission areas for church members to pray for specifically.

Third, I urge members to support a church in the mission field financially. In the former Soviet Union, the economic situation makes it almost impossible for locals to start a new church by themselves. So I recruit sponsors for new churches from our church members and even from others outside the church. I challenge them to cut down on their necessary living costs and to send $200 a month for one church for two years.

Tasting the Fruit
Finally, I make sure that my church members taste the fruit of our mission work. The sense of achievement is important in motivating people.

CONCLUSION

I have shared here many principles and items for consideration. I would also like to invite your prayers for our continuing vision for world evangelization through missions.

We eventually want to send 2,000 missionaries who have full financial support; we want to establish a training institute in Korea for missionaries and seminary graduates; we want to open a similar institute for second-generation Korean-Americans; and we want to cooperate with other mission groups.

Mission work is not an easy task. Because it is the heart of our Lord and the ultimate purpose of all churches on earth, however, and the ultimate purpose of Christians living in this world, let us invest our best efforts to carry on this sacred command until our Lord Jesus returns in glory.

David Kim
Grace Korean Church
P.O. Box 8040
400 W. Freedman Way
Anaheim, CA 92812-8040
Phone: 714-780-5800
Fax: 714-780-5811

PART TWO:
Based in Other Nations

15

FAITH COMMUNITY BAPTIST CHURCH

Pastor Lawrence Khong
Singapore

Reverend Lawrence Khong graduated with a degree in business administration from the University of Singapore in 1976 and received his master's degree in theology at Dallas Theological Seminary in 1981. Rev. Khong is deeply committed to a strong pulpit ministry of expository preaching as well as to the ministry of healing through the supernatural work of the Holy Spirit. Filled with a consuming zeal to reach the lost for Christ, Rev. Khong preaches as would a Bible teacher, but projects through the fervor of an evangelist. Presently, he is the senior pastor of Faith Community Baptist Church and also the chairman of the Spiritual Warfare Network, Singapore.

On August 17, 1986, I stood on the platform in a rented auditorium in Singapore to preach in the first worship service of a brand new congregation. As I approached the pulpit, the Holy Spirit spoke clearly to my heart: "Son, today the new baby is born!" Then the words of Haggai 2:9 flooded into my mind: "'The glory of this present house will be greater than the glory of the former house,...And in this place I will grant peace,' declares the Lord Almighty" *(NIV)*.

I was too emotionally worn out to be excited about the "greater glory." I simply took comfort in the fact that in this new church there will be *peace*. I had just emerged from more than a year of leadership struggle in my former church. I had grown up in this church—a Bible-believing congregation that had been growing consistently. This had been my spiritual home throughout my teenage years. The leadership of the church had clearly and lovingly affirmed my calling into the ministry. They sent me to pursue my theological training in the United States. I returned to be the pastor of the church. Within five years, it grew from 350 to 1,600 under my pastoral leadership.

A CAREER-CHANGING EXPERIENCE

During the fifth year of my pastorate, I had an unexpected encounter with the Holy Spirit that opened my heart to the reality of God's power. In that encounter, I began speaking in a new tongue. It was something I had always told my congregation would not and should not ever happen in this day and age. I clearly taught them that this particular gift, together with other power gifts of the Holy Spirit, had ceased at the end of the apostolic age. I taught them so well, in fact, that the leadership of the church rejected the validity of my experience and its theological implications immediately. I realized they were doing the very thing I would have done if I were in their shoes.

I was confused. My experience completely devastated my neat and tidy theology. I could not at that point give a clear biblical understanding about what happened. On the other hand, I could not deny the reality of that experience without compromising the witness of the Holy Spirit in my heart. Meanwhile, my ministry began falling apart. Before long, theological differences within the leadership degenerated to attacks on my personal integrity. After many months of painful struggles, I was finally asked to relinquish my role as the senior pastor of the church.

In the midst of this agonizing process, the Lord gave me a clear word from Scripture:

> "A woman, when she is in labor, has sorrow because her hour has come; but as soon as she has given birth to the child, she no longer remembers the anguish, for joy that a human being has been born into the world" (John 16:21).

The Lord told me He was bringing forth a "new baby" in my life that would launch me into a new ministry. The painful struggles I was going through were the labor pains needed to bring forth this new birth.

THE NEW BABY IS BORN

When the Lord said, "Son, today the new baby is born!" on August 17, 1986, Faith Community Baptist Church (FCBC) began. It brought unspeakable joy to my spirit. Since then, the promise of God has been true. The glory of this ministry has far exceeded what I would ask or think. Indeed, in the last 10 years of our church, there has been peace. As I am writing this, the baby has grown considerably. The attendance in our weekly worship services has reached close to 8,000. In the past 10 years, we have baptized more than 6,400 new believers. During the same period, some 16,000 persons have made professions of faith for the first time. Most significantly, in my mind, almost every person who worships with us is also part of a cell group ministry during the week. In these small groups, we train every member to be a minister of the gospel, calling forth a higher-than-average level of commitment.

A recent survey of our congregational stewardship has revealed that the giving averages more than 25 percent of the total income of all our members. This explains our annual budget of U.S. $12 million—20 percent of which goes to world missions, and another 10 percent to community services. In addition, the church owns two auditoriums costing a total in United States currency of $20,000,000, fully paid!

As I reflect upon the grace of the Lord in Faith Community Baptist Church during the last 10 years, the Lord has impressed me with four major factors that have contributed to the phenomenal growth in this local congregation. These four factors include (1) a clear vision and strategy for growth; (2) a cell church structure; (3) a reliance on the supernatural work of the Holy Spirit; and (4) one strong and anointed leader.

A CLEAR VISION AND STRATEGY FOR GROWTH

During the first 12 months of FCBC, I had the leaders of the church join me in seeking the Lord for a clear vision and strategy for growth. We were determined not to be another church that religiously maintained traditional programs. With all our hearts, we sought the Lord for a blueprint that would enable us to take our city for God. The Lord showed us that to do this, we must move in unity, we must share a common vision and we must agree on the appropriate strategies to fulfill the vision. As early as 1987, we developed a three-part vision that

215

has guided our programs ever since. This three-part vision has seen refinements through the years. Today, it stands as follows:

By God's grace, we will, by the year 2000 (1) establish integrated ministries of outreach, discipleship and service that encompass the whole of Singapore; (2) be a model cell group church that provides quality pastoral training and equipping resources for transitioning cell group churches in Singapore and around the world; and (3) establish 50 cell group churches around the world by sending out teams to reach hidden or responsive people groups.

To achieve this vision, we have adopted the following strategies:

1. Develop an exciting and meaningful celebration every Sunday through music and the pulpit ministry;
2. Minimize committee meetings by decentralization of operations to full-time staff;
3. Commit to active staff recruitment to establish a multiple-staff ministry;
4. Establish a discipleship network for evangelism, prayer and Bible study;
5. Provide lay leadership training for all leaders of the church;
6. Develop and establish specialized ministries of outreach;
7. Train, equip, send and fully support missionaries from the church to the mission field;
8. Build a "Touch Center" consisting of an auditorium seating some 3,000, including other ministry facilities for both the church and the community;
9. Develop within every member a deep commitment to regular, disciplined and intense warfare prayer for spiritual revival in Singapore and around the world;
10. Strengthen the family so as to provide a solid base for reaching the unsaved with the love of Christ.

From the beginning, we were filled with a sense of excitement that God was going to fulfill these visions among us. In FCBC, everyone of us is given a corporate challenge to fulfill the vision the Lord has given us. We believe that "everybody's job" becomes "nobody's job." Members of FCBC believe that if no one else will do it, we will assume the responsibility of winning our nation to the Lord. Before long, most of us would begin to realize that we could no longer possess this vision. Rather, this vision has now totally possessed us with a consuming zeal from the Lord!

COMPLETELY STRUCTURED AS A CELL GROUP CHURCH

In the last five years, FCBC has organized an annual "International Conference on Cell Group Church." Thousands from around the world

> **There is a heaven and earth difference; an east and west difference between a CHURCH WITH CELLS and a CELL GROUP CHURCH.**

have come to learn the principles and operations of a cell group church. Every year, I begin the conference by proclaiming a statement that has become a major landmark of my teaching about the cell church. My statement is: There is a heaven and earth difference; an east and west difference between a CHURCH WITH CELLS and a CELL GROUP CHURCH.

Just about every church in the world has some kind of small groups. Some of these groups are Bible study groups, fellowship groups, counseling/therapy groups, prayer groups and many others. However, these are churches with cells and not cell churches. The major difference between the former and the latter is a structural one. Hence there is a *fundamental*, not a *superficial*, difference between them.

In a church with cells, the cell ministry is only a department within the total ministry of the church. Members of the church have many options. They can choose to serve in the missions department or the prayer department or the Christian education department or the fellowship department. They can choose between the Sunday School or the adult fellowship. The cell ministry is just another one of the options.

This is not so in a cell group church. In a cell group church, *the cell is the church*. No menu of options is open to every member except that they be in a cell group. Every department of the church is designed to serve the cell ministry. Departments do not have any constituency of their own. All are designed to support the ministry of the cells.

In FCBC, every believer is assimilated into cell groups, similar to military squads. Each cell is trained to edify one another and to evangelize so that it will multiply within a year to a maximum size of 12 to 15 people. These cell groups are not independent "house churches," but basic Christian communities linked together to penetrate every area of our community. Approximately three to four cell groups cluster to form a sub-zone, and a volunteer zone supervisor pastors the five cells and its cell leaders. Five sub-zones cluster to create a zone of about 250 people pastored by a full-time zone pastor. Five or more zones cluster to form a district, and a seasoned district pastor shepherds as many as 1,500 people.

From the start, we created zones that were geographical (north, east, west) and generational (children, youth, military). Later, we added our music zone for those participating in our choirs, bands, orchestras, drama and dance. Even these music cells are constantly winning people to Jesus Christ. Every year, more than 2,500 make first-time decisions for the Lord in the cells.

FOUNDATIONS FOR MINISTRY

In the early years, we worked hard to create the foundations for our ministry. Pastors who had no previous experience with cell church structures were trained and cell leaders were equipped. Nonexistent equipping materials had to be written. Soon we had a nickname: "FCBC—Fast Changing Baptist Church"! Every experimental step helped us learn how to equip and evangelize in the new paradigm. We were determined to discard anything that did not help us achieve our goals, so we revised our strategy again and again as we gained experience. Indeed, we are still doing so!

Like other cell churches, our life involves three levels: the cells, the congregations (a cluster of five zones) and the celebration on Sunday. We quickly had to go to two and then three celebrations of 1,000 people to accommodate the growth in the cell groups. We presently have one evening service on Saturday and four services on Sunday of two hours duration each.

A completely different congregation of people worships in the Saturday evening service. We have studiously avoided advertising "seeker-sensitive services," choosing instead to grow through the ministries of our members in the cells. Our cells are seeker-sensitive, but our celebration is not. For us, the celebration is an assembling of the Body of Christ rather than a means of attracting the unconverted. Nevertheless, many profess faith in Jesus Christ as a result of the intense anointing that comes through worship, as well as my pulpit ministry that focuses on down-to-earth life issues.

THE YEAR OF EQUIPPING

What we call "The Year of Equipping" has become an important part of our cell group life. Each incoming member is visited by the cell leader, who assigns a cell member to be a sponsor for the new person. A "Journey Guide" is used to acquaint the cell leader and sponsor with the spiritual condition of the person. Guided by private weekly sessions with the sponsor, this person will complete a journey through the "Arrival Kit" and then be trained to share Christ with both responsive and unresponsive unbelievers.

Another major part of The Year of Equipping consists of three cycles of training for evangelism and harvest meeting in the cells throughout the year. One such cycle begins in January, where new members of the cell are sent for a weekend of evangelism training. This is followed by further practices during the cell meetings, leading up to the Good Friday weekend.

In these months, every member of the cell is asked to pray for unsaved people whom they would invite to a special Good Friday evangelistic cell meeting. On that one Good Friday evening, we will have as many as 4,000 unsaved people in all our cell groups spread throughout the city. More than 10 percent of them will give their lives to the Lord for the first time. In that meeting, every member of the cell shares the gospel with unsaved friends. We do this three times a year. In this way, equipping for evangelism is an ongoing lifestyle of every cell. It is my intention that every cell become a fit fighting unit in the army of the Lord!

COMMUNITY SERVICE

Because of our strong desire to penetrate the society around us, we have formed the Touch Community Services. This is the neutral arm of our church designed to relate to the community. Through this separate corporation, we conduct child care, legal aid services, after-school clubs, marriage counseling, a workshop to train the handicapped and many other social ministry areas. This has earned the respect of unbelievers around us and has provided openings for the gospel we would not otherwise experience. It has established good will for us among the many racial groups that live together in harmony in our nation.

Our community services have found so much favor with government authorities that much of our service ministry is actually funded by the government. As of now, the juvenile courts make it mandatory for their offenders to seek counseling from our youth counseling services. The registry of marriage has invited us to conduct premarital counseling for all who are getting married in Singapore! This is our "root system" into the unconverted world.

RELIANCE ON THE SUPERNATURAL WORKS OF THE HOLY SPIRIT

The structure of the cell church is nothing but a conduit for the power of the Holy Spirit. Unless the living water flows, the cells are lifeless. A major spiritual breakthrough came for us in those early years as we began to recognize the place of the gifts of the Holy Spirit in our midst. As our cell groups were confronted by the need for spiritual power in caring for people, we saw a gracious outpouring of His presence in our midst.

I shall never forget a certain Sunday when the Lord visited us powerfully. We were then conducting four worship services in a rented auditorium that seated about 800. On that particular Sunday, I preached a message about repentance. Many came forward to repent of their sins. As I prayed for them from behind the pulpit, the Holy Spirit came into our midst. Most of them fell under the power of the Spirit. This was something we had never experienced in our church. It surprised everyone in the auditorium, especially the people who found themselves lying on the church floor for the first time in their lives, completely unable to move.

The presence of the Lord was so overwhelming that by the beginning of the third service, members who were just walking into the auditorium for worship fell under the power of the Spirit, having no idea what had been happening in the preceding services!

This visitation of the Holy Spirit brought about a six-month period of deep repentance among the members of the church. The anointing of the Spirit filled every cell meeting. The sick were being healed. The demonized were set free. The church grew rapidly as our cell groups learned to minister in the power of the Spirit.

ONE STRONG AND ANOINTED LEADER

At the risk of misunderstanding me as being arrogant, I have always told audiences around the world that one of the main factors that has contributed to the growth of FCBC is the gracious gift of leadership the Lord has entrusted to me. FCBC has grown rapidly because of my strong and anointed leadership. In the early years of the church, the leadership team carefully studied a chapter written by Oswald J. Smith in his book *Building a Better World*. He began his chapter with these words:

> "Behold, I have given him for a witness to the people, a leader and commander to the people" (Isa. 55:4). God's plan is that His flock should be led by a Shepherd, not run by a Board. Committees are to advise, never to dictate. The Holy Spirit appoints men. To Bishops and Elders is given the care of the churches, never to Committees. They are to be the Overseers, the Shepherds. Each one has his own flock. Because men have failed to recognize this, there has been trouble. When God's plan is followed, all is well.[1]

The cell group church is vision driven. It needs a strong leader to rally the people toward a God-given vision. It is also structured like the military. It calls for a strong commander to instill a sense of strict spiritual discipline needed to complete the task. At the inception of the church, my core leaders asked, "Pastor, what sort of leader will you be?"

My answer was unequivocal, "I believe I will be a strong leader, one who believes what the Lord wants me to do and who pursues it with all my heart."

Traditionally, the church has been suspicious of strong leadership, especially when it is centered in one person. As a result, many man-made systems of checks and counterchecks have been built into traditional church polity to ensure that there can be no one-man rule. Although I agree that there is a need for mutual accountability, these

> **Many lay leaders have expressed great fear of so-called "dictatorship" behind the pulpit. After 20 years of ministry, however, I must say that I have seen more "dictators" sitting in the pews than those standing behind pulpits.**

checks have more often become major roadblocks for God's appointed leaders to lead His people into victorious ministry. Many lay leaders have expressed great fear of so-called "dictatorship" behind the pulpit. After 20 years of ministry, however, I must say that I have seen more "dictators" sitting in the pews than those standing behind pulpits.

WHAT IS LEADERSHIP?

One day I was praying about this issue of leadership and the Lord impressed upon me to write down these words about leadership:

Leadership Is Not Dictatorship

Leadership is rallying people to pursue a vision. A leader successfully instills in those he is leading a deep desire to fulfill that vision. He gains the trust of his people by virtue of his character, his integrity, his resourcefulness, his zeal, his good judgment, his people skills and, most importantly, his anointing from God. As a result, the people grant him the freedom to decide and the authority to supervise and control. Such leadership can never be provided by a committee or a board. If, indeed, such leadership is provided by a group, it is because within that group someone can provide such strong leadership first to the group and through that to the rest of the people.

We often talk about New Testament leadership as if it is completely different from Old Testament leadership. I believe that biblical leadership is consistent throughout the New and Old Testaments. *Whenever God wants to do a work, He chooses a man.* We have leaders such as Moses, Gideon, David, Elijah and others in the Old Testament. In the New Testament, we have leaders such as Peter for the Jews and Paul for the Gentiles.

In FCBC, I assert my clear leadership in three areas:

Casting the Vision

I lead the people by casting a clear and concrete vision for the church. In the early years, I spent countless hours sharing, discussing, praying and formulating the vision and strategies of the church. I realize that a vision is only powerful when it is fully owned by the people. Our vision and strategies were clearly set by the third year. Since that time, I have constantly shared and reinforced this for my leaders and members. I speak to every new member of the church about this vision in our new member orientation called "Spiritual Formation Weekend." I challenge every member to consider seriously our vision before joining our church. If someone is not able to subscribe to the vision, I strongly recommend that the person join another church.

Once the vision and strategies have been forged, I expect every leader in the church to support them. This is especially so for pastoral staff. They are selected on the basis that as lay cell leaders and group supervisors they have demonstrated their commitment to the vision of the church. Today, the church has a paid staff of almost 200. In the last 10 years, we have had a staff turnover of fewer than 10 persons. There is a tremendous sense of unity on the team. The reason for this is that I have clearly provided leadership in casting for the people a clear vision and articulating specific strategies from the Lord.

Creating an Environment for Growth

As leader, I am concerned about creating an environment conducive to growth. We have written a clear mission statement and we have agreed upon specific core values that define the uniqueness of FCBC, both in terms of belief and of practice. I will reproduce the mission statement here:

> We seek to fulfill God's role for us in bringing the gospel to the world by developing every believer to his full potential in

Jesus Christ within a vision & value driven environment and a God-centered community.

Preaching and Teaching from the Pulpit

The main vehicle by which the growth environment is established comes through dynamic teaching and preaching during the celebration. Some think that the cell church consists of only cells. This is not true. Although the cell is the church, the church is more than just cells. The cells come together in the celebration meeting, absorbing the apostolic teaching that shapes the direction, commitment and spiritual atmosphere for the whole Body. The church in Acts 2 met in homes, but they came together to listen to the apostles' teaching. I spend some 20 hours every week preparing my sermon. The sermon each week is more than teaching the Bible. Every sermon conveys a passion for God and communicates His purposes for His people.

There is no doubt that the growth of FCBC is the result of God's special grace in and through my life. As long as I walk humbly before the Lord in intimacy, the Lord will lead us from glory to glory. I realize that as I promote and support strong apostolic leadership, there is always the danger of abuse. It is altogether possible for apostles to abuse the authority God has given us as His apostolic leaders. Nevertheless, this apparently is a risk God is willing to take with us because, in His grace, He has chosen to do just that. God is more than able to bring down His erring servants just as quickly as He raises them up. Meanwhile, I believe in affirming God's appointed leadership over His people.

AFFIRMATION WITH HUMILITY

I believe that God's leaders need affirmation and encouragement as they agree to take positions of leadership. Yet they must have the humility to serve. Strong leaders have often been misunderstood to be dictatorial and proud. For my part, though, I would rather affirm them, pray for them and release them to become a blessing to the Body of Christ.

When FCBC started, my heart was completely shattered by the rejection of the leaders of my former church. The issues that finally brought about the split of the church turned personal. I was attacked for being controlling, dictatorial and even dangerously influential. At the inception of FCBC, I had lost my confidence to lead. Thus I became laid back, relinquishing the leadership to my core leaders who, together with me, started the church. In the beginning of 1987, a few months after the church had started, we invited Pastor Bill Yaegar from the First Baptist Church of Modesto, California, to speak to us about leadership. Pastor Yaegar was in his 60s and since then has retired.

In his visit with us, Bill Yaegar noticed how discouraged I was. I could never forget his parting words to me at the Singapore airport. He said, "Son, I was praying for you this morning. The Lord told me He was giving you a new name. Your name shall be called 'Ari.' This is a Jewish name that means 'lion.' Lawrence, the Lord tells you that you are the 'Lion of Singapore.' You are to stand up and roar. And whenever others forget that you are the 'Lion of Singapore,' stand up and roar again!"

No one had ever previously affirmed me that way. It was an extremely important moment in my ministry career. I realized in that instant that through all my years of Christian ministry, people were constantly warning me to go slower, to be more cautious and to be more "humble." This was the first time a seasoned servant of God had actually encouraged me to take charge, to lead and to press on. Something burst forth within the depths of my spirit. I have been roaring ever since for the glory of God and the advance of His kingdom!

Note
1. Oswald J. Smith, *Building a Better World* (London, England: Marshall, Morgan Scott, n.d.), p. 50.

Rev. Lawrence Khong
Faith Community Baptist Church
66/68 East Coast Road
#06-00 GRTH Building
Singapore 428778
Phone: 440-8821
Fax: 440-5205

Resource List—Audiotape Series
Role of Senior Pastor
Principles of Cell Group Church
Equipping in the Cell Group Church
Vision of the Cell Group Church
Work of the Holy Spirit in the Cell
Group Church

Resources may be ordered through:
TOUCH RESOURCE PTE LTD
8 Kaki Bukit Road 2 #02-07
Ruby Warehouse Complex
Singapore 417841
Phone: 7448627
Fax: 7448632

16

His People
Christian Ministries

Pastor Paul Daniel
Cape Town, South Africa

Paul Daniel and his wife, Jenny, founded His People Christian Ministries in 1988 at the University of Cape Town. Since then, their church has expanded rapidly and currently has about 6,000 members. In keeping with the His People motto "His Commission, Our Mission," Bible schools have been established on 20 university and Technikon campuses both nationally and internationally. More than 2,000 students are enrolled for the current year. His People churches are also flourishing in seven cities in South Africa, three in Europe and one in Namibia, Zambia, the United States and Australia. Paul is the founder and president of His People Christian Ministries, and his ministry is marked by a strong apostolic anointing.

I came to Christ in July 1981, during my final year at the University of Cape Town in South Africa, in a dramatic experience. My entire life changed in an instant as I walked out of agnosticism and almost total spiritual darkness into what felt like brilliant daylight. Two weeks later I was filled with the Holy Spirit and, as the waves of God's glory flashed through my spirit, I began speaking in tongues. At that time, I clearly heard God's call to the ministry.

Up till this point, I had been determined to be a success in the worldly sense and to achieve my personal goals and ambitions. God, however, had other plans for my life. I believe He started to implement these plans through my grandmother, an "old Pentecostal" who was saved through the ministry of John G. Lake and who diligently followed the ministry of Oral Roberts. She prayed for us daily and she often told the family that God had called one of her grandsons to the ministry. We all thought this would be my younger brother, Christian, who truly lived up to his name and who loved God with all his heart.

My foundations were first shaken in my final year of high school when I read a poem by Thomas Gray entitled "Elegy Written in a Country Churchyard." Gray had attended a funeral where a great man was buried, receiving full pomp and ceremony, and then reflected on another time when he was in a country churchyard beside the simple grave of a man who died unknown and unremembered. His remark, "The paths of glory lead but to the grave," brought me face-to-face with the futility and emptiness of life without God and challenged me to consider what was truly important.

Finally, the tragic death of my younger brother, Christian, who suffered a critical injury, arrested my full attention and need for God. During his last few days in the hospital, I was deeply moved by Christian's absolute assurance in God and his knowledge of where he would spend eternity.

SHARING THE GOOD NEWS

Following my conversion, I returned to university determined to share the good news. I led many of my friends and colleagues to Christ, and soon a small prayer group developed where we prayed nightly from 10:00 P.M. right through to 3:00 A.M. the next morning. Revival came to our campus, and the group grew so fast that it eventually became a church, and then one of the largest churches in town.

After graduation, God told me to return home and attend Bible school. I had a seemingly unquenchable thirst for the Word of God and I enrolled in both local and correspondence Bible schools. I was subsequently invited to teach at the local Bible school and went on to hold the position of full-time dean of the school. I was commissioned to write a Bible School curriculum to train Christians for ministry and for greater influence in the community. Thus, I spent much of the first five years of my ministry studying God's Word extensively, and researching a wide range of Christian material from throughout the world. Today, this curriculum forms the basis of the His People Bible School curriculum and is taught on campuses around the world.

TAKING "GOOD HOPE" TO THE NATIONS

A short while later, I met my future wife, Jenny, and we soon were married. After six months of marriage, we knew it was time to move on and prayed earnestly about exactly where God wanted us to go. We were willing to go anywhere in the world. While reading a book about revival, I saw a vision of a fire breaking in Cape Town, South Africa, and spreading to the nations of the world. I knew God was speaking to us about moving to Cape Town and that we would take the "good hope" of the gospel from there into the nations.

I use the phrase "good hope" because historically Cape Town was called the Cape of Storms, but its name was later changed to the Cape of Good Hope. I saw the ministry as a ship carrying a precious cargo, the sail of the ship representing the vision. The higher we lifted the vision, the more the wind of the Holy Spirit filled the sails and took us to the ports God would show us. As long as we had direction and held the vision before us, we would be able to do what He had called us to do.

THE BEGINNINGS OF "HIS PEOPLE"

In obedience to the call of God, Jenny and I sold our house and moved to Cape Town. In March 1988, the first His People service was held in our home, including one other person. As the weeks went by, more and more students came to these meetings, until they were literally hanging out the windows. At about this time, we formed a society on the University of Cape Town campus. While fasting and praying with the students, God clearly told me to keep on pursuing the vision of His People that He had given, as He wanted to take it into the nations of the world. The ministry grew rapidly, and soon the biggest lecture hall at the University of Cape Town was unable to hold the congregation.

We moved in 1993 into Cape Town's second largest theater, and within three years we were conducting four full-capacity meetings every Sunday. During this period, the ministry began to expand rapidly to other campuses within South Africa and internationally. Recently, God has opened the door for us to move into one of Cape

Town's most prestigious venues, the Nico Theater Centre. Situated in the heart of the city, this move enables us to influence the people of Cape Town to an even greater extent. It also provides the perfect stepping stone for our next move to our own property. There, God has given the vision for an apostolic center for His People Christian Ministries International.

GROWING BY LEAPS AND BOUNDS

A pioneering spirit has been at the heart of His People ever since its inception. In nine short years, it has grown from a local to an international ministry. In keeping with our motto "His Commission Our Mission," we now have Bible Schools and churches established in seven cities in South Africa—Cape Town, Johannesburg, Pretoria, Port Elizabeth, Grahamstown, Durban and Kimberley. They are also established in seven cities internationally—Windhoek (Namibia), Lusaka (Zambia), London (UK), Innsbruck (Austria), Stockholm (Sweden), Perth (Australia) and Miami (United States).

Our strategy is to place one foot on the local campus by establishing a Bible School, and the other foot in the community itself by establishing a local church. We currently have 2,616 students enrolled in 18 Bible Schools, and to date 6,326 students have graduated worldwide.

A VISION AND A COMMON DESTINY

I value the great sense of unity, vision and common destiny among the leaders of our churches worldwide. Cape Town, known in South Africa as the "Mother City," is the first of what we hope will be many His People apostolic centers worldwide. Leaders come to this apostolic center to be trained before being sent out to start new His People works.

My church in Cape Town conducts five Sunday services and has between 5,000 and 6,000 people attending regularly. A full-time staff of about 35, including 7 pastors, keeps the wheels moving and the office is a delightful hive of activity. During the week, nearly 300 cell groups meet across the Western Cape, covering a radius of more than 50 kilometers, and providing the "love net" of the local church where members can be cared for and where they build friendships.

A MULTICULTURAL CONGREGATION

Significantly for post-apartheid South Africa, our churches have managed to span cultural divisions, and people of all races are experiencing the reality of their oneness in Jesus Christ. Should you visit one of

> *Many people have described South Africa as a microcosm of the world and the problems we experience and address are reflected in many other nations.*

our Sunday services, you would be hard pressed to tell whether we have more white, black or colored folk in our congregation. Many people have described South Africa as a microcosm of the world and the problems we experience and address are reflected in many other nations. Issues such as crime, poverty, racism, conflicting political ideologies, cultural and political diversity, constitutionalism and the secular state have been uniquely profiled because we are in a real sense a nation in the process of transformation.

These challenges have galvanized us as a church toward being reformed and determined to bring the many practical benefits of our Christian heritage to the disenfranchised and underdeveloped communities. Throughout South Africa, our churches sponsor effective programs to bring healing, restoration and upliftment to the disadvantaged, providing a wide range of educational and entrepreneurial skills, ministering to the homeless and working also on a practical level to provide health care and counseling.

An important part of the international ministry is the His People Institute based in Cape Town. The Institute is distinctive in that it equips leaders to participate in and bring a biblical Christian worldview into the spheres of church ministry, education, politics, business, media, arts and sciences. Many students have testified that the Institute has stretched them, questioning many of their former presuppositions and igniting a new passion in them to be relevant and uncompromising Christians in the contemporary world.

OUR GUIDING PRINCIPLES

I can best describe the ministry as evangelical in doctrine, charismatic in expression and reformed in our understanding of family, church

> **It is only to the extent we have revival and self-government in our hearts that we can bring true reformation to the communities around us.**

and civil government. I believe it is only to the extent we have revival and self-government in our hearts that we can bring true reformation to the communities around us. To do so, we need to develop a biblical Christian worldview, having a clear understanding not only of what we believe and why we believe it, but also of what we do not believe and why we do not believe it.

My philosophy of church as it relates to the kingdom of God is that God uses the Church (Body of Christ) as His agent to bring His kingdom into the earth. This is not a physical but a spiritual Kingdom whose influence can and should be seen in every area of society. I believe that this Kingdom extends far beyond the four walls of our church, and it comprises everything submitted to the rule of Christ and is obedient to His lordship.

KEEPING FOCUSED

I am convinced that people are our greatest resource and that good relationships form the foundation of all we do. As a result, we have a strong sense of "family" and emphasize the importance of keeping our relationships pure. Our vision is also multi-generational—we labor not just for the benefit of our generation, but also for the generations to come, recognizing that we are only ultimately successful to the extent that we pass on our Christian heritage to our children, grandchildren and great grandchildren.

University campuses are miniature representations of nations and cultures, where students from all communities come together. As such, universities and colleges have been rightly identified as "the rudders of the nations." The prevailing ideas taught in these institutions will inevitably be the predominant philosophy in society in later years. Consequently, I do not treat students as "youth," but as young adults and future leaders. Our priority is to reach them by presenting a biblical Christian worldview and by nurturing them in their gifts, callings and leadership. As we are both campus and community based, we are able to present our ministry in such a way that they will continue to identify with and relate to the broader church, community and society. My dream is to see young leaders take the way and will of God into all of life.

OUR LONG-RANGE VISION

My main objective of our 1996 International Leadership Summit was to finalize our vision and strategy for the next 5, 10 and 20 years. God is calling us to keep on expanding into the nations: "Enlarge the place of your tent, and let them stretch out the curtains of your dwellings" (Isa. 54:2).

As such, the vision of His People Christian Ministries is to establish Bible Schools and local churches on 1,000 campuses worldwide within the next 20 years. By planting one foot on the campus through establishing a Bible School, and one in the community by starting a local church, we not only bring the students and community together in one Body in a local church setting, but also inundate both the campus and city with the gospel.

I have not only written down the vision so that those who read it can implement it, but I also pray into it and preach and proclaim it. We are a purpose-driven ministry and are careful to keep our vision before us. I recognize that God has given us stewardship about the vision. As we expand into the nations, it becomes an increasingly important part of my apostolic role to encourage cohesion and sound working relationships so that we remain focused on what He has called us to do. We measure ourselves in terms of this call rather than comparing ourselves to other ministries. Consequently, our primary concern is to obtain the necessary skills to do the task more effectively to the glory of God.

OPERATIVE PRINCIPLES

In establishing the form of government for our ministry on an international, national and local level, we have combined elements of the Episcopal, Presbyterian, Congregational and independent forms of church government. Every individual is valuable and precious to the ministry, and we have endeavored to establish a form of government that enables the contributions of all members of the congregation to be considered as part of the decision-making process.

The ministry operates within the legislative framework of our Constitution, our Statement of Faith, our Manifesto and, of course, the Word of God. The government of His People separates the legislative, executive and judicial powers in the church according to Isaiah 33:22. I recognize that no one but God is able to exercise all three areas of authority with absolute justice. As a result, no individual or group of people has all power in the church.

By separating the executive from the judicial functions, the administration of the local church is separated from the spiritual aspects of church life. The job description of the executive of the ministry is based on clear business principles, hiring staff who are employed on a contractual basis, and who work normal "office hours." We view the church as an institution of society, and we are careful to present ourselves in an appropriate way to the broader business and political communities.

THE SENIOR PASTOR LEADS THE CHURCH

The senior pastor of each His People church exercises headship in the local church. Although he may hold both executive and judicial powers, he is still required to operate within the legislative framework of the ministry and he is accountable to those he leads. As a senior pastor, I have associate pastors who work with me to care for the spiritual life of my local church. Each associate pastor has a pastorate, comprising an area of the city that is cared for with the assistance of the members of the congregation, who act as area leaders and who in turn have cell leaders to assist them. Apart from their pastorate, associate pastors oversee a directorate, or an area of specific interest or ministry. These directorates can include areas such as media, missions, music, campus and so forth.

His People Christian Ministries is the umbrella and covering body for all our churches and Bible Schools worldwide. When a new church is planted in a city, providing it operates within the parameters of the legislative framework that governs every His People church, the senior pastor has the flexibility to set up a church that responds uniquely to the local needs of that city.

The senior pastor and eldership have the liberty to set the vision for their local congregation, to employ their own staff and administer their own finances free from external interference in the day-to-day running of their church. If they experience problems, however, they can call upon the His People International Leadership for counsel and assistance, thus providing each church with spiritual covering and the security of being part of a greater whole.

HIS PEOPLE BIBLE SCHOOLS

Although the churches are self-governed, all the Bible Schools remain the property of His People Christian Ministries International to ensure that consistent standards are maintained in what is taught. The Bible School and curriculum materials are freely given to every church planted as an inheritance of the His People "family." Our Bible Schools have their own constitutions, and each cchool has a dean who cares for the staff and oversees the Bible School's academic teaching.

CORPORATE IDENTITY

His People Ministries has developed a strong corporate identity. This ensures that wherever we may be established in the world, there is an immediate identification with the greater vision of the ministry and a reminder of the importance of relationships with others who are following the same calling and vision. Managing our corporate identity and how we present ourselves to the community is very important in terms of our public relations. I believe this plays a valuable role in streamlining and keeping open the lines of communication both internally and externally. Communication is the lifeblood of our ministry, and our unity is strengthened by ensuring that we have a clear understanding of one another and our commonly shared goals and objectives.

ACCOUNTABILITY AND TEAM BUILDING

As Christian leaders, I believe we are stewards of the mysteries of God and we are accountable for what we preach and teach, and how we

> *A primary principle of team building and accountability is that people are only given authority to the extent that they accept responsibility.*

communicate with people. Realizing this, His People leaders are held accountable for their ministry by the parameters set out in our Constitution. Should these parameters ever be transgressed, correction would be necessary. A primary principle of team building and accountability is that people are only given authority to the extent that they accept responsibility.

I also place great value on team dynamics, and it is taught as part of leadership development and training. All team members learn to play their part in a team, to clearly understand their areas of responsibility and accountability, to know where their borders of authority lie and what decision-making powers they have. In a growing church, it is important for this to be understood so that everyone can pursue a common goal.

As a church, we have made ourselves accountable to both our congregation and to the local community by holding a public Annual General Meeting. At this meeting, our financial director accounts for the income and expenditure of the church, and these figures are externally audited. At the same meeting, all department heads present reports about their previous year's activities and their vision for the following year.

Accountability is built in at every level of leadership, and as the founder and president of His People Ministries, I fully realize the need for me to be in relationship with other apostolic figures, and to keep my life accountable to them in a meaningful way that runs deeper than mere friendship.

LEADERSHIP IN SERVING

Leadership training is one of the hallmarks of the ministry. Identifying and training leaders is central to our successful growth and functioning. Leadership forms the base of our ministry because the more leaders we have, the more people we can serve and the more people we can reach. I understand that for our church and ministry to grow, to continue planting churches and Bible Schools in the nations and to continue sending young people into all spheres of life, we consistently must identify, equip, train and release leaders.

I consider true leadership to be leadership in serving, and believe that every leader must be a servant leader. To me, the measure of a leader is not how many people serve him, but how many people he faithfully serves. God has called the "fathers" of the ministry to identify the gifts and callings on young people's lives and to serve that calling so they may become everything God wants them to be. If these young people do greater things for God in their lives than we ourselves accomplish, we will rejoice. Fathers, I believe, should never be threatened by sons, but should rejoice when they excel.

HIS COMMISSION, OUR MISSION

The His People motto "His Commission, Our Mission" encapsulates the value we place on fulfilling God's command to reach our community, city, nation and the world with the full-orbed gospel of Jesus Christ. To increase our effectiveness, I think it is important that we study the culture of the people we are trying to reach, and seek to understand and meet their needs in a spirit of serving.

Much of the outreach into our cities is therefore of a practical and servant-oriented nature. This is accomplished through community involvement in projects such as literacy training, hospital visitation and caring for the homeless. I encourage involvement in police and community forums, prison ministry, civic associations and local authorities as part of our outreach to the community. We also use drama, clowning, mime and dance in a variety of venues such as shopping centers and arts festivals as methods of outreach.

His People has a unique missions strategy, and has at least two major mission initiatives taking place every year. The first mission to a city is a scouting trip. His People students use their university vacations to visit other campuses in their own and neighboring countries to seek opportunities to establish a Bible School and to build relationships. When scouting trips and follow-up visits have opened a door for ministry onto a campus, ideally a fully trained married couple is sent to plant our Bible School on the campus and a His People church in the community.

Our Bible Schools are set up as "boot camps" to release each person's gifts, calling and leadership potential. Furthermore, our campus ministries are structured to equip young people for involvement in teaching, leading cell groups, student government and other areas of leadership on the campus. We have set in place training programs to equip young people for leadership in society.

I believe, however, that a person who completes our Bible School or Institute should not automatically be ordained for ministry. I look for fruitfulness, proven character and faithfulness in a person and part of my role as an Apostle is to identify young and emerging leaders and give them the opportunity to be discipled for leadership and ordination.

According to our constitution, we have two kinds of ordination for ministry. In the context of an established local church, the senior pastor has the liberty to appoint associate pastors to assist him in the work of fulfilling the vision of his local church. He will present the person concerned to the local congregation, then ordain him by prayer and the laying on of hands to release him to his assigned task. As this is in a sense an "internal matter," it does not need to involve the International Leadership or me. If a new senior pastor needs to be appointed to an existing local church, however, this person is identified by the existing leadership of that local church and then presented to the International Leadership for ordination into this office.

In the case of a couple who have a clear calling to pioneer a local church and Bible School in a nation, they may be invited to come behind the scenes of the Cape Town church to work with the leaders in all the various departments. In this way, they gain the benefit of becoming well acquainted with a good working model of a local church to guide them as they pioneer their own His People Church and Bible School. After completing a period of training, and at the discretion of the International Leadership, the couple will be ordained by the laying on of hands and sent out to pioneer a new His People Church and Bible School.

In my role as an Apostle, I nurture and support every new work up to the point where it is established and able to stand on its own. This support takes a variety of forms, but it invariably involves assisting those sent out with our His People Bible School and other materials. We also provide financial support and I give apostolic oversight, covering, counsel, encouragement (and even correction where necessary) to new and emerging works. One of the most valuable roles I play is to offer advice about specific situations that arise as the couple works to establish its church and Bible School. My door is always open, and these young men and women have access to me any time.

The covering of an international organization is a great advantage to those pioneering a new church and Bible School, as it is clear to the local community that they are part of something greater than themselves. This in turn helps to generate confidence. I also arrange for one of the senior international leaders or me to visit each new church to help lay strong apostolic foundations and help ensure the desired results of the ministry are achieved. Each new work receives at least one visit annually, which plays a valuable role in nurturing relationships and in maintaining our unity and focus as a ministry.

PRAYER AND POWER MINISTRIES

Prayer is a vital part of the ministry and we endeavor to saturate every aspect in prayer. At the beginning of each year I call the leadership to an annual fast, which can last for up to four weeks. This is a special time of consecration when we wait upon the Lord to seek Him, and receive His word and specific direction for what He wants us to pursue in the year ahead. Within the church, instead of only having a weekly intercessory prayer group, we have what we call "beach heads" in all the pastorates and departments. Literally hundreds of people pray regularly in groups during the week for the church, the leaders, for South Africa, Africa and for the nations of the world. People are also encouraged to have "prayer friends" to whom they are accountable and with whom they can share their lives.

One feature of our church services is that we often have times of corporate prayer when the whole congregation prays together for a specific issue. I have noticed tremendous results spring from these times of prayer. One notable example was when South Africa was going through its time of transition leading up to the 1994 elections. People from diverse cultures representing both the oppressed and the oppressors came together, took communion, wept together, asked one another for forgiveness and prayed for reconciliation in our nation. Today, we can notice the results of these times of prayer both in our nation and in the healing and reconciliation that has taken place within our congregations.

I have often seen the manifestation of God's power in our services and I encourage people to operate in the power and gifts of the Holy Spirit. Healings and miracles frequently occur, and these have played a key role in drawing people to our services to hear and to see what God is doing.

My understanding of power ministries, however, goes beyond the working of miracles and signs and wonders in our meetings. For example, one of the greatest sources of encouragement for me has been the obvious way in which God has providentially and repeatedly, against all odds, intervened in the circumstances of our progress. For this no man can be given credit, except God alone! I believe that the presence of God can be demonstrated in all of life, and hence my teaching and prophetic thrust is to send young pioneers into every area of society as agents of change.

FINANCIAL PRINCIPLES

I insist that all our churches and Bible Schools be "squeaky clean" when it comes to their financial dealings. There is considerable sensitivity today in much of the world concerning the church and its dealing with finances. Every church operates on sound business accounting principles. Although not required by law, we ourselves require external audits of our accounts, and we present the results to our congregation and to the greater community at our Annual General Meeting.

Annual budgets and actuarial models are created to project income and expenditure accurately and to ensure that funds are available for effectively implementing the work in which we are involved. We operate debt free. Individual projects or special events are run against separate budgets and a full accounting is made for all income and expenditures.

The majority of the finances that come into the ministry is raised from members of the congregations, and until now we have done little external fund-raising. I actively encourage church members to give not only to the work of God in tithes and offerings, but also to the poor and to support our community outreach. By giving financially, members of our congregation have gained a sense of oneness and ownership of what we are achieving.

COMMUNITY FAVOR

The growing profile of our church and the changes our nation has experienced have led to our involvement in many aspects of life—areas in which other churches might not be involved. We have developed proposals on constitutional development for the nation, have been in public debates on human rights issues and have publicly addressed the issues of crime, unions, taxation, abortion, homosexuality and pornography. I am careful to present our position to ensure we are not viewed as being reactive, but rather as being proactively involved in formulating the solution to the current problem. As a result, our ministry has found great favor with a broad sector of the community.

Paul Daniel
His People Christian Ministries
P.O. Box 275
Rondebosch 7700
Cape Town
Republic of South Africa
Phone: 27-21-686-9015
Fax: 27-21-686-9017
E-mail: mail@cpt.hispeople.org
Internet: www.hispeople.org

Resource List—Course Book
New Foundations Course (Order from the ministry)

17

DEEPER CHRISTIAN LIFE MINISTRY

William F. Kumuyi, General Superintendent
Lagos, Nigeria

William F. Kumuyi is pastor of Deeper Life Bible Church, acclaimed to be the largest single congregation in Africa as well as one of the fastest growing churches on the continent. The church has an adult membership of more than 85,000 at its international headquarters in Gbagada, Lagos, Nigeria. Kumuyi attended the University of Ibadan, Nigeria, where he obtained a degree in mathematics in 1967. He has also done post-graduate work at the University of Lagos. He is an international evangelist who moves in the miraculous. Including the church, his ministry—Deeper Christian Life Ministry—has a total of 700,000 members and about 5,000 churches in Nigeria.

It was not easy for me to decide to write this chapter. The challenge of telling one's story at middle age, when many trials, tests and traumas of life may have subtly given birth to triumphant tones, involves the risk of being written with an undertone of self-exaltation. However, my friendship with Peter Wagner, spanning a period of eight years, leaves me confident that he knows my heart, my lifestyle and especially my insistence on the Christian principle of self-effacement. My Wesleyan background from the early days of my Christian life has shaped this fundamental principle I hold so dearly.

Agreeing with Peter's vision that a book like this would be used by God to strengthen the Church and uplift the Body of Christ has motivated me to launch out in an effort I would not easily have undertaken on my own initiative. I now regard the assignment to write a chapter about our church as a most welcome one, especially when viewed in the light of the overwhelming interest of the Church of Christ in some of the new moves of the Spirit of God.

MARVELS OF GOD'S GRACE

It was sunset on Christmas Day, 1985. The tropical African sun, in its phosphorescent splendor, glowed brightly. The 80,000-capacity National Stadium in the sprawling city of Lagos, Nigeria, was already stretched beyond its limits. The crusade, in its third day, began at 6:00 P.M., but at 5:00 P.M., the stadium was jam-packed. Outside tens of thousands more were glued to loudspeakers. Many of them came in their uniforms—soldiers, policemen, traffic wardens, students and all. They came from offices, schools, factories and homes. Several of them came in their cars. Others came in buses, trucks, and a few on motorbikes. Not a few came on foot.

It turned out to be an illustrious spiritual concourse in a sports arena. Some had to be carried into the arena because of their infirmities. Others were led in. Many more walked with hearts laden with guilt and sorrow of sin. They all came expectant, expecting to receive the miracle of their lives. Hopes and assurances rested on their faces. They came to drink from God's new apostolic spring!

Excitement pervaded the stadium arena. The air was electric. The worship songs were thunderous—loud, clear and inspirational. The Spirit of God was on the move. Miracles were on the way. Even *unusual* miracles (see Acts 19:11) were on God's agenda for that evening. Many in the crowd had already witnessed the ease and simplicity of experiencing the miraculous during the past two nights.

My Christmas message was entitled "The Wonders of Christ's Birth." It was a remarkably short and simple sermon.

After the message, a sound like rushing waters filled the air as multitudes in the arena rose to pray. The young and the old prayed. The men prayed. The women prayed. Finally, the preacher prayed for all.

At the end of my prayer from the podium, I simply said, "All lame people here should rise up and walk in Jesus' name." An initial air of silence pervaded the stadium. Then shouts of joy followed. In the midst of those joyous thousands, a boy, Aliu, was led down to the track, walking, hopping and smiling. His mother followed closely behind, dancing, waving a stick (the boy's stick) in the air with careless abandon.

Aliu's mother told the crowd: "Aliu's right leg was not only lame, but it had no femur (leg bone) at all. I have borne this burden and cared for my son for more than nine years. While the prayer for the lame was going on, Aliu began pulling me and saying he was feeling some strange sensation in his leg. I asked him to be silent and allow the prayer to end. At the end of the preacher's prayer, I opened my eyes to find Aliu walking about without his sticks! I was overwhelmed with excitement. I could not control my emotions. I yelled for J-O-Y!"

That same evening a young man named Sunday, who had been incapacitated by a near-fatal accident years earlier, later recalled: "On December 25, 1985, the preacher at the crusade in the sports arena said: 'This is Christmas Bonanza Night! Whatever your problem is, you can begin to do now what you were not able to do.' My stiff leg was there. It could not bend beyond 10 degrees without a serious, sharp pain. But all of a sudden, my muscles became relaxed. I sat down, stood up and sat down again. My leg moved freely without any pain. God had healed it!"

Pa Alozie, who had been totally blind for 33 years, also recalled how he received his sight at the crusade. "I did not know where we were until the ministry time, when the preacher said, 'I am going to pray a miracle prayer, and the blind will begin to see. If you are blind, open your eyes and you will begin to see.' I never saw anything like that in my life before. It was like a sudden flare of match in darkness. I saw light!" Seeing any light at all was very strange to Pa Alozie because he had spent more than three decades in complete darkness. "My first reaction was to shout: 'Praise the Lord!' I was glad!"

After the six-day crusade, we did intensive follow-up. Church workers and members searched throughout the city and combed every nook and cranny visiting the crusade participants. The result was outstanding exponential church growth! Membership grew by eight thousand! Excitement filled the church. Workers enthusiastically continued to labor for the conservation of the fruits. Home cells grew significantly. The people's hearts were endeared to the Lord and the church. It was the evidence and fruit of the new move of God in a rebirth of an apostolic era.

OFF TO A FALTERING START

As an adult, whether in the pulpit or on the crusade podium, I am a far cry from my person at boyhood. I was born in 1941 into a religious family, and my father was of the strict, unsparing sort. As a disciplined Anglican, he was firm in raising me. Both my academics and church attendance were always under his watchful eyes. Perhaps because I was his firstborn, he was most impatient with my boyish pranks.

My restlessness met with his stiff resistance and reprimand. I grew to be known as a dull, unpromising boy. I could barely gain admission to high school. Life became complex as my schoolmaster, an unrepentant and avowed atheist, took time every morning to indoctrinate the students with his godless ideology. Each morning, he did his utmost to dim the smoldering flame of faith in my heart. My heart yearned for something, though, that I could not really express in words. The religious instinct within seemed to drive me into a search for some tangible expression of my obscure faith. So in my adolescence, I turned to the syncretistic churches adulterated with African traditional religion. I continued in this until 1964, when I had a personal encounter with the Lord in a full gospel denomination in western Nigeria.

In those early days of my conversion, I sensed the call of God upon my life. A deep unshakable and unquenchable interest in sharing the gospel, a burden to see souls saved, the ease with which my meager resources and property were committed to gospel work, my love for the people of God and my ministers, all pointed, at that time, to the possibility of a higher commitment and call to service in the future. I began reading voraciously, and I plunged deep into the worlds of John Wesley, Charles G. Finney, Charles Spurgeon and the Puritans. I studied biblical interpretations as well as many biographies and autobiographies.

DIGGING DEEP

The more of Wesley I studied, the greater my thirst for holiness became. In my early years at the university, I could teach and convincingly show other Christians the scriptural position on the subject of holiness. I was yet to have this as a personal experience, though. One day, in 1965, I locked myself in my room and knelt down to pray. My burning desire was to have a personal, deep and intimate walk with

God; and God did it! Since that day, I have never been the same! My heart was prepared to sacrifice everything for God, if need be. Though I obtained a first-class degree in mathematics and was acknowledged as the best student at the university the year of my graduation, I decided to reach forth and dedicate my life to the service of God.

A LILY FROM THE MUD

Coincidentally, the year of my graduation, 1967, was the year the Nigerian civil war started. Nigeria, the most populous black nation in the world, had attained independence from British colonial rule in 1960. However, the geopolitical, social and economic realities in Nigerian society gave rise to ethnic rivalry and suspicion, distrust, religious bigotry and tribal intolerance. These pervasive negative factors in 1967 erupted into a bloody civil war that lasted almost three years.

At the end of the war, Nigeria was still embroiled in problems of ethnicity, disunity, poverty, disease and misery. The spiritual climate of the country was dry and dreary. The prevailing circumstances, however, seemed to create the right environment for instituting various government-sponsored development programs as well as birthing many serious, Bible-based Christian movements. Thus, along with others, the Deeper Christian Life Ministry was born out of the adversity of the times, like a lily springing up from the mud.

HUMBLE BEGINNINGS

When I moved to Lagos for postgraduate studies, little did I realize God was preparing to launch me into full-blown public ministry. Christian students on campus and others outside sought my counsel and help in their spiritual lives and I attended to them. The increasing demand for counseling led to the decision to meet together one evening every week to study the Bible. Only 15 people were in attendance at the first Bible study in my residence in 1973. This was the humble beginning of Deeper Christian Life Ministry.

Within a short time, I was being invited as a guest speaker to other universities in Nigeria, and I began attracting a loyal following from those who turned to Christ through my ministry, as well as from members of various denominations who valued my straightforward Bible exposition. The initial core membership continued with the Bible study, and this little ember grew far beyond my expectation. I began gathering my followers in annual camp meetings, which, 10 years later, were drawing 70,000 participants.

SETTING THE CAPTIVES FREE

As our ministry grew, the demographic spread of the membership changed. The congregation, which had attracted mostly singles, began to swell, but now included older people, couples, retirees and others. Some came bearing peculiarly spiritual problems. So in response to their needs, we prayed and the Lord launched us into power evangelism. The gifts of the Spirit fully blossomed. The result was tremendous growth. Revival broke forth. People were saved in large numbers. Captives of Satan were loosed and victims of demonic yokes were delivered.

THE DEEPER LIFE BIBLE CHURCH

The growth of the ministry brought in its wake some pastoral problems that needed attention. Many of those to whom I was ministering found themselves ostracized by their own churches. Some were denied baptism and the Lord's Supper. A strong wave of criticism came against my movement. It was a painful season, but the Lord used it for good, and I was forced to decide to start a church.

The first Sunday service of Deeper Life Bible Church was held in November 1982. It took care of the prevailing problems amongst the brethren and placed their commitment in proper perspective. Other significant developments followed shortly after. To create a meaningful spiritual home for every member of the church, the Home Caring Fellowship system was introduced. By starting this system, evangelism, caring and fellowship were taken nearer the people.

A turning point came in 1985 with the crusade I described in the first part of this chapter. The National Television Authority of Nigeria stunned the nation by reporting a seven-minute news story about Deeper Life Great Miracle Crusade, highlighting the unprecedented attendance at the sports arena, the miracles, the preacher and the ministry. Many families were awakened to the presence of a church through which God would channel His power into their homes if only they would believe.

The local Deeper Life Bible Church in Lagos grew dramatically, and in a few years we reached an attendance of more than 70,000 adult members, and 30,000 children meeting in a separate building. This forced me to decentralize, and now we have 735 district churches in Lagos. Besides that, we have planted Deeper Life Bible Churches in every government district in Nigeria, totaling more than 5,000 local churches. We sponsor church-planting missions in more than 35 African countries and a growing number in Europe, the Americas and Asia.

A recent syndicated article by Nkiry Asika appeared in newspapers across the United States, saying, among other things, "For generations,

> **The gospel,...needs to change our lifestyle deeply and impressively in whatever ways may be appropriate to our context.**

Christian missionaries from the United States went to Africa to teach their religion. Now, amid an explosion of Christianity in Africa, churches there are sending thousands of missionaries overseas to preach the Christian message in their unique style. And many of those missionaries are coming to the United States....Some of the churches are affiliates of larger bodies such as the Nigerian-based Deeper Life Bible Fellowship, while others..." God is working in wondrous ways!

FOUNDATIONS OF DEEPER LIFE MINISTRY

The Deeper Life Bible Church is essentially a teaching ministry. The prop and hub of our ministry is holiness of life and conduct. The pivot of our daily activity is evangelism. Thus the tripod on which the church rests is the Word, holiness and evangelism. In relation to the Word, we take the Bible as the final authority in all matters concerning Christian conduct and work (see Prov. 30:5,6; 2 Tim. 3:16,17; Rev. 22:18,19). In this vein, we study the Bible weekly, corporately, expositorily and systematically.

The church's desire is for every member of the ministry to be thoroughly Christian and uncompromising with the world. The gospel, we affirm, needs to change our lifestyle deeply and impressively in whatever ways may be appropriate to our context. Sunday services focus on the exposition of the Scriptures, and miracle ministries take place on Thursday nights.

ORGANIZING OUR OPERATION

From the outset, traditional hierarchical structures have not been part of our administrative design. At the apex of Deeper Life is the General Superintendent who oversees the church globally from the international headquarters in Lagos. In the various Nigerian states, State Overseers are assigned to keep the work going. The same applies to the Regions and Districts. In other countries, one National Overseer leader is assigned to take care of the work in the nation. The major role of each leader is service and ministry.

When we started the Home Caring Fellowship system, we developed a well-defined organizational structure. Every geographical area in which Deeper Life operates is divided into regions. Each region is further mapped out into districts. Each district is delineated into zones. The zones are further divided into units of houses, and Home Caring Fellowship (HCF) locations are planted for fellowshipping, witnessing and caring in each unit. Every Home Caring Fellowship is supervised by a house leader.

Deeper Life has developed a substantial women's ministry, led by the National Women's Coordinator. Each state and district has its own Women's Coordinator as well to carry the responsibility of checking on the welfare of women.

ACCOUNTABILITY AND FINANCIAL PRINCIPLES

We have put in place effective control mechanisms—administrative, financial and relational. These provide probity, discipline, honesty and integrity in managing the finances of the ministry at all levels. Auditing committees are established by the ministry, and they are responsible for the internal control of the finances of the church at various levels—branch, district, region, state and international headquarters.

LEADERSHIP TRAINING

Training is an integral part of the programs and work of Deeper Life. The ministry trains its members at various levels: Home-caring Fellowships, zones, districts, regions, states, national and international. Training commences for individuals who make a commitment to Christ, using basic teachings in Christian living, Bible ordinances and Bible doctrines. Thereafter, training is provided to prepare them for the work force in the church. From the point of admission into the

> *Members are appointed to various positions of leadership on the basis of their gifting, calling, competence, experience, exposure and maturity. They are encouraged to pray for a fruitful ministry and effective evangelism.*

work force, they attend a regular weekly training session. This exposes them to the precepts of Christian service, witnessing and Christian living. Periodically, at various levels in the regions and states in Nigeria and nations in Africa, concentrated training sessions lasting four to five days in retreat settings are organized.

A Deeper Life Leadership Strategy Congress is held once a year at the ministry's International Bible Training Center in Lagos. It is attended by 12,000 to 15,000 participants drawn from many African countries. At the congress, we concentrate on teachings about strategies of evangelism and church planting, Bible doctrines, leadership, discipleship and family life. This event also affords the leadership the opportunity to build relationships, to plan and to set goals for the coming year.

We put little emphasis on formal licensing or ceremonial ordination. Members are appointed to various positions of leadership on the basis of their gifting, calling, competence, experience, exposure and maturity. They are encouraged to pray for a fruitful ministry and effective evangelism.

REACHING OUT

The growth of Deeper Life is directly tied to its unflinching obedience and commitment to Jesus' Great Commission: "Go into all the world and preach the gospel to every creature" (Mark 16:15). We use personal evangelism, literature evangelism, friendship evangelism, carriage evangelism, specialized evangelism, media evangelism and mass evangelism.

We have divided Nigeria into several groups based on geographical and linguistic contiguity for the purpose of reaching out to specific people groups. For instance, in Western Nigeria, the Yoruba group, made up of five states, launched out in cooperative evangelism to villages in 1996 and planted close to 700 churches that year. The North East Group (Hausa speaking) planted 50 churches. Other groups set targets on a regional basis and have crossed language barriers and planted churches throughout their regions.

Specific outreaches to the various subregions of the African continent have been under way for some time. We have spread from Kenya throughout the East African subregion, from Ghana throughout Anglophone West Africa, from Côte d'Ivoire throughout Francophone West Africa, and from Zambia and South Africa to the whole Southern Africa subregion.

Many of these leaders came together in Lagos in 1992 when we organized a Church Growth Conference for the continent in connection with the A.D. 2000 Movement. This attracted more than 12,000 church leaders from 42 African countries and represented more than 2,000 denominations. Participants from West, East, Central and Southern African countries learned principles of church growth from our guest speakers C. Peter Wagner and Luis Bush.

DISCIPLING THE NEXT GENERATION

Deeper Life maintains a full-fledged children's ministry, which we call Children for Christ. Presently it has grown to more than 150,000 children in Nigeria alone. Most Deeper Life Bible Churches outside of Nigeria have followed suit. Children for Christ has now grown into a full-blown ministry organizing children's crusades and other evangelistic programs through which children effectively reach out to and win their peers to Christ.

Our vision to "catch them young" led to the Deeper Life School Outreach to high school students, which now has a membership of about 25,000 in Lagos. Special monthly youth revival services held in the headquarters in Lagos are regularly attended by 20,000 youths. Camp meetings across the nation also attract thousands of students. Every Sunday evening in Lagos, 23,000 students cluster in many homes hosting Home Cell Fellowship meetings.

In the institutions of higher learning, the Deeper Life Campus Fellowship seeks to lead students, faculty, staff and graduates to a personal encounter with Jesus Christ. Its membership is about 10,000 now and it has been established in some other African countries—notably Zambia, Ghana, Namibia and Côte d'Ivoire. We consider this the church of the future across the continent, and the world itself will be its parish.

PRAYER AND POWER

Our efforts to come to grasp with the necessity of addressing felt needs of the people eventually launched us into power evangelism. I always had known Jesus can heal and I knew that God has the power to do all things. Our prayer emphasis in the early days, though, merely reflected our strong bias toward consecration, holiness, fruitful Christian service and witnessing. Not much prayer effort and time was expended on the miraculous.

In 1982, I attended a conference at Caister, in Britain. There I saw others minister to the sick, and it was a little bit new to me. I then began to study the Scriptures about healing and to pray that God would show me if He wanted me to move in that direction. During a regular Sunday morning service in 1983, the Lord revealed to me a specific problem of a lady in the service. I took the risk of mentioning it and praying for her. The following week, she came up to the stage and gave her testimony of miraculous healing. The incident encouraged me to believe that the gifts were available, but I still needed to develop them.

As I did, the Thursday revival service in our church began to take on the character of a crusade, having several thousands in attendance weekly. The ministry time became the high point, and the miracles that followed were used by God to attract more who were in need. This became a regular feature of ministry in Deeper Life, creating a public reputation and awakening interest in the deeper things of God among the members. Ministries of the miraculous are particularly relevant to African situations, especially needs for deliverance, healing and material provision.

HOPE FOR THE HOPELESS

A lady in Kinshasa, the Democratic Republic of Congo (Zaire), who had been seriously infected with HIV came to our meeting. Both her doctors and her relatives were merely buying time. Death was certain. Some concerned friends, however, had reached out and invited her to the crusade we were conducting in Kinshasa. She was brought in on a stretcher. Her demeanor and general frame reflected the typically gaunt features of an AIDS patient.

After the sermon, we started the ministry time. Several miracles took place. The high point of the crusade, though, was this AIDS patient who got up from her stretcher and walked around the football field in the stadium. It was incredible! The National Television Authority of the Democratic Republic of Congo was most impressed and intrigued. They followed up the story and used it as a news item on the network news. The nation was awakened to the reality of miracles, even for those inflicted with incurable illnesses such as AIDS!

OUR VISION FOR THE FUTURE

As a church, we cherish the vision and privilege of service. First of all, we see an ever-widening field in Africa that must be reached. The unreached people groups in Africa have been and continue to be our primary target. We will mobilize our resources to reach them and saturate them with churches.

The vision of Deeper Life is not confined to Africa, though. We want to build relationships and network with other international organizations and mission agencies for global evangelization.

Each local church is a vital part of the vision. We want every local church to spend and be spent for edifying, strengthening and equipping Christian communities for reaching the lost of Africa and the world.

The message of holiness will continue to be the focus of our doctrinal persuasion. If He gives us strength, and if His people obey His mandates, God's name will be glorified and His kingdom will come in all the earth!

This is God's work. We are His witnesses. As we look forward to the year 2000 and beyond, we yearn for more of God's gracious presence, power and manifestation in His Church.

Pastor William Kumuyi
Deeper Christian Life Ministry
Gbagada, Lagos
Nigeria
Phone: 234-1-823264
Fax: 234-1-822990

Resource List—Books
Key to Happiness
Complete Bible Study Series
My Message to Christian Workers
The Key to Revival and Church Growth
Power as of Old

Resources may be ordered through:
LIFE PRESS LTD.
6 Ayodele Okeowo Street
Gbagada, Lagos
P.M.B. 1004, Yaba, Lagos
Nigeria

18

JESUS IS LORD CHURCH

Bishop Dr. Eddie C. Villanueva
Manila, Philippines

Bishop Eddie Villanueva was born in Bunlo, Bocaue, Bulacan, Philippines. After graduating from Polytechnic University of the Philippines, earning a bachelor of science degree in 1969, he began teaching in the Department of Economics and Finance. From Roman Catholicism to becoming a committed Marxist, he finally found the Lord in 1973. His ministry—Jesus Is Lord, or simply JIL—was started in September 1978. The ministry has grown from about 15 students 19 years ago to about 2,000,000 today in the Philippines and elsewhere around the world.

But God has chosen the foolish things of the world to put to shame the wise, and God has chosen the weak things of the world to put to shame the things which are mighty; and the base things of the world and the things which are despised God has chosen, and the things which are not, to bring to nothing the things that are, that no flesh should glory in His presence (1 Cor. 1:27-29).

I grew up as a strong-willed defender of the poor and the oppressed among my people, and a spokesperson for my nation's rights and freedom. I understood later that God would choose to use such traits to further His divine purpose for my life.

During the martial rule of then President Ferdinand Marcos, the city streets became my home. Leading protests against social injustices, graft and corruption, and political despotism became my primary occupation. The returns for my dedication to such a cause were not that rewarding, however, as I eventually found myself behind bars for allegedly inciting rebellion. For me, though, that was nothing compared to my burning passion to see the Philippines emancipated from political tyranny.

I was so disillusioned about our nation's predicament that the idea of a "callused" God only enraged me day after day. Because of this, I converted from Roman Catholicism to communism. As a committed Marxist, I devoted much time and effort implanting into the hearts and minds of my students at the Polytechnic University of the Philippines (PUP) the importance of fighting for their freedom and rights, even through bloody revolution. I taught them more about the principles of Mao Tse-Tung than my assigned lessons in commerce, economics and finance. Unknown to the university administration, many of my students were converted to communism and atheism, too.

It was a great source of satisfaction for me. After all, reforming an exploited country was too great a task for a single person, and our ranks were swelling.

FINDING THE
ANSWERS IN JESUS

"I have even called you by your name; I have named you, though you have not known Me. I am the Lord, and there is no other; there is no God besides Me. I will gird you, though you have not known Me, that they may know from the rising of the sun to its setting that there is none besides Me. I am the Lord, and there is no other" (Isa. 45:4-6).

In 1973, two years after I married Dory, I grew even more defiant of our despotic political system when my family turned victim to a powerful land-grabbing syndicate. Despite my expositions about the syndicate's illegal activities, pinning them down was very difficult because the judges could be bribed easily. Even the few conscientious government officials who believed in the legitimacy of our lawsuit against the said unscrupulous people could do nothing.

Although I was growing increasingly defiant toward our judicial system, I also felt terribly helpless. It was then I began to face my human frailty realistically. Then one evening, after a frustrating day attempting to follow up our case, I found myself reading one of the letters my older sister, Leni, had sent to me from the United States. Being an ardent born-again Christian, she kept on urging me to try God as the solution to our mounting legal problems.

My sister wrote:

> I know, Eddie, that you are in deep crisis. I know of your burning compassion for the masses. I know of your great personal sacrifices for our family's case. But, believe me, even your well-intentioned friends in the military, even your friends in the government cannot help you if God does not want to help you.
>
> Please, heed my advice! Receive the Lord Jesus Christ into your heart as your personal Lord and Savior. After doing this, then lift up in sincere prayer our family land problems to the throne of grace in heaven, and believe at this time there will be miracles on behalf of our family.
>
> Please heed my advice.

After exhausting all efforts, I decided to heed her *spiritual* advice. I prayed the sinner's prayer, I received Jesus into my heart, and then I hungrily fed on every word written in the Gideon Bible she had sent to me months before. I was totally amazed how a single book could just smash my long-held political ideologies, such as my lofty thoughts about existentialism, revolution and communism I had fanatically embraced all my life.

Still somewhat a skeptic, I couched my relationship with God upon the condition that He should prove to me the reality of His omnipotence. I demanded that He work on behalf of our family regarding the land case.

Five days after I said that prayer, members of the syndicate were arrested and detained in the military stockade! My skepticism vanished, and the following days were days of my new beginning in the Lord Jesus Christ—the God of a second chance!

A NEW BEGINNING
FROM A LOVING GOD

"You did not choose Me, but I chose you and appointed you that you should go and bear fruit, and that your fruit should remain" (John 15:16).

My young faith was first nourished at Bocaue Baptist Church, then at the Foursquare Gospel Church. As I went on studying the Bible

> **Like a pot that can never question the design of its maker, I found myself powerless before God.**

day and night, God turned my love for the masses during my atheist days into a burning compassion and burden for the lost souls. The early years of my Christian walk were never easy, particularly as I began to hear the call of God on my life for full-time ministry. For three years I desperately tried to escape His call, promising Him my fullest financial support should He just bless me as a Christian businessman instead. Like a pot that can never question the design of its maker, though, I found myself powerless before Him. In 1978 I finally yielded to His call.

That same year, I reapplied as a professor at Polytechnic University of the Philippines, but with an entirely different goal. I wanted to share God's plan of salvation through faith in the Lord Jesus Christ to the youth of my nation. So I shared the gospel with my students at the start of every class. Afterward, we began to meet in Bible studies during our free time.

Those who knew me as a radical political activist wondered whatever happened to this once bitter man. Some turned against me and opposed the "different message" I preached. God's work could not be stopped, though, and many students were born again in just a few months' time.

CHOOSING A NAME

The Bible study ministry on campus grew to the point where some people began suspecting we were another budding subversive political movement. This was obviously the time to find a name for the ministry so we could establish our true identity.

Suggestions for names began to pour in: "Charismatic Youth Encounters," "Crusaders on Campus" and the like. At that time, I also went through a season of prayer and fasting specifically seeking God for the name of the movement.

Then God led me to John 12:32: "'And I, if I am lifted up from the earth, will draw all peoples to Myself.'"

The Lord clearly impressed on my mind that our name should be something that would *lift up the name of Jesus*. What should it be, though? Clearly the Lord showed me that He had written it in Paul's Epistle to the Philippians:

> Therefore God also has highly exalted Him and given Him the name which is above every name, that at the name of Jesus every knee should bow, of those in heaven, and of those on earth, and of those under the earth, and that every tongue should confess that Jesus Christ is Lord, to the glory of God the Father (2:9-11).

On September 9, 1978, our ministry was formally named "Jesus Is Lord Fellowship" or simply, "JIL."

How 19 years ago a handful of about 15 students could multiply to about 2 million souls today in the Philippines and elsewhere around the world is indeed the Lord's exclusive doing.

THE PAINS OF PIONEERING

> "And now I say to you, keep away from these men and let them alone; for if this plan or this work is of men, it will come to nothing; but if it is of God, you cannot overthrow it—lest you even be found to fight against God" (Acts 5:38,39).

During the early years, it seems we experienced every kind of hardship imaginable. The most furious attacks of the devil failed to shake us from under His mandate.

Working with my students as co-pioneers of JIL, we somehow endured on the meager resources we had—eating candies in place of regular meals, jam-packing about eight people in a four-seater Volkswagen Beetle for kilometers of missionary trips to nearby provinces, and just making do with whatever was available to us because we had to.

Owning no permanent place of worship, we were continually forced to move from one place to another. Moreover, envious religious and insecure political leaders, who had witnessed the phenomenal growth of JIL, became formidable adversaries of the gospel of the Lord Jesus Christ.

Like the descendants of Jacob in the land of Egypt, though, the more we got hard pressed on every side, the more God multiplied us! The Holy Spirit descended like wildfire upon us, and started a contagious nationwide revival. JIL ministry chapters simultaneously sprouted in a multitude of communities, companies, universities, towns, provinces, cities and even jails.

OUTDOOR SERVICES IN A HIGH SCHOOL QUADRANGLE

In 1981, JIL started holding worship services in the outdoor quadrangle of Araullo High School, one of the biggest public schools in the heart of Manila. There, more than 20,000 people gathered every Sunday afternoon to experience the reality of God through manifold healings, signs, wonders and miracles. Souls were saved by the hundreds. Soon, JIL became recognized as one of the 10 most rapidly growing churches in the world.

By the grace of God, Jesus Is Lord now has 105 Sunday worship services in 26 districts of Metro Manila alone. It also has 37 Sunday worship services in 25 towns of Bulacan. Aside from these, it also has 258 provincial Sunday worship services nationwide. All in all, the church has more than 2 million regular Sunday attendees in the Philippines and elsewhere around the world.

SPREADING OUT TO THE WORLD

"Enlarge the place of your tent, and let them stretch out the curtains of your dwellings; do not spare; lengthen your cords, and strengthen your stakes" (Isa. 54:2).

For lack of better employment opportunities at home, many Filipinos have sought greener pasture in foreign lands, only to open themselves to abuse and exploitation. What the devil meant for evil, however, God used for our good (see Gen. 50:20). These seemingly displaced Christian overseas Filipino contract workers eventually became *God's ambassadors*—His missionaries—to wherever He caused them to dwell. We also saw the hand of God carefully working to fulfill His redemptive plan for every human being, regardless of nationality, language, color and belief.

Because of the blessing of the heavenly Father, JIL today has 67 Sunday worship services in 34 chapters across Africa, Australia, United States, Canada, Middle East, Europe and Asia. Almost every worldwide chapter of JIL becomes the largest and fastest-growing Filipino full gospel church in that particular place. JIL Hong Kong, for instance, has more than 12,000 attendees, which makes it the largest Filipino Christian church in China.

JIL workers' fervent commitment to turn the kingdoms of this world to become the kingdom of our Lord Jesus Christ (see Rev. 11:15) has not waned throughout the years.

HOW WE ORGANIZE

JIL operates on the principle we call "theocratic governance," where the head of the church is the Lord Jesus Christ Himself (see Eph. 5:23). We also recognize His calling upon chosen and gifted individuals whom He has entrusted as faithful stewards of His ministry, such as the minister of the local church and the members of the board of trustees.

The JIL Church, as an international movement, is supervised by a Spiritual Director/President and an Executive Director. They are the two individuals who are the most accountable to God for expanding the ministry and realizing His vision for the church. Meanwhile, the day-by-day management of the church is handled by three major departments. They are Administration, National and International Operations, and Finance.

1. **The Administration Department** is composed of a management board responsible for the planning, facilitation, transaction, implementation and evaluation of all pertinent matters concerning the ministry. The board consists of mature, God-fearing, respectable church leaders. They contribute wise counsel and sound judgment in the appointment and ordination of pastors, execution of church discipline, formation of church policies, acquisition of church possessions, dissemination of church information and guidelines, and attendance to legal matters and research concerning the church.

2. **The National and International Operations Department** is headed by a director who has exemplary administrative anointing because it is the very heart of the church's "towel and basin" ministry. It encompasses all the major ministries of the church such as the pastoral, ministerial, evangelistic, educational, provincial, local and international outreaches, as well as the educational and tri-media (TV, radio, print) ministries. Each ministry is supervised by a ministry head who works with special staff members.

3. **The Finance Department** is headed by a director of unquestionable integrity because it is in charge of the general financial management of the church funds and assets. It is also responsible for all major financial transactions and disbursements. Aside from these, it supervises the total church expenditures, prepares and allocates budgets for church programs and projects, and monitors the financial affairs of faithful church partners through the tithers' information cards. Thus, aside from the Finance Director, the department also has a certified Christian accountant. To further safeguard the integrity of the church, a nonmember public auditor regularly monitors the ministry's financial status.

ACCOUNTABILITY

The leaders, workers and members of the church are bound by the principle that "no one is indispensable in the ministry but God." Thus, everyone is responsible for preserving personal integrity and faithfully performing assigned duties. Commitment to serve God's interest is held above all else. Accountability to adhere to the church's Declaration of Faith and Principles is absolute. All workers comply with these policies as they fulfill the Lord's vision for the church. Any deviation from this is appropriately handled by the church leadership.

When human failure does occur, a Committee on Church Policy and Discipline handles the matter according to the Lord's standards of mercy and justice.

TEAM BUILDING ON ALL LEVELS

The church operates on the principle of team ministry. This is an integral topic in every leadership training program of JIL. All levels in the

> *The church's [JIL] central teaching for leaders revolves around personal integrity and moral uprightness, character beyond reproach, purity of heart, good courage, godly vision and genuine compassion, meekness, humility, selflessness and servanthood as emphasized by the Lord Jesus Christ.*

church leadership work as a team because regionalism or parochial mentality is strongly discouraged and discarded. Interdependence and synergism are instead encouraged and promoted.

Any plan, program or project, and its implementation, therefore, are discussed at a monthly team meeting first. These consultations and collective "meeting of the minds" are largely responsible for the consistent growth of the church. For it is only when brothers and sisters dwell together in unity that the outpouring and empowering of the Holy Spirit's anointing manifest in their strongest dimensions (see Ps. 133:1)!

TRAINING OUR LEADERS

The quality of the leader as a person is of supreme importance. Hence, the church's central teaching for leaders revolves around personal integrity and moral uprightness (Joseph), character beyond reproach (Daniel), purity of heart (David), good courage (Joshua), godly vision (Caleb) and genuine compassion, meekness, humility, selflessness and servanthood as emphasized by the Lord Jesus Christ.

The church also believes that not all leaders are born. Thus, leadership qualities can be learned and enhanced by constantly developing and equipping our leaders and potential leaders.

Starting right with the congregation, each chapter of the church offers basic Bible seminars before the start of every Sunday worship service. Aside from this, home and cell group Bible studies are also conducted. These teachings focus on sound doctrinal foundations of faith for every church member. From the congregations, the individuals on whom God has placed His hand for service and leadership begin to surface.

To equip these potential leaders, each chapter of the church offers specialized training called the Leadership Enhancement and Advancement Program (LEAP). It involves three levels: fundamentals of leadership, management and ministerial skills.

On a broader scale, annual leadership training and workers' conventions for national and international leaders are held at JIL Praise Valley Campsite in Norzagaray, Bulacan. These provide continuing education for the entire church as it keeps all leaders focused on the vision.

On more advanced levels, the church provides a formal school program through the School of Ministry. The School of Ministry offers courses on prayer, evangelism and certificate courses in specialized fields. Church ministers also receive spiritual nourishment from the Pastoral Training Course, the Missionary Intensive Training Course and the Bible Teachers' Training Course.

CRITERIA FOR ORDINATION

Divine appointments come from the Lord alone. However, it is usually not difficult to recognize one who has been "marked" by God for service.

The church's moral qualifications for ordination to full-time ministry are clearly set forth in 1 Timothy 3:1-7. Those aspiring to be ordained must be above reproach (person of integrity); husband of one wife or wife of one husband (keeper of covenant); temperate and self-controlled (rational); respectable and hospitable (compassionate); able to teach (skillful); not given to drunkenness (sober); not violent and quarrelsome but gentle (humble); not a lover of money (honest); manages his/her own family well (able manager); his/her children obey him/her in proper respect (able leader); not a recent convert (spiritually mature); and has a good reputation on the outside (exemplary testimony).

Aside from these basic qualities, a proven and fruitful ministry led by the candidate bears witness to God's high calling upon his or her life.

REACHING OUT

The JIL church maintains both nationwide and worldwide outreaches. The nationwide outreach ministry consists of two main ministries: the Provincial Missions Ministry (PMM) and the Pastoral Care Ministry (PCM).

The Provincial Missions Ministry operates at the forefront of church planting and evangelism in provinces throughout the Philippines. Missionary teams are sent to barrios, towns or cities of specific provinces to conduct crusades and other ministerial activities. Afterward, when the place is finally ready for sowing the Word of God, a JIL home church is established.

Meanwhile, the Pastoral Care Ministry is in charge of the outreach programs in the Metropolitan Manila area where the largest concentration of people is found. Because of its dense population and strategic location, PCM has divided each major city into several districts to monitor church growth effectively. Presently, regular Sunday worship services are established in every district of the city, some districts having up to eight Sunday worship services in their area. Aside from these, midweek services, Bible study groups, prayer meetings, cell groups and family devotional meetings also are held regularly during a given week.

The Worldwide Outreach Ministry (WOM) is in charge of the international outreaches of the church. These international outreaches are usually pioneered by JIL Christian Filipino overseas workers already established there. They do the initial plowing of the foreign land before it finally is ready for sowing the Word. When such a time comes, the leadership in the Philippines makes proper legal arrangements with the host country and sends a missionary overseeing pastor to that nation.

Teaching teams follow to offer the training necessary for the new church chapter to operate on its own. The church headquarters in the Philippines, however, takes responsibility in supervising the affairs of the international outreaches while the anointing of the Holy Ghost serves as a corporate covering over the entire JIL church.

PRAYER AND POWER MINISTRIES

The JIL Church is born through prayers. Only by powerful prayer does the church continue to thrive and grow. Like Jesus, who agonized in prayer until blood came forth from Him as drops of sweat, the church never neglects its own "Garden of Gethsemane." For there the JIL people constantly rededicate themselves to the very will of the Father and to the very passion of His heart.

Each day is welcomed by prayer from intercessory groups in what the church calls "Dawn Prayer Watch." In some chapters, a daily "Dusk Prayer Watch" is observed instead. Aside from these, weekly prayer meetings and monthly overnight prayer gatherings are held in every church chapter. Meanwhile, every third Saturday of each month is sanctified unto the Lord as a whole day of prayer and fasting. From time to time, prayerwalks and prayer on locations are likewise conducted.

As surely as there is liberty where the Spirit of the Lord is, gifts of healing, words of knowledge, prophecy, signs and wonders are very much at work in every worship service of the church. In fact, conducting the church's Sunday worship service in the open-air athletic ground of Polytechnic University of the Philippines in Manila has familiarized us with the casual display of God's awesome power. In uncounted numbers of occasions, thunderstorms and raging rains just instantly stopped by just a word of simple prayer unto the living God!

WHAT IS JIL'S SECRET TO GROWTH?

Being confident of this very thing, that He who has begun a good work in you will complete it until the day of Jesus Christ (Phil. 1:6).

I never fail to stand amazed at the wonder of God's faithful commitment to keeping His calling and election to every individual steadfast and sure. I may never have been literally thrown into a lions' den like Daniel; nor thrown into a furnace heated seven times over like Shadrach, Meshach and Abednego; nor mandated to lead a stubborn and murmuring crowd out of slavery (Thank you, God, for a wonderful, loving JIL family!). I did, and still do, however, have my own share of potentially fatal close encounters with the fiery darts of the enemy.

The greatest truth I have discovered in all my 19 years of service to Him is this:

> My total abandonment to Jesus Christ my Lord is my firmest security. My total surrender to Jesus Christ my Lord is my surest affluence. My total submission to the will, plan and purpose of my Lord Jesus is my greatest joy. For only in totally dying to myself can I completely live in Him!

Indeed, questions will continue to be asked of me—ranging from the church's framework to operations procedures to methodologies to leadership styles. To all these things, I will find myself giving this one response: The secret to dynamic Christian ministry is in *lifting up the name of Jesus*. Because in His name, every creature in heaven, on earth and under the earth bows down and pays reverence. Because in His name, demons tremble and cower in fear. Because in His name, diseases are healed. Because in His name, signs, wonders and miracles happen. Because in His name, the chiefest of all sinners find salvation and new life. Because in His name, Abba Father grants even the most impossible of all petitions and desires.

Thus, in His name and for His name alone, the Jesus Is Lord Church will ever be established. In His name and for His name alone, an obscure Bro. Eddie C. Villanueva, whose only credential is being a recipient of God's abundant mercy and grace, will live and move and have his being.

JESUS IS LORD OVER ALL THE WORLD!

Bishop Dr. Eddie C. Villanueva
Jesus Is Lord Church
1832 San Marcelino Street
Malate, Manila
Philippines
Phone: 632-524-18-31
Fax: 632-522-42-46

19

HOPE OF
BANGKOK CHURCH

Dr. Joseph C. Wongsak
Bangkok, Thailand

The Hope of Bangkok Church was started in 1981. The church first met on the ninth floor of a hospital building where the elevator was occasionally out of order. Nevertheless, God caused us to expand. In a few months, we had outgrown the small meeting room and moved to the second-floor chapel. The next few years were a time of training disciples. In 1985, a second church was started in the northern part of Thailand.

THAILAND AND BEYOND

Now, in 1997, more than 800 Hope of God churches have been planted, covering most districts of Thailand. Another 40 churches have been established internationally in 19 countries, including the United States, Canada, Europe, Australia and most of the countries in Southeast Asia.

Although most of these churches emphasize a schedule of regular weekly activities, some of the larger churches have also been able to devote a part of their resources to community projects. Some of the churches operate centers to help the underprivileged and medical clinics to serve the poor.

THE HOPE OF BANGKOK PHILOSOPHY OF MINISTRY

The main tenets of our philosophy of ministry are outlined as follows:

- Obedience to the Great Commission of Jesus Christ;
- The importance of the local church;
- The need for every Christian to serve God fully according to the giftings and endowment God has given;
- The recognition that church leaders are appointed by God, not by people;
- The importance for every Christian to be under spiritual covering;
- The understanding that a church is both an organization and an organism;
- Strong commitment of the members to their local church;
- Unity within the members of the local church, and cooperation between the local churches in recognition of the universal Body of Christ;
- The role of the church as salt and light within its communities, cultures and nations;
- Establishing the church as a place of security and blessing to people.

Before people formally become members of our churches, they have a chance to learn about our philosophy of ministry so they can thoroughly understand us. In turn, they also learn of our expectations for membership in the local church.

Our vision is to continue to be in total obedience to the Great Commission. We want to play a significant part in having this fulfilled. As an outworking of this, we would not be satisfied to make only a token effort. We want to be involved in planting churches worldwide.

Nonetheless, we know that the task of fulfilling the Great Commission in its entirety is beyond the capability of any single church or family of churches. Therefore, we hope that our declared intention to do so inspires many other churches to do likewise. Collectively, then, we will be able to finish what our Lord first commissioned His Church to do.

OUR ORGANIZATIONAL STRUCTURE

The smallest component of the typical Hope of God church is the care group. People are divided into groups ranging in size from 5 to 10 individuals who are supervised by a leader. The grouping is done in as homogeneous a manner as possible. Thus, student care groups may meet on campus, encourage each other in the midst of their studies and reach out to their classmates together.

Those in the medical profession group together to build strong fellowship links, serve the church and reach their colleagues. Because of their small size, care groups are an excellent forum for personal teaching and pastoral care. In addition, care groups offer visitors an informal setting where sharing needs, testimonies and the Word of God can be done in an atmosphere of love and concern.

To preserve a good balance, we provide opportunities for fellowship among people of various backgrounds during larger-scale church activities.

The tiered approach found in our churches originates from the principles found in the Bible. Two or three care groups form a unit. One level higher, two or three units are grouped together and headed by another leader. This configuration extends upward to the pastoral team, which is headed by a senior pastor.

Although our people participate in many decentralized activities of their respective care groups throughout the week, they are all brought together on Sundays for a celebration meeting.

Sundays are strategically important in the growth of our church. They are the times when we can worship God, reach out and plan together for the coming week.

ACCOUNTABILITY SYSTEMS AND TEAM BUILDING

We believe that proper spiritual covering is biblically essential. To facilitate this, each member of our church is accountable to a more mature member through a network of relationships within the church. For example, members are accountable to their care group leader, care group leaders to their unit leader and so on.

In each of the relationships involving any pair of individuals, the more mature Christian spends some time with the less mature Christian regularly each week. Such time is spent getting to know one another, studying the Word of God, praying, discussing the work of the ministry, working through problems, and various other activities that benefit the care receiver and help him or her grow. Such individual attention facilitates rapid spiritual growth for the care receiver. These weekly one-on-one meetings are a good forum for deep sharing, ensuring that individual problems are handled with proper care and concern.

To avoid potential problems, care giver-care receiver relationships are established between individuals of the same gender. Furthermore,

> *We view upright character as essential for leadership, using Paul's Epistles to Timothy and Titus as the basis for this conviction.*

to prevent abuses of the system, those receiving care are given ready access to higher-level leaders should the more mature Christian's behavior or teaching ever become questionable.

In this way, strong ministry teams are built because the individuals in groups have already been together for some length of time, facilitating team building. This is also a practical way of incorporating every member of the church into ministry, as all the members of each care group are given responsibility in the support structure to help them successfully fulfill their duties. Care groups foster strong interpersonal ties as members serve together for several years and help each other through periods of great success as well as times of barrenness in ministry.

TRAINING OUR LEADERS

Church leaders must normally be trained and selected from within, not from without. Leaders who have been converted and matured within a local church are well versed in the preferences of that church as well as with its philosophies of ministry. At the same time, their giftings, abilities and character are apparent to the leaders appointing them. They also have already established relationships with the members and gained their acceptance. In this way, appointing leaders can be based solidly on an in-depth discernment of their gifts, strengths and callings.

We believe people should be functioning as leaders before they are appointed as such. In this way, we can recognize God's anointing on their lives. We view upright character as essential for leadership, using Paul's Epistles to Timothy and Titus as the basis for this conviction.

We also recognize that leadership is key to the growth of a church. The size of a church depends on the quantity and quality of its leadership at every level. Vital churches must always be developing leaders because growing churches always seems to have an insufficient number of leaders.

TRAINING PROGRAMS

To handle this need, regular leadership training programs are a part of our churches. Some of the programs are formal, others are less structured. At the same time, we seek to balance acquiring theory with on-the-job experience. Seminaries have been established in several of our churches. They offer courses that combine rigorous academic standards and biblical teaching along with practical character development and ministry training. Because of the great need for leaders at all levels of ministry, we seek to meet the needs of students from a wide range of academic backgrounds.

Our seminaries offer a variety of programs, each having different entry requirements for a candidate's academic background, Christian maturity and ministry potential. While in seminary, students are discipled by pastors. A strong emphasis is placed on practical service. The placement of such seminaries within the local church provides a ready-made laboratory where students may apply their acquired knowledge in real-life situations.

The second form of leadership training is more informal through groups we call David's Mighty Men. Here people within the group study Christian doctrine, character development and ministry practices. Informal training is prevalent at all levels of leadership formation. Potential leaders develop by watching their own care group leaders lead worship, teach and counsel. The leader at each level is responsible to train those for whom he is responsible.

HOW WE REACH OUT

To ensure that the Great Commission is fulfilled, each member of a church is required to be involved in evangelism regularly. It would not make sense for churches to rely on transfer growth, especially in countries that have low percentages of born-again Christians. At the same time, the churches themselves must be obedient to the Great Commission. Thus, evangelistic activities are planned on a variety of levels, from the individual to the entire church. Evangelism is the means of establishing new churches in order to fulfill the Great Commission.

Our churches are started in a variety of ways. Many times, when a member moves to a new locality we seize the opportunity to plant a new church. If those who move away are not ready to start a church themselves, we send others along to help them. When the churches are

> *We realize that we are only instruments of the Lord and that we need to rely fully on the Lord to help people mature in their relationship and service to God.*

started, the whole process of sharing the gospel, welcoming new members and discipling them is set into motion. In turn, some go out from there to new locations and start additional churches.

To ensure quality of all these churches, regional pastors travel frequently to their regional daughter churches to make sure the new pastors receive sufficient help and understand how to run their church. Likewise, regional churches support the smaller churches in their care.

At the international level, the process is very much the same, but with an added dimension. Some churches have been started when God brings individuals to us from new countries who want to join us and start churches in their own home countries. Administratively, they are coordinated by a central missions office, helping to ensure they are all moving synonymously in a biblical direction.

To make sure the pastors receive sufficient input, Hope of God International organizes a quarterly conference for pastors and leaders within its family of churches. These leaders gather for intensive Bible teaching and practical training as well as for spiritual input, fellowship and strategic planning. It is also a time when they can share their joys and sorrows, and usually after a few days they are refreshed so they can continue their ministry with renewed zeal and enthusiasm.

PRAYER AND POWER MINISTRIES

We emphasize prayer at both the individual and corporate levels. Members are regularly encouraged to have a consistent private relationship with the Lord. We realize that we are only instruments of the Lord and that we need to rely fully on the Lord to help people mature in their relationship and service to God.

Prayer activities take various formats. Every Sunday morning we meet for a corporate prayer meeting. Some of our churches sponsor a church-level prayer meeting some other day of the week. In other churches, especially those in large cities, it has been more practical to decentralize these meetings.

Although the time set aside for prayer is given importance, we seek to inculcate a spirit of prayer into the lives of our people. They are taught to pray before, during and after each meeting, even if it is only between two individuals. It is not uncommon for our people to plan a regular schedule for fasting and prayer each week. Members regularly spend their lunch hours praying for their friends, relatives and acquaintances.

In response to our prayers, signs and wonders are often visible in our midst. Healings of people who were sick beyond medical aid are documented regularly. We have documented cases of paralytics and cancer patients who were miraculously healed after prayer. Our people are taught about the empowerment of the Holy Spirit soon after they are converted. Because of this, boldness in proclaiming the gospel is often the result.

In many cases, healings are powerful evangelism tools in the countryside where people already have worldviews recognizing spiritual reality. Demonstrations of God's authority help villagers realize that our God is real. Sometimes God works in amusing ways. One of our pastors was able to start a church when some sick cattle were healed. The owner's testimony convinced other farmers to give their lives to the Lord.

Leaders teach our people that everybody can move in the power of the Holy Spirit. For example, in our church in Bangkok, we pray for the sick in quarterly prayer meetings. Very often, we celebrate miraculous healings when a group of young believers earnestly prays for the sick.

FINANCIAL PRINCIPLES

Our understanding of the Bible leads us to believe that the local church should be self-sufficient. We teach our churches that from day one, they must support themselves. Nonetheless, some special circumstances could arise where help from other churches is warranted. For example, when a church building is damaged by a natural disaster, other churches rally around to help, not unlike the situation when Christians in the Antioch church sent help to their brothers in Judea during a time of famine.

In this way, the members of the church have a greater sense of involvement. The success of the local church depends very much on each and every individual member's support and giving sacrificially. Initially, the pastor is a tent maker, working for a living while serving the Lord, the same as the other members in the church. When the church grows larger and a need exists for a full-time pastor, then the pastor is paid by the church.

We also teach our people to financially honor the pastor and other full-time workers. They should be paid reasonably and as much as the church can afford. At the same time, good-hearted people normally do not make demands on the church for their salaries.

Within the local church, the pastor and his leadership team make the decisions about expenditures within the limits of the church income and budget. The pastor himself does not handle money, however, to avoid any possible accusations. Counting the money is normally taken care of by a team to avoid embezzlement of funds. Proper financial, accounting and auditing procedures are instilled into our churches.

CONCLUSION

Operating a church is a complicated matter. Although many of us know what it takes to grow a church, applying and maintaining all the factors is a challenging task. We do not want to make a mistake by building strongly in some areas, but missing out in others. To be successful in building the kind of church Jesus stipulated, we need to build according to the various facets suggested in the Bible.

At the same time, when so many components are involved, effort must be made to ensure that the right balance is maintained. Much wisdom is needed to build with the right emphasis according to the biblical pattern. We need to "major on the majors" and "minor on the minors."

For example, we cannot seek to organize our church without recognizing that it is also an organism that has its own life force. On the other hand, if a church is only treated as an organism without us making any attempts to coordinate its efforts, chaos could result. A fine balancing act between organizing the organization while preserving the inherent life of the organism has to be coordinated adroitly.

Joseph C. Wongsak
Hope of God International
Hope Place
1200 Rama IV Road
Bangkok, Thailand 10110
Phone: 662-24-2865-75
Fax: 662-240-1289

INDEX

Visionary Resources from
Bill Hybels and Willow Creek

Rediscovering Church: The Story and Vision of Willow Creek Community Church, by Lynne and Bill Hybels, Zondervan Publishing House.

The God You're Looking For, by Bill Hybels, Thomas Nelson Publishers.

Becoming a Contagious Christian, by Bill Hybels and Mark Mittelberg, Zondervan.

Becoming a Contagious Christian Evangelism Training Course, by Mark Mittelberg, Lee Strobel and Bill Hybels, Zondervan.

God's Outrageous Claims: Thirteen Discoveries That Can Revolutionize Your Life, by Lee Strobel, Zondervan.

Inside the Mind of Unchurched Harry and Mary, by Lee Strobel, Zondervan.

Inside the Soul of a New Generation: Insights and Strategies for Reaching Busters, by Tim Celek and Dieter Zander, Zondervan.

Student Ministry for the 21st Century: Transforming Your Youth Group Into a Vital Student Ministry, by Bo Boshers, Zondervan.

The Journey: A Bible for Seeking God & Understanding Life, NIV, Zondervan.

Sunday Morning Live (drama sketch books and videos), edited by Steve Pederson, Zondervan.

Show Me the Way: An Inside Look at the Willow Creek Seeker Service (video), Zondervan.

The Life You've Always Wanted: Spiritual Disciplines for Ordinary People, by John Ortberg, Zondervan.

Community 101: Reclaiming the Local Church as a Community of Oneness, by Dr. Gilbert Bilezikian, Zondervan.

Leading Life-Changing Small Groups, edited by Bill Donahue, Zondervan.

Network: Understanding God's Design for You in the Church (training course), by Bruce Bugbee, Don Cousins and Bill Hybels, Zondervan.

• • • • •

To order these and other Willow Creek Resources®, including the church's audio teaching tapes, call Willow Creek Direct at 1-800-570-9812.

For information on Willow Creek Association's conferences for church leaders, to subscribe to the Association's publications, including WCA News, or to learn about the many benefits of joining the Association, call the WCA at 1-847-765-0070.

To access Willow Creek's on-line resource, WillowNet, or to send WCA an E-mail, log on to: www.willowcreek.org.

Prophetic Materials from Bill Hamon and Christian International Ministries Network

Books by Dr. Bill Hamon

Apostles, Prophets and the Coming Moves of God	$ 12.95
Prophets and Personal Prophecy	10.95
Prophets and the Prophetic Movement	10.95
Prophecy—Pitfalls and Principles	10.95
The Eternal Church	11.95

Teaching manuals and workbooks are also available

Prophetic Destiny and the Apostolic Reformation	6.95
Fulfilling Your Personal Prophecies	3.95

Books by Evelyn Hamon

The Spiritual Seasons of Life	3.95

Audio Teaching Tape Series

Prophetic Pitfalls (Dr. Bill Hamon)	35.00
The 10 M's (Dr. Bill Hamon)	15.00
Plugging Into Your Gifts (Dr. Bill Hamon and others)	30.00
Handling Life's Realities (Evelyn Hamon)	20.00
Dealing With Life's Challenges (Evelyn Hamon)	20.00

Prophetic Praises Cassette Tapes and CDs

NEW. *Show Your Power* by Dean Mitchum (cassette)	10.95
NEW. *Show Your Power* by Dean Mitchum (CD)	14.95
Here's My Heart by Dean Mitchum (cassette)	10.95
Fan the Flame by Robert Gay (cassette)	10.95
Fan the Flame by Robert Gay (CD)	14.95

Other Materials

Manual for Ministering Spiritual Gifts

Many more audios, videos, cassettes, CDs and books are available by other prophetic and apostolic ministers.

To order call: **1-800-388-5308**

Have your Master Card, VISA or AMEX ready when you call, or write:

> CHRISTIAN INTERNATIONAL, P.O. BOX 9000
> Santa Rosa Beach, FL 32459

Phone: 850-231-2600 / Fax: 850-231-1485 / E-mail: cinpm@arc.net

Shipping costs: (based on retail value) 10% of order ($3.00 minimum).
Outside U.S.: 15% of retail order ($5.00 minimum) for regular surface mail.
Contact shipping for exact costs of airmail.
Prices subject to change without notice.

More Exciting CI Programs and Resources!

Manual for Ministering Spiritual Gifts

A teaching and activating manual consisting of 300 pages, two videos of two hours each, portraying the 18 activations used to teach, train, activate, mentor and mature the saints in their spiritual gifts. Divided into 13 weekly sessions. More than 25,000 saints and 6,000 leaders have been trained in the United States and many nations on several continents.

Christian International School of Theology

Undergraduate and Graduate Bible College

Distinct education courses offering credit toward graduate and undergraduate degrees. Ten different majors to choose from, including our anointed major in the prophetic and apostolic ministry.

Christian International Network of Churches

A networking organization for ministers and churches who have a vision for the full restoration of all truth and ministries—especially the restoration of prophets and apostles, the equipping of the saints in their weapons of warfare—the gifts of the Holy Spirit. For those who want to receive the anointing of the prophet and apostle; to be related to those of like vision for accountability and fulfilling divine destiny. CINC is committed to building strong, growing prophetic-apostolic local churches.

Christian International Business Network

Established with the divine vision and commission to teach and equip Christian businesspeople to succeed with biblical principles and supernatural gifts of the Holy Spirit, prophetic ministry and apostolic miracle-working faith. Raising up a last days Joseph/Daniel, Deborah/Esther prophetic company of businesspeople that will bring the wealth of the world into the Church to help reap the great harvest of souls and establish God's kingdom business and divine principles throughout the earth.

Christian International Healing House (Prophetic Counseling)

Hundreds of individuals, married couples, ministers and saints have been inwardly healed and restored through this special prophetic counseling. People are taken through 20 to 30 hours of intense counseling and deliverance; also special training for Christian leaders who want to become counselors. Four areas are covered: (1) Forgiveness and release from sins of the fathers and resulting causes. (2) Ungodly beliefs—false concepts of oneself. (3) Soul-spirit hurts revealed and healed. (4) Deliverance from any demonic involvement.

Christian International Ministry Training College

Our residential college on CI Campus. First semester covers 10 courses in Bible and theology for establishing a biblical foundation. Second semester, all students are trained in prophetic ministry and then choose the special ministry area in which they want to be mentored: Counseling, arts and worship, pastoral, prophet or business. Credit is earned toward undergraduate or graduate degree. Two- to four-year programs are offered, as well as advanced education and activation for all adults.